INDEX
ON CENSORSHIP

VOLUME 33 • NO 1 • JANUARY 2004 • ISSUE 210

GW00725461

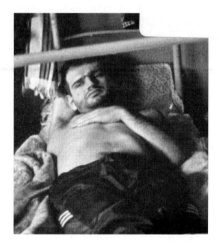

WEBSITE NEWS UPDATED WEEKLY
WWW.INDEXONCENSORSHIP.ORG • CONTACT@INDEXONCENSORSHIP.ORG
TEL: 020 7278 2313 • FAX: 020 7278 1878

CONTENTS

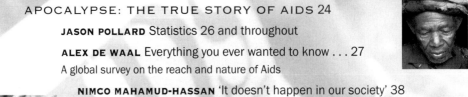
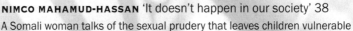

TELLING IT LIKE IT IS

URSULA OWEN

Illness and denial often go hand in hand; in the case of Aids, denial is as much an epidemic as the disease. The silences are profound and damaging – silences on sexual practices, on gender inequalities, on the social and economic effects of Aids. Cultural traditions, religious beliefs, relations between men and women and political expediency have all been crucial in suppressing vital information in the fight against Aids. And this is as true in rich countries such as the US as in poor ones, though poverty is a malign influence.

In Africa, the numbers affected are almost unimaginable (p27). The Zambian Ministry of Health expects that half the population will die of Aids. Life expectancy in Zambia is now 33 years – the lowest in the world. In Zimbabwe, up to 25 per cent of the population is HIV-positive and half a million children have lost one parent to Aids. In Botswana, the infection rate among pregnant women is about 40 per cent. Swaziland may cease to exist. The UN reports that 6,000 adolescents worldwide become infected with HIV every day – the equivalent of one every 14 seconds.

Index reports, too, on Aids epidemics more rarely discussed – the next wave. In China (p120), where official denial and silencing is common, experts warn that 15 million people might be infected in the next five years if the government does not respond more effectively. In India, where the admitted official infection figure is 4 million, set to rise to an astounding 20 million by 2010 (p108), information on Aids is politically massaged; while news of the scale of the illness in Russian prisons (p162) is only just beginning to filter out. Meanwhile, there has been a 20 per cent increase of HIV-positive cases in the UK since 2001, and Aids is one of the top three causes of death for black men and women between the ages of 22 and 45 in the US (p66).

True, more governments are recognising the need to put money and education into combating Aids, international aid is increasing and the supply of drugs is improving. But there have been decades of stigmatising, denial and pretence, and there are huge barriers to overcome: deliberate disinformation on contraception from the Catholic Church (p84); the silencing powers of sheikhs and imams (p91); the stigma attached to discussions of sexuality (p38); the hypocrisy of governments; ignorance about the nature of the threat (p42). In this issue of *Index*, people report frankly and honestly – some in defiance of their own institutions (p80) – about the facts, the issues and personal experiences (p94). Without such openness the battle has no hope of being won. ❏

PRIVACY ON PARADE

SANDI TOKSVIG

Part of my job is that I have to read all of the British press every day. This is frankly a dispiriting experience as I find I am easily confused. Not being much of a television watcher I often mistake the lurid tabloid headlines about a soap opera storyline for fact. I wake up to what seems to be a world of murder, bigamy and the occasional bit of incest to liven things up. I temper this confusion by playing 'spot the news item' in the cheaper tabloids, which is just like the old 'spot the football' game except marginally more difficult.

It is said that the British public read more newspapers per capita than any other country in the world. Consequently, you might think that we are spoilt for choice and that the entire country is awash with free information. Sadly, this is far from the case. My other morning occupation is to play the truth test. This involves reading the same story in a selection of papers and seeing how many facts they all agree on. I have yet to read a piece about anything where the informational content was the same in every paper that I perused. It's not just that some papers take a clear political slant on certain matters, but that there seems to be a truly cavalier attitude by present-day journalists when it comes to fact checking. There used to be an old rule of thumb that no journalist would publish anything he or she hadn't verified from three separate sources. Now it would seem hardly anyone can be bothered with one. Someone in the news can find they have aged ten years by simply switching newspapers, their income can vary wildly and what they did or did not say is frankly a matter of conjecture.

As if that were not bad enough, in addition to failing tests of accuracy, many journalists, bored with having to do anything like legwork, have simply taken to making things up. Wild fantasies are attributed to 'an anonymous source'. If I had done all the things the tabloid press claim I have, I'd be medically incapable of sitting down. Dare to put your head above the parapet about this, or call the scribblers to task, and the media moguls simply cry 'press freedom' and go back to printing nonsense. The libertarian such as myself is caught in a dilemma. Should we bring in some kind of privacy legislation that would act as a brake on the worst of these excesses, or would such a law severely hamper freedom of information? Do

Arlington National Cemetery, USA, 2003: the last thing the president needs . . .
Credit: Sipa Press / Rex Features

we actually need some kind of censorship in this country to get us back on the path of true and honest reporting? Of course, the argument against a privacy law is that it might inhibit investigative journalism; and if anyone could give me an example of good investigative journalism in the last ten years that would have been inhibited then I might agree.

There is an easier solution. If the press is so keen on freedom then it should be a two-way street. If they make a mistake the correction should be placed in the same prominence and size as the original error. If someone calls you a swine on the front page of their *Daily Error* and you are not a swine then the front page is the place for the apology.

The trouble is the whole issue of privacy is rather complex. I think it is right and proper, for example, that funerals should be an entirely private matter. I dislike intensely long-lens grainy photographs of grieving parents or widows snapped after some tragedy. You might think, therefore, that I applaud the fact that the President of the United States, the man elected by no one but marching forward anyway, George Bush, has banned all news coverage and photography on military bases of dead soldiers' homecomings from Iraq. I might indeed put my hands together if it weren't for the fact that he didn't do it out of respect for the deceased.

When I was a kid growing up in the 1960s in the United States, we were in the midst of the increasingly unpopular Vietnam War. Each evening the main news team of Huntley and Brinkley would announce the numbers of US personnel lost in the conflict so far. Television pictures would show the slow transport of coffins draped in red, white and blue and borne on the shoulders of achingly young marines. It was these images more than anything that brought the ignominious end to America's involvement in Vietnam.

Having gone through a period of successful brainwashing by the Bush administration that to be against the Iraq war was somehow to be un-American, the US media are now coming out the other side. Questions are being asked about the validity of the war and the reasons given for entering the Middle East arena in the first place. The last thing Bush needs is pictures of dead young men. So far he has not attended a single ceremony as the fallen heroes return to the Dover military base in Delaware. This is hardly in keeping with tradition when we recall footage of both Presidents Reagan and Carter attending moving ceremonies for soldiers lost during their terms of office.

The Pentagon has not been shy in the past of acknowledging the effect on public opinion that a casket draped in the Stars and Stripes can have on the public. In 1999, the then chairman of the Joint Chiefs of Staff, Army General Henry H Shelton, stated that a decision to use military force is based in part on whether it will pass 'the Dover test', as the public reacts to fatalities.

So there is a dilemma — how much should privacy be on parade? As a person in the occasional spotlight I wish to defend my right to a private life, but I would hate to find myself on the side of those who invoke privacy as a useful catch-all to manipulate the truth. Answers on a postcard please. ❏

Sandi Toksvig is a writer and broadcaster

BAD HABITS IN BAGHDAD

ROHAN JAYASEKERA

THE MANIFEST UNFAIRNESS OF MEDIA
CONTROLS IN IRAQ AND THE FAILURE OF
US-SPONSORED IRAQI MEDIA TO WIN A
RATINGS WAR AGAINST THEIR ARAB RIVALS
SET A BAD PRECEDENT FOR THE FUTURE

What's on the telly tonight in Iraq? Pretty much the same kind of things you might see on any state-run TV network in the Middle East: football, bought-in Egyptian soap operas, a *Sesame Street*-style puppet show for kids from the Gulf, re-re-run folk music shows from the 1980s. As for the news, there's a blank acceptance that it's all just propaganda, and that the real truth is, as ever, elsewhere.

The new Iraqi state TV is not hated, even if the country's mainstream Islamist SCIRI Party takes umbrage at the flirty California blondes in the straight-to-video action movies it shows late at night. By and large, the worst thing Iraqis can say about it is that it's sometimes boring and a bit amateurish.

Very familiar stuff indeed. Even Saddam Hussein's successor, US civilian chief L Paul Bremer III, has his predecessor's habit of pitching up on screen twice a week to deliver portentous speeches about the courage of the Iraqi people and their will to defy their enemies.

'You must not lose hope, because you have seen the evil one go,' Bremer told his audience in the week before Ramadan. 'You, the Iraqi people, whom the evil one was bound to protect, he instead tortured, he instead murdered. You, the Iraqi people, whom the evil one was bound to feed, he instead starved.'

Bremer's voice was overdubbed with Arabic and he was talking about Saddam, but you might have closed your eyes and wondered exactly who was speaking and who on earth was the 'evil one now gone' he kept citing. George Bush Sr perhaps?

The point is, of course, is that it's not supposed to be bad business as usual at Iraqi state TV. After the end of 'major combat operations' in Iraq, the US Defense Department hired one of their favourite contractors,

Science Applications International Corp (SAIC) to turn Saddam's state TV into George W Bush's.

Renamed the Iraqi Media Network, the new state TV was supposed to bring Western journalistic values, professionalism and independence to the country's media landscape. SAIC's failure to do that is well documented and, for all its scale, hardly surprising given that it had no relevant broadcast experience. For if you gave the contract to equip US Special Forces to the British Broadcasting Corporation, no doubt they would make as much of a pig's ear of that job as SAIC did of the job of running Iraqi TV and radio.

But the media has become *the* battleground in Iraq. A US State Department survey in October warned that audiences for Arab satellite channels were growing at the expense of the US-funded IMN. Among Iraqis reliant on terrestrial broadcast only 59 per cent depended on IMN for news. Where they had the dish and the choice they went for either Qatar-based al-Jazeera or the Saudi-financed al-Arabiya network for their news, a combined 63 per cent against just 12 per cent who tuned in to IMN news programming.

Economic crisis has left the average Iraqi very hard up, yet the US$200 dishes and kit are literally rolling out of the electrical goods shops that flank Baghdad's Karrada Dakhil boulevard; scores of dishes daily out of scores of stores. The US survey showed that a third of the country already had access to satellite TV and al-Jazeera, al-Arabiya and Abu Dhabi TV, plus the Iranian-based station al-Alam, and Hezbollah's al-Manar in Lebanon, the latter two firmly critical of the US-led occupation. If the paucity of the US-run alternative is not tackled, all their audiences look likely to go up.

So the media managers at the CPA are under orders to do better. Defense Secretary Donald H Rumsfeld told the *Washington Times* in October that the US had to contest extremist views directly and reverse the collapse in public support that the US has endured across the Middle East since 2000. 'We are in a war of ideas, as well as a global war on terror,' Rumsfeld said, adding that 'ideas are important, and they need to be marshalled, and they need to be communicated in ways that are persuasive to the listeners'.

US pollsters – the Pew Research Center for the People and the Press, Gallup, Zogby International – showed that despite their generally favourable view of democracy and globalisation, Muslim populations in the Middle East, Asia and Africa have deeply unfavourable views of the US, especially since this year's conflict. Disapproval of the US reached 95 per cent in Saudi Arabia, 91 per cent in Morocco and 99 per cent in Jordan.

Why? It's the policies, stupid. 'When we polled in Islamic countries a year ago,' John Zogby, president of Zogby International, told the US *National Journal*, 'we essentially found that a majority of Muslims still generally liked Americans, and many aspects of our culture – especially the younger generation under 30 years of age, who comprise 70 per cent of the Arab population – but they disliked our policies. When we poll in those same countries today, we find that they just don't like America, period. Muslim opinion of the US has just dropped off a cliff.'

Long before the US-led war on Iraq and 'regime change', US calls for democracy in the Middle East were tainted by long support for repressive regimes there. Rumsfeld's own shift, from Saddam's one-time oil trade partner and ally in the war on Iran to his vengeful foe, with the cruelty of sanctions in between, only underlines those double standards. And that's even before considering Washington's pro-Israeli stance in the conflict that really defines and defiles the region.

The roots of Islamic frustration are tangled and run too deep to be shifted by public relations, yet the determination of Washington to have a go regardless is fuelled by self-delusion. For example, David Abshire, president of the Center for the Study of the Presidency, writing in the foreword to his think tank's report, *An Initiative: Strengthening US–Muslim Communications*: 'Will America be labeled an invader and occupier, as well as a new target for converging terrorists? Or instead will America be called a liberator and become the bridge to a world of democratic ideas?'

Not been keeping up with current events? Or watching the Iraqi Media Network, perhaps? Unfortunately, since the policy is not up for negotiation, it is its presentation that has to change. 'Despite the best efforts of American officials, [Iraqi] media are not getting the US story,' says the State Department in its report on what it calls 'public diplomacy' in the Muslim world. It also urges the White House to 'provide for more coherent messaging and better overall coordination'. And more money too. 'In this time of peril, public diplomacy is absurdly and dangerously underfunded, and simply restoring it to its Cold War status is not enough. First and foremost, public diplomacy requires a new strategic direction.'

The State Department-commissioned report, issued in October, said it spent about US$600 million annually in promoting the US and US$540 million on broadcasting, but only US$25 million on programmes to influence the estimated 1.5 billion people in the Muslim world.

This is now going to change, starting with Iraq. The Pentagon, the State

Department's foe in all things to do with US policy in Iraq, has already blown over US$70 million on IMN alone so far, according to a highly placed media expert with the Iraqi Governing Council. Now the Pentagon has allocated another US$97 million for 2004 on new contracts to improve the professional standards at IMN (renamed al-Iraqiya by the CPA in November in a move that spoke volumes for the power of wishful thinking).

According to the call for interests, the proposed private contractor would have as 'objectives' the creation of 'quality' radio and television programming for the stations, television and film production facilities in 'each major region of Iraq' and training of an indigenous Iraqi workforce that would take over independent operation of the network within two years. One additional objective for the bidder, the proposal said, would be to show that the new IMN leads 'all mass media in providing comprehensive, accurate, fair and balanced news and public affairs to the Iraqi people'.

Some 29 international broadcasters, including the media development divisions of Britain's ITN and BBC TV networks, initially expressed interest in tendering for the contract to hold this particular poisoned chalice for up to two years. The lucky winner was due to be announced as *Index* went to press.

There may be an equally generously stuffed bag of cash on offer from the US State Department as it puts its plans for a 'public diplomacy' blitz into action under the direction of former State Department spokeswoman and US ambassador to Morocco Margaret Tutwiler, who took over the department's public diplomacy division late last year.

That will mean yet more money for what will almost certainly be a more professional operation, possibly even popular, if the Voice of America's existing Radio Sawa Arabic-language programmes are anything to go by. But independent? They'll never convince the Iraqis. The CPA's hands are on everything and that's the way it will stay.

The Iraqis are told: you are either with us or against us. It colours the entire debate on the future of Iraqi journalism with perceptions of collaboration. As Iraqis increasingly come to see the anti-US insurgents as resistance fighters, those who work for the CPA or with them have to come up with ever more ardent defences of their actions.

Western concepts of journalistic balance and independence, ideas of the kind that are traditionally central to most internationally organised media training programmes, are failing to take hold in the face of this reality.

Israa' Shakir, the personable and clever editor of the Baghdad weekly *Iraq al-Youm*, worked hard for six months to find imaginative ways to maintain balance and independence for her paper, which unlike so many other new Iraqi papers lacked the support of a political party or a millionaire with political ambitions. She took US military press releases and marked them up like paid-for ads to distinguish them from her staff's own work and she challenged the US press spokesmen to come out from their bunkers and put their side of the story to the reports of abuse and incompetence the paper was carrying.

But the US press releases, news of good deeds in orphanages and friendly football games, grew ever more disconnected from the reality around them. It got harder to get the US official comments that her paper needed to add the journalistic balance that the US demands but fails to take the steps to facilitate.

The US officials themselves, inaccessible to Western journalists, let alone Iraqi ones, further retreated behind the CPA HQ security walls in the face of the worsening security situation. Now even the routine journalistic practice of 'getting the other side of the story' looks dangerously like tolerance of an occupation that a growing majority of Iraqis want to end sooner rather than later. At worst, to a well-armed and murderous few, it looks like collaboration.

The collaborator's tag is a powerful weapon in the hands of the unscrupulous. The gaggle of unreformed Ba'athist era hacks who dominate the country's Journalists' Syndicate have held up reform of the one body that should be taking a lead in the development of an independent, professional Iraqi media. The creation of an alternative new and independent journalists' union is being guided by Ismail Zayir, editor of *al-Sabah*, the US-financed national newspaper produced under the aegis of the IMN. He endures pages of poisonous abuse for this perceived 'crime'. His claims to independence are hopelessly qualified by his connections.

Worse, Zayir's supporters have to strike a balance between negotiation with the old union and making a declaration of independence. The Iraqi media urgently needs a system of self-regulation to allow its best people to deal with their bad journalists and protect their good ones. Led by Simon Haselock, the UK official who ran a similar system in Kosovo, the British officials within the CPA initially lobbied for the creation of some sort of press council to do just that.

But in Iraq, the responsibility for media self-regulation is enshrined in law and clearly given to the existing syndicate. It is bad news for Zayir's allies to be seen to flout Iraqi law, no matter how badly it was abused by the old membership. Haselock and the CPA may not be able to reform it; by accepting the mantle of occupiers, they also accept the authority of the Geneva Convention, which limits changes in the occupied nation's laws to the minimum necessary to maintain public order.

Issues such as this have led to a degree of soul-searching by the non-governmental organisations – *Index on Censorship* included – that normally take the lead in supporting independent media development in post-war societies. Normally, the burden of duty is shared between these non-profits or public charities – generally US, British, Dutch and Canadian – funded by private trusts, semi-governmental and fully governmental agencies from around the world. This was the case in the Balkans and Afghanistan.

Al-Sabah *editor Ismail Zayir pilloried in a paper supporting the Iraqi Journalists' Syndicate. The passer-by is saying: 'Now that's what I call an American union.'*
Credit: al-Zawra'

In Iraq, the security problems that effectively drove out stalwarts such as the Red Cross and the United Nations have also kept most media development NGOs out of the country. One of the largest and most experienced, the US NGO Internews, started the process of guiding the reform of the Iraqi media with a major conference in Athens supported by funding from USAID, only to find the process quickly stymied by the realities on the ground in Iraq. BBC training programmes in the southern Iraqi city of Basra, considered by the average Baghdadi a haven of peace, good shopping and reliable public utilities, were suspended during the autumn on security grounds.

There are still plans in hand. Haselock's team have drafted a proposal for a media training strategy while the United Nations Development Fund has already financed the opening of a well-equipped centre under the direction of Iraqi journalists (though it is not clear where the wherewithal for its actual training activities will come from without the active participation of other donors and foreign media development NGOs).

The University of Baghdad's journalism faculty, once no more than a rest home for deadbeat Ba'athist lecturers (mostly graduates from the University of Moscow, class of '74), is re-establishing its credentials as a future seedbed for a new Iraqi media under the new guidance of former political prisoner Hashim Hassan. And the London-based Institute for War & Peace Reporting is elaborating a proposal to establish a centre, with funding from the UK Department for International Development, that it hopes will emulate a centre for media development run with great success in Afghanistan in the year after the US war there.

There are all too obvious dangers in the operation of such venues in a city where the men that George W Bush calls 'suiciders' drive truckloads of explosive looking for soft targets. But the dangers of guilt by association present more complex obstacles to media development.

Index on Censorship runs its media development projects in Iraq in the context of its longterm programme to establish an independent edition of the magazine in Arabic, *Marsad Hurriyat Atta'beer*, published in the Middle East. Its emphasis is on freedom of expression as a right that is at the centre of professional journalistic responsibilities in the Middle East. The courses are led and primarily devised by Arab journalists with strong track records in both the media and in the active defence of human rights at home. They are living proof that free expression is as relevant and important to the Arab journalist as to anyone else.

Media assistance programmes in Iraq, indeed anywhere, must pay more attention to the newsroom than the classroom, must support independent professional bodies, must encourage self-regulation and self-criticism and must defend journalists against unbridled censorship. But maintaining the credibility and the viability of Western media development initiatives is wholly dependent on the ability of NGOs to separate themselves in practice and principle from the occupation authorities, and to be seen to do so.

Index on Censorship has in the past called for UNESCO to assign an official, working independently of the CPA and the coalition governments, to take the lead in facilitating consensus on strategy between the various media development NGOs planning work in Iraq. Another useful innovation might be a newswire service in Arabic and Kurdish for the optional use of the Iraqi media. Such a news source, even if funded by a coalition partner state, need not be totally compromised. An Arabic version of the Reuter Foundation's online Alertnet bulletin for aid NGOs, covering civil reconstruction in Iraq in all its forms but not shying from hard criticism, could inspire Iraqi journalists to better work in different areas.

Meanwhile, the British Foreign Office, which partially supports *Index*'s work in Iraq through its Human Rights Programmes Fund, is looking seriously at the problems of NGOs that have to work alongside the military there.

This is not a new debate – for emergency aid NGOs in particular – but it is complicated in Iraq by the fact that the troops on whom they may depend for protection are not UN-mandated Blue Berets, but troops of their own or allied nations that are still in combat. The use of armed guards – some Westerners who are virtual mercenaries, and some who are associated with specific Iraqi factions – by a few US journalists and even one or two NGOs further blurs the distinction.

But the biggest hurdle facing media development NGOs in Iraq is the problem of double standards. For all their work advocating professionalism, independence and freedom of speech is undone daily by the continuing bad example set by the CPA itself.

Citing the CPA's Public Order 14, the coalition has already come down hard on half a dozen of the scores of newspapers that were set up in Iraq after April. Papers found guilty of incitement to violence face closure and seizure of equipment, and their staff face possible detention.

Naturally, the targets deny the charges. Baghdad staff from al-Alam satellite TV, which also broadcasts terrestrially from Iran, complained to *Index* of a series of raids on spurious grounds on their office by US forces in Iraq. Among the restraints, they were banned from doing pieces to camera from the office roof, with its pleasant view of the River Tigris, in case US forces on the other side might be seen in the background.

Two Iranian journalists working for state-run television spent four months in US detention on suspicion of espionage. Meanwhile, Reporters Sans Frontières notes that the detention of Iraqi journalists by US troops is becoming routine, the allegations are always left vague and the detainees are usually released after a few days without charge.

Another lesson learned from the US is that political muscle works. Iraqi journalists watched as al-Jazeera's staff, too often the target of deadly fire from the US military, bowed under the weight of diplomatic pressure on its

home government in Qatar and chose not to air several Osama bin Laden tapes. It also pulled website cartoons that the White House said were offensive; this followed the dismissal of al-Jazeera general manager Mohamed Jassem, apparently engineered by the US a few days after Bush's visit to Qatar in May.

Unsurprisingly, the US-endorsed Iraqi Governing Council, which has expressed its desire to exert more control over the Iraqi media, also took a lead from the CPA's example by issuing their own unfair and legally suspect orders against al-Jazeera and al-Arabiya TV. Both were told that they were 'endangering stability and democracy' and 'encouraging terrorism' by their reporting, and that their work in Iraq would be controlled for a two-week period in October. The orders were delivered in person by the Governing Council's Ahmed Chalabi, a sworn foe of al-Jazeera. This reinforced the view that personal agendas were at work.

On 24 November, the council again banned al-Arabiya from reporting from Baghdad, in punishment for what it called 'incitement to murder', after the station broadcast an audiotape on 16 November purportedly made by Saddam Hussein.

Front page of Al-Mustaquilla, *Baghdad,
July 2003. Top headline:
'Saddam's head found near
Jordanian border.' Lower
headline: 'What is really
happening in Falujah?
Does the toppled regime
have anything to do with
the resistance?' This edition
led to a US Army raid,
the temporary closure of the
paper and a two-week spell
in detention for the editor
Abdulsattar al-Shaalan,
under the CPA's Order 14.
Credit: al-Mustaquilla*

The wider allegation was that the Arab satellite stations were in cahoots
with the insurgents. Rumsfeld alleges he has seen evidence to that effect but
has declined to produce it. He told reporters that anti-coalition forces had
called al-Arabiya and al-Jazeera to say: 'Come and see us, watch us; here is
what we are going to do.' However, he added: 'I'm not in a position to
make a final judgement on it.' The problem is, no one is. Whatever
happened to due process? Where was the networks' right to hear the
evidence that supported the charge that their journalists incite terrorism?
Where was their right to appeal?

International Federation of Journalists secretary-general Aidan White
warns that such moves only 'play into the hands of the enemies of democracy by imposing the sort of censorship that was a hallmark of Saddam
Hussein's odious regime'.

It also sets a precedent that may never be reversed, a bitter gift to the
people of Iraq from the nation that drafted the First Amendment. ❑

Rohan Jayasekera *is associate editor of* Index on Censorship *and is currently
directing the charity's independent media support programmes in Iraq*

PLAGUES WE HAVE KNOWN
FELIPE FERNÁNDEZ-ARMESTO

THROUGHOUT HISTORY, HUMANITY HAS BEEN
BEST BY PLAGUES THAT HAVE DEVASTATED
POPULATIONS, RUINED ECONOMIES AND
BROUGHT STATES AND RULERS TO THE VERGE
OF COLLAPSE. IS AIDS DIFFERENT? OR DOES
HISTORY HAVE SOMETHING TO TEACH US?

Aids is 'the worst calamity to hit mankind since the fourteenth century', says the Secretary-General of the United Nations. The language is meant to evoke the horrors of the Black Death: 'medieval plague' is a phrase calculated to shame us into action over Aids, rather as Michael Buerk's 'biblical famine' helped conjure a response to starvation in Africa in the 1980s.

But is the image coined by the Secretary-General more useful than that? Does it point towards an instructive precedent, with lessons for our present plight, or a helpful context, which might enable us to understand what is happening? Historical precedent is no consolation to the dead and dying. But a little historical perspective might help the living to cope.

There are some striking parallels between Aids and the Black Death – above all, in the way they were perceived when they struck. Both cued instant *Schadenfreude* from moralists. They were scourges of God: in Christendom, the Black Death was a general summons to repentance; in Islam, a reward for wickedness. Voices from America's 'moral majority' actually welcomed Aids with something sickeningly close to glee, as a 'judgement' on practitioners of promiscuous and perverse sex. Both diseases excited millenarian fantasies of a world winnowed of the wicked and improved for those meritorious enough to survive. Both visitations tethered scapegoats for sacrifice to popular anxiety. In the case of the Black Death, Jews supposedly poisoned wells. With Aids, blame bloomed like buboes. Homosexuals were victims of its first eruptions: there were better grounds for linking Aids with gays than the Black Death with Jews, because gay sex lives genuinely multiplied the chances of contagion. But the tendency to identify Aids as a gay affliction proved exaggerated and seemed unfair, so the accusations switched targets. Aids got reclassified as a curse 'out of Africa', supposedly originating in bestiality and spread by sexual slavery. Its diffusion and perpetuation – to even out the arraignments – were the fault of Western drugs companies, who withheld cures or ratcheted up costs. Or the governments of the worst afflicted countries were to blame – South Africa especially – for defying medical counsel and declining to get involved in their citizens' sex lives.

All these reactions were understandable; some even had some utility. It is true, for instance, that chastity is a useful preventive against Aids. Repentance – though no cure for the Black Death – must have helped some of its victims to die happily or to lead better lives on recovery. But in both cases, scientific urgency to find causes and cures soon displaced sententious outrage about grievances and guilt. As Samuel K Cohn has shown in a brilliant recent book (*The Black Death Transformed*, Hodder Arnold, 2003), moralistic explanations of disease were hardly more convincing to most people in the fourteenth century than they are today, and dispassionate medical enquiry soon took over from the self-indulgence of the breast-beaters. Every culture had its cure. In Cairo, they smeared the boils with Armenian clay. In Andalusia, Ibn Khatib advised abstention from corn, cheese, mushrooms and garlic. Decoctions of barley water and syrup of basil were widely prescribed. The Turks sliced off the heads of the pustules and extracted green glands. Prayer was a universal placebo; but professional responses were markedly different from place to place. Only rigorous quarantine measures really worked, most famously when the infected village of Eyam in Derbyshire undertook voluntary isolation to prevent the spread of plague to the neighbouring communities.

In short, no one really understood the pathology of the Black Death: we still don't. Books have been devoted to a fierce, inconclusive and probably pointless controversy among historical epidemiologists about whether it can properly be classified as a form of what we now call bubonic plague. Again the parallels with Aids are irresistible. The deficiencies of our attempts to treat it arise from our uncertainty about what it is. With Aids, too, prevention has been the most effective strategy. Yet the Black Death receded. The likelihood that it was conquered either by prevention or cure seems negligible. So what did happen to check it?

There are three plausible explanations on the table. First, most scholars in the field tend to think it raged unchecked for hundreds of years and that many or most of the episodes called 'plague', in densely populated areas of the globe, from the fourteenth century to the eighteenth, were recurrences of the same pestilence. This seems improbable. 'Plague' was a catch-all name for a startlingly diverse array of syndromes, which occurred in widely differing environments, at widely separated seasons. After the Black Death, no visitation ever again rivalled it for reach or virulence. In any case, the claim that the same plague recurred at intervals until the eighteenth century only postpones the problem. What was special about the eighteenth century? The usual answer is that improved nutrition, hygiene and medical expertise drove pestilence away. This must be false. Urbanisation bred ever more insanitary conditions, even in the most technically ambitious and sophisticated societies, until well into the nineteenth century. An age of typhus and cholera succeeded the 'age of plague'. Nutrition did improve over much of the world in the relevant period, thanks to the worldwide 'ecological exchange' of biota, which increased farmers' options and extended the amount and yield of cultivable land; but early industrialisation marked a backward step for the diet of the poor of the West, while increased food production could not keep pace with population growth in China and India. As for medical improvements, there were some of enormous benefit in containing specific diseases – most significantly, in combating smallpox – but most medicine remained bodged and ignorant, and nothing that was new affected the plague.

Natural immunisation is the second explanation for the retreat of plague. This is plausible. Lethal diseases kill off those susceptible to them and spare those with a genetic disposition to resistance. So each generation grows in immunity. Sammy Cohn argues that the Black Death was a one-off disease, too successful for its own survival. It killed off so many of its human hosts that it was left with no one to attack. The Black Death died.

This raises a third possibility. The demise of plague could be like most other forms of species extinction: a product of evolution. The micro-organisms that bear disease are more volatile, more mutable, than other, bigger organisms because they are individually short-lived. They go through many generations in a relatively short space of time. So species come and go with far greater rapidity in the microbial world than among the great, lumbering organisms whose evolution we normally observe. We think of evolution as a slow-working process. Microbes experience it fast. Those that kill off their hosts are obviously not adaptively successful: they need to find new eco-niches to ensure their own survival or they are self-condemned to disappear. For reasons we do not know – but which must be connected with their own evolutionary advantage – hostile micro-organisms may

1348, The Black Death: English School. Credit: Bridgeman Art Library

sometimes switch their attention away from one set of victims and find another. Or evolve less virulent strains, as did syphilis. Historically, our improving health may owe less than we suppose to our own cleverness and more to the changing habits and nature of microbes.

One of the great merits of this theory is that, if true, it explains an otherwise puzzling feature of historical epidemiology. Historians used to mislead their readers by assuming that we ought to be able to identify the plagues of the past in terms of modern diagnostics. (In reality, it is usually impossible to recognise diseases from historical records. In most cultures, in most periods, it is misleading to suppose that the symptoms people noticed were of the sort physicians would emphasise today. They might describe them differently. What is presumed to be the same disease looks and sounds different in different cultural contexts.) In any case, the microbiology of disease defies historical analysis. We do not know – or, at least, specialist scholars cannot agree – what the plague of Athens was, or the Black Death, or the disease that enfeebled the Aztecs at the time of their conquest by Spain. Maybe these – or some of them, or others equally hard to identify – were one-off visitations by micro-biota which then became extinct or mutated unrecognisably. There certainly have been historically documented cases of the disappearance of old diseases and the sudden appearance of new ones. The waning of leprosy and the rise of tuberculosis in late medieval and early modern Europe are the most thoroughly studied examples. Syphilis is another possible candidate: neither the theory that it is of great antiquity in Europe nor the claim that it was transmitted from long-established heartlands in the New World quite matches the evidence now available. The epidemiology of influenza is full of cases of new strains arising and mutating too rapidly for medical science to keep up. Type II diabetes may be another case of a disease without long-term historical precedents. We are always creating new eco-niches in which new diseases can develop or old ones grow in virulence: salmonella in chicken batteries, legionnaires' disease in air-conditioning systems, Type II diabetes in over-nourished populations, West Nile Fever in New York. Lhasa fever, Ebola and Sars have all shown remarkable agility in leaping the limits of their environments of origin. To judge from the history of BSE and new-variant CJD, prions seem even more subject to sudden change than bacteria and viruses.

Aids seems to be such a case. Historians have tried to track it into the remote past without success. It is a product of rapid and sudden evolution – a disease extemporised by history. Its profile seems to have changed while we have had it under observation. Is this a cause of comfort? Can we rely on plagues always to recede, glutted with victims, or yield to growing human immunity? Rather than rush to answer those questions, we should ask another: how ready are we to cope with the threat of rapid microbial evolution? Aids does not, at present, look like a disaster on the scale of the Black Death, though in some regions its demographic effects could yet be comparable. But it has shown us how vulnerable we are to new diseases, or old diseases in new forms, which can take us unawares and for which we are ill-prepared by the current research strategies favoured by governments and industry – for electoral politics and the profit motive both concentrate effort on reacting to disease rather than on fundamental research into the obscurities of microbial evolution.

If a new Black Death were to hit us, what would we do? It could happen. If the next pestilence were no more virulent than that of the fourteenth century, we might fare better than our predecessors six and a half centuries ago, because our information-sharing technology is so efficient, our means of response so much more rapid; or we might fare worse, because our means of imposing quarantine are so much more leaky in our interconnected world. ❏

Felipe Fernández-Armesto is the author of Civilisations *(Macmillan) and teaches at Queen Mary College, University of London, where he is professor of global environmental history*

APOCALYPSE
THE TRUE STORY OF AIDS

WE ALL KNOW THE SHOCKING STATISTIC:
40 MILLION PEOPLE AROUND THE WORLD
LIVING WITH HIV/AIDS. THE STORIES OUT
OF AFRICA, THE PRESENT EPICENTRE OF
THE DISEASE, ARE TRAGIC AND OFTEN
COLOURED BY A SENSE OF HOPELESSNESS
IN THE FACE OF OUR MODERN PLAGUE:
'THE BLACK DEATH OF OUR CENTURY'.
BUT SO MUCH REMAINS UNKNOWN,
UNSPOKEN. 'INDEX' GOES BEHIND
THE STATISTICS, BREAKS THE
SILENCE AND HOLDS
CULPRITS TO
ACCOUNT

GUEST EDITOR
ALEX DE WAAL

Uganda: Aids orphan and grandfather.
Credit: Giacomo Pirozzi / Panos Pictures

STATISTICS

The statistics running along the bottom of the pages in this issue of *Index* give a general picture of the global impact of the HIV/Aids pandemic. However, the value of such data is tempered both by the limitations of inferring general statistics from at-risk groups when these do not 'officially' exist, and by the paucity of monitoring, or sentinel, sites in regions where the epidemic is acknowledged. Aid organisations in the regions affected in the first wave of the epidemic, such as southern Africa, have established a network of sentinel sites, located mainly in maternity centres, where women are tested for the virus and, if proved HIV-positive, can be questioned about their sexual history to indicate primary modes of infection. In contrast, India's failure to acknowledge its high number of sex workers and intravenous drug users has resulted in official figures underestimating the number of infected, possibly by as many as 6 million. Political and cultural sensitivity in China has led to outright denial of practices such as unlicensed blood selling that generated China's own rise in cases. As a result, estimates of the full scale of the Indian and Chinese epidemics can only be inferred from reported cases. ❑

Compiled by Jason Pollard

40m people live with HIV/Aids: women 19.2m, children under 15 years 3.2m | WOMEN: in Western Europe in 2001 women represented c26% (140,000) of all HIV cases; North America 20% (190,000); Latin America 31% (430,000); South

EVERYTHING YOU EVER WANTED
TO KNOW...

ALEX DE WAAL

. . . ABOUT AIDS TODAY AND TOMORROW.
HIV/AIDS THREATENS THE SURVIVAL
OF ENTIRE SOCIETIES IN AFRICA
AND IS MOVING ON TO CREATE NEW
EPICENTRES IN RUSSIA AND ASIA

HIV/Aids is destined to be an ineradicable part of the human condition for the next hundred years. Unlike recent historic epidemics and wars, which kill for a period of time and then recede, HIV/Aids will be akin to the devastation of a war in each and every generation. It is much, much more than a humanitarian tragedy. Future historians will draw a line at the last decades of the twentieth century, when the world passed from 'pre-Aids' to the era of Aids. But the subject of this unpleasant and stigmatised disease has, for the most part, drawn at best humanitarian responses and at worst indifference and outright denial.

At the very dawn of the pandemic in 1983, the American gay activist Larry Kramer opened a column:

> If this article doesn't scare the shit out of you we're in real trouble. If this article doesn't rouse you to anger, fury, rage and action, gay men have no future on this earth. Our continued existence depends on just how angry you can get.

In the 1980s, America's gay community was devastated by Aids, but its angry mobilisation forced a scientific and political response. The doomsday scenarios projected by some UK and US public health officers didn't materialise. Today, when entire societies in southern Africa are imperilled by HIV/Aids and tens of millions are likely to be infected in Eastern Europe

and South-East Asia 37% (2 million); Caribbean 53% (210,000), sub-Saharan Africa 58% (15 million) | 90% of women with HIV do not know that they are infected | Women are statistically more likely to die from HIV/Aids; more than

A hospice in Uganda, the only country in sub-Saharan Africa to provide palliative patient care within its health servcies. Credit: Penny Tweedie / Panos Pictures

and Asia, the worst really is coming true. But there is astonishingly little anger, fury and rage; and far too little action.

Human immunodeficiency virus and acquired immune deficiency syndrome (HIV/Aids) is the first global pandemic of an inscrutable acronym. For many people, confusion over the disease begins with its nomenclature. The label 'Aids', still less 'HIV', carries none of the resonance of words such as 'plague'. It is also well disguised, carrying off its victims through a panoply of familiar conditions such as tuberculosis and pneumonia. In southern Africa, where about one-quarter of all adults are currently living with the virus – giving today's teenagers a worse-than-evens chance of contracting HIV and dying of Aids during their lifetimes – the epidemic is still only rarely publicly announced as a cause of death. In September 2003, South Africa's President Thabo Mbeki said he did not know of anyone who had died of Aids.

In Uganda, the first country where HIV/Aids reached epidemic proportions among the general population (perhaps 12 per cent in 1992), and where war and dictatorship have bred an ironic sense of humour, it was

50% of those who have died are women | HIV/Aids now ranks as one of the leading causes of death among women aged 20–40 in several cities in Europe, sub-Saharan Africa and North America | In 2002 2.5m adults died of HIV/Aids:

popularly known as 'slim'. In Swaziland, which vies for first place in the league of stricken countries (adult prevalence estimated at 38 per cent), many people refer to it as 'the Beast'. The drawback of seeing Aids as 'the Beast' is the apocalyptic religious resonance it holds. On the other hand, a secular 'Beast' is a challenge to our species of a Darwinian nature. In *The Songlines*, Bruce Chatwin hypothesised that in our early evolution, *Homo sapiens* had confronted a specialised big cat predator on humans, perhaps co-inhabitor of the caves that were our domestic niche, against which we struggled for millennia and ultimately prevailed.

HIV is a specialised parasite of an unusually cunning kind. At the level of cell, organism and collectivity, it subverts our basic mechanisms. Micro-biologists understand only too well how the virus uses the human body's own defences as its mechanism for reproduction. Together with its tendency to mutation and recombination (different clades of HIV present in the same individual producing new strains), this means it is free from evolutionary pressure towards less virulent strains. It utilises our most basic drive – sex and reproduction – for its own transmission. It infects rich and poor alike, but poor and dislocated countries are more vulnerable to the epidemic.

Because of the average eight- to ten-year lag between infection and developing Aids, HIV has the capacity for reaching saturation in a human population without killing its host so quickly that it endangers its own survival – thereby neatly avoiding another evolutionary pressure towards lower virulence. And it is now becoming clear that HIV at epidemic level also creates the conditions conducive for it to be sustained at saturation level. Although the sociological epidemiology of HIV/Aids is still a rudi-mentary science, it is clear that social inequality, migration, high levels of transactional sex and poor educational achievement are all factors that leave a society more susceptible to an Aids epidemic. Unfortunately for us, a high-prevalence generalised HIV/Aids epidemic creates secondary effects – hunger, large numbers of orphans and pressure to take children out of school – which have precisely this impact on the affected society.

This is possibly the future of Swaziland. From the point of view of the virus, prevalence is close to the optimal level at which the great majority of the population will contract it during their lifetimes. Most adults will die in

1.2m were women; 610,000 children | HIV/Aids kills more adults in their economically active years,15–49, than in any other age group | Every minute six people under the age of 24 become infected with HIV | In 2002 5m new

their twenties or thirties, making it extraordinarily difficult, if not impossible, to sustain the institutions essential for a modern society. The poverty, disorder and demoralisation this entails will, in turn, create more receptive conditions for the onward transmission of HIV. For Swaziland, tackling HIV/Aids is a question of national survival. But the government is still half-hearted and bewildered. And how can it mount an effective response when its health workers are dying more quickly than they can be trained?

One of the many peculiar ironies here is that the funds needed for Africa's health services to prevent HIV and treat Aids, while bigger than all existing health budgets, are tiny in global terms. US$20 billion a year would double international assistance to Africa, but is minuscule compared to the budget of the Pentagon (US$400 billion) or what US women spend on cosmetics (higher still). This disparity is 'a grotesque obscenity', in the words of Stephen Lewis, UN special envoy for Aids in Africa.

In short, the HIV/Aids pandemic is a question of the survival of some entire societies, but is still just a blip on the charitable radar screen of the rich world. Will this change as the numbers of people living with HIV and Aids in Russia and Asia surpass today's epicentre, Africa? Or will Europe and the US be content to 'manage' the pandemic, trying to make it as little a threat as possible to themselves?

It has been tempting for political leaders to declare 'war' on Aids. For example, stirring commitments were made by African leaders meeting in Addis Ababa, Ethiopia, for a conference on 'Aids: Africa's Greatest Leadership Challenge' in December 2000. Mark Malloch-Brown, administrator of the United Nations Development Programme, was committed to putting his agency on 'a war footing' in the struggle against HIV/Aids. Three years on, there is no doubt who is winning this war. If today's string of inglorious and mostly unacknowledged defeats continues, the next generation in Africa will be Aids' dominion. Major epidemics are developing in India, China, Russia and Ukraine, each with its own characteristics. Thus far, though large numbers are involved, these epidemics have been confined to certain groups such as intravenous drug users and commercial sex workers; but it would be an act of reckless optimism to assume that they cannot spread to the general population (Aids in Russia p162).

HIV/Aids infections occurred, 800,000 in children under 15; 75% of new infections are sexually transmitted | More than 13m children under the age of 15 have been orphaned by HIV/Aids; this is projected to double by 2010 | Only

The global numbers living with HIV and Aids have risen from about 36 million in December 2000 to over 40 million today. They are still rising and, as the Asian epidemics begin to accelerate, it is quite possible that we may be contemplating numbers in the hundreds of millions in a decade or so. Even if everything is done right – medical progress, 'best practice' prevention policies, a flood of new resources – these figures will get considerably worse before they improve.

On the scientific front, HIV has been more intensively studied than any pathogen in history. There have been impressive advances. The development of simplified anti-retroviral drugs (ARVs) has reduced the death rate from Aids in rich countries and could potentially do the same in poor countries, given the dramatic drop in their price in the past 12 months. ARVs do not cure Aids, they merely lengthen the lives of those infected. They have unpleasant side effects. They require complicated monitoring for viral loads. But in rich countries, ARVs have transformed Aids from a death sentence to something akin to a chronic ailment, like diabetes.

A cure or a vaccine for HIV/Aids remain elusively just over the horizon of realistic medical expectations. In the epidemic's early years, there was blithe optimism that a magic bullet would quickly be found. And, once a reliable test for the virus was discovered, the screening of blood supplies almost completely eradicated transmission through blood transfusions, so that the mass infection of haemophiliacs and surgical patients became a tragic but transient episode in the pandemic. Faith in medical science may have retarded investment in humbler preventive technologies (such as microbicides, which reduce the risk of a woman absorbing the virus through her vagina), needle-exchange programmes for injecting drug users and inventive ways of promoting the still humbler condom. Medical research continues to consume the great majority of funds devoted to the intellectual struggle against HIV/Aids. Much more is known about the virological complexities of HIV than the sexual networks and practices that have created the conditions for a generalised epidemic in sub-Saharan Africa.

Many believe that no vaccine will ever exist; others that, in time, a partially effective vaccine may be developed. Even if there are medical breakthroughs, we can be confident they will be available first to the rich

5% of those in need of anti-retroviral (ARV) therapy currently receive the treatment | In southern Africa only 1% (c50,000) receive ARVs | In southern Africa HIV/Aids medications can cost up to US$400 per month in a region where

and well connected, and only later, if at all, to the poor and remote. This pattern is clear already in the distribution of anti-retroviral treatment. The moral case for ARVs focuses first on equity – life should not be beyond the purchasing power of people who happen to be poor – and second on the social benefits that follow from keeping the productive population of an affected country alive for longer. For example, the prevention of mother-to-child transmission of HIV (PMTCT) is of limited value if the HIV-positive mother of the infected child falls sick and dies, leaving the child an orphan. Hence 'PMTCT plus' is currently the 'best practice' for HIV/Aids programmes: provide the mother with ARVs to keep her alive and prevent her child from becoming an orphan. In reality, however, mothers, especially poor women in rural areas, are at the end of the queue for treatment. It is the skilled staff of multinational companies, army officers, senior civil servants and professionals who are first in line. As the World Health Organisation rolls out its '3 by 5' initiative that aims to get 3 million people in the developing world on ARVs by 2005, equity will loom large.

Visitors to the website of the Joint UN Programme on HIV/Aids (UNAids) will find a section dedicated to 'best practices'. This gives a reassuring impression that not only are there tried and tested methods of HIV prevention, but that some of them have proved to be 'best'. An abiding theme of any institutional audit of Aids-prevention policies and programmes will be that such policies and programmes can be assessed and evaluated, but there is very little evidence that any of them have had any demonstrable success at bringing down rates of HIV transmission. It is a sad reality that, except in Uganda, national policies aimed at Aids prevention have failed to make an impact in any high-prevalence country. And Uganda's success is solitary, intriguing and controversial: was it because of President Museveni's outspoken frankness about the disease? Because of promoting abstinence and faithfulness (as today's religious right in the US insists)? Or chiefly because the end of the war in 1986 stabilised society, causing people to leave the cities for villages and enabling young women to stay in school? Only in the past two years have social scientists and epidemiologists begun to test these hypotheses. Meanwhile, programmes are designed and projects implemented on the basis of an amalgam of project experience, a handful of

290m live on less than US$1 per day | Of the 5m infants born with HIV/Aids since 1990, 90% have been born in sub-Saharan Africa | In 1984 only 1% of women in Brazil were HIV-positive – in 1994 the rate was 25% | There are an

studies and ideological preference. Much 'best practice' means little more than redefining 'success' to mean 'where we're at'.

Ironically, it's extraordinarily simple to prevent HIV transmission: tackle the highest-risk factors such as untreated sexually transmitted infections and the early age of sexual debut for girls, and make condom use universal outside mutually faithful long-term sexual partnerships. But it has proved extraordinarily difficult to get men to put on a condom. While ignorance is a factor, especially in rural areas, many men who know perfectly well how they may contract the virus still refuse to use a condom. Some HIV-positive men, protected by their right to privacy, are knowingly putting their partners at risk.

In a court case in Britain in October 2003, an HIV-positive man was found guilty of 'biological' grievous bodily harm after deliberately infecting two women, having made specious arguments as to why he should not use a condom. He was sentenced to eight years' imprisonment. This was the first such case to reach the courts since a conviction for deliberately spreading a venereal disease in 1866, and has proved instantly controversial. Opponents of the decision to prosecute argue that 'the real crime is the stigmatisation of people living with HIV'.

Certainly, there are real fears of deterring people from being tested and admitting HIV-positive status whenever someone living with HIV is prosecuted. But in sub-Saharan Africa, where the overwhelming responsibility for HIV transmission rests with heterosexual men who are abusing their position of power over women, there is a powerful argument that the duty of not infecting should prevail. They may be victims of adverse global power relations, but in the specific situation in which the virus is transmitted, heterosexual men are not victims.

A recent book by Cathy Campbell, *Letting Them Die: Why HIV Prevention Programmes Fail* (James Currey, Oxford, 2003), addressed this question of why so many people knowingly engage in sexual practices that run a serious risk of leading to a slow and painful death. Campbell studied a South African mining township, working among miners, commercial sex workers and schoolchildren. For most women, the answer is simple: knowledge counts for nothing when women have no power in sexual encounters, and

estimated 6–10m intravenous drug users worldwide | In countries with an adult prevalence rate of over 15%, 33% of 15-year-olds will become infected with HIV/Aids | The Global Fund To Fight Aids, Tuberculosis and Malaria has

when sex with a condom commands a significantly lower price than sex without. For miners, the dangers of unprotected sex may be an irrelevance – death in a decade's time may seem remote compared with the risks and hardships borne every day underground; the risk-taking may even be part of what constitutes their masculine identity. Meanwhile, migrant workers' lives are rough and lonely, leaving 'skin-to-skin' sexual contact – even in a brief, commercial, open-air encounter – the sole marker of intimacy. And for both sex worker and client, alcohol increases the tolerance for day-to-day life but decreases the practice of safer sex.

A last reason for the difficulty of containing Aids in high-prevalence countries is that HIV transmission is over-determined. When one-quarter or more of the adult population is HIV-positive at any one time, the chances are that any single individual will contract HIV not once but several times in her or his lifetime. The level of behavioural change needed to stop the epidemic is extraordinarily high, and infection so widespread that most people treat HIV simply as an occupational hazard of life. Indeed, they ask, is it worth living to a lonely old age if all one's peers have died?

We are not facing a one-off loss of adults, as might occur with a war. We are facing a sustained truncation of life chances, in which most young people cannot expect to live to see their grandchildren, save enough money to own a house, build a career. Complex societies and economies rest on the unexamined pillar of a 'normal' adult life. Four decades of adulthood provide opportunities to save, invest, acquire and transmit skills; two decades of adulthood don't. Shorter careers mean staff with less experience and skill, and narrower networks. Companies in southern Africa are finding that they need to train two (or more) people for every post they need filled, expecting a large number to fall sick and die of Aids. This doesn't only increase training and payroll costs, it also demands new management styles. Running an Aids-impacted institution may be more akin to mobilising students for union activism than administering a university, relying on people with a lifetime of experience and a wide-ranging peer group to match.

One of the simplest and most basic lessons to learn from the HIV/Aids epidemic is that the past is not a reliable guide to the future. The reasons for this are simple: we are on the upward slope of two curves. The first is HIV

awarded grants totaling US$2.1bn to 224 programmes in 121 countries over two years, 60% for Africa to combat HIV/Aids | The Global Fund has attracted

Zambia: Aids orphan
Ndola. Credit: Jeremy
Horner / Panos Pictures

prevalence and the second, lagging almost a decade behind, is Aids deaths. Although we are 20 years into the HIV pandemic, we are only at the beginning of global Aids deaths. We have an increasing array of scholarly studies on the impact of Aids at community level, but we have yet to learn what it means to try to run a country when the majority of its adults can expect to contract HIV.

Unlike the microbiologists, the institutions mandated to 'fight' Aids are not doing well. Ministries of health, aid donors, World Bank, UNAids have all scored successes in building their infrastructure, but on the battlefield itself the tide has been virtually one-way.

The World Bank's Multi-country Assistance Program for HIV/Aids (MAP) is a case in point. Initiated in January 2001 to provide funds for African governments, it had disbursed about US$800 million by the middle of 2003. Of this, less than 15 per cent had actually been spent. The main problem is the capacity of African ministries of health. After decades of austerity measures and low salaries, exacerbated by the loss of staff due to the brain drain and Aids itself, the human infrastructure simply isn't in place to

US$4.7bn for 2001–8 | US$7–10bn pa is needed to address the global HIV/Aids epidemic | *Sources: UNAIDS, WHO, World Bank*

develop the programmes needed. The situation is worsened by similar short-ages in ministries of finance (where staff need to spend inordinate amounts of time and energy on processing grants) and education. In response, the Bank is now setting up a Treatment Acceleration Program (TAP) aiming to bypass health ministries in selected countries, using the private sector and civil society as the preferred route. But will it find enough capacity there? And what are the implications of transforming much of African civil society into a conveyor belt for internationally funded ARV programmes?

Two years ago, the WHO's Commission on Macroeconomics and Health, headed by Jeffrey Sachs, put the case for hugely increased interna-tional spending on health. Now, with lower prices for ARVs, the establish-ment of the Global Fund To Fight Aids, Tuberculosis and Malaria (the additional two diseases added to mollify Thabo Mbeki) and President George W Bush's promise of US$15 billion for international Aids programmes (most of it probably new money), the availability of funds will soon no longer be the key obstacle. Sachs's experiment is being played out. Can money solve the HIV/Aids epidemic in poor countries?

The numbers are beguilingly small by global standards. But if we shift the focus to African budgets, the problems become huge. Aids funding on the scale envisioned by Sachs would double aid flows to Africa. Countries like Uganda and Mozambique are already close to saturation point in terms of official aid, with about half their national budgets externally funded. A big increase in aid flows might be too much for these governments to handle and, if not spent well, might end up by fuelling inflation and under-mining economic prospects. Or funds might be purloined from poverty reduction, environmental protection or education.

Africa's biggest ever service delivery initiative needs to do massively better than decades of development assistance. In rushing to scaled-up Aids treatment, there is a danger of throwing away decades of experience in development and social protection, which consistently demonstrate the importance of starting with locally designed programmes and slowly taking them to scale, rather than designing grand blueprints from outside. With the avalanche of funds now becoming available, for most governments and NGOs the priority is to rush out a funding proposal tailored to the donor's requirements, not painstaking study of how the problems might be solved.

The treatment programme could also have far-reaching implications for democracy. What will it mean for African governments' already much-emasculated discretion over policymaking, if they are dependent on indefinite foreign largesse for keeping a large proportion of their populations alive? Perhaps Africa's biggest public policy decision for the decade is being made without any significant public discussion.

International institutions dealing with Aids speak eloquently of 'new ways of doing business' and 'thinking out of the box'. They talk the talk. But in reality, performance is not measured against outcomes. First, any real results in combating HIV/Aids will take at least a decade to show, and they need to demonstrate success within a year or two. Second, we don't properly know what constitutes a good outcome. The best measure for prevention programmes is HIV incidence – the number of new infections – and that is extremely difficult to measure. For programmes aimed at minimising the wider impact, we don't have measures of success at all. But ministers and heads of agencies don't want to be confronted with a problem for which there is no solution ready to hand: having given HIV/Aids their five minutes' attention, they will move on to a more pressing problem. Third, because every institution needs to claim some success, we are befogged by wrong or unverifiable pretences of success, which means we miss the chance of studying what is really happening, what to expect and what might actually work. And last, there's an obligatory optimism that pervades discussion of Aids, especially in Africa. Speaking frankly is considered bad taste and presentations and papers are often assessed not by the rigour of their argument but by the temperature of their optimism.

The struggle against HIV/Aids entails a level of honesty that has been at best intermittently present during the past 20 years. Our starting point should be an admission that the epidemic is ruthlessly exploiting every denial, hypocrisy and pretence. Reckless complacency has helped bring us to this impasse. It would be tempting to call for the mass dismissal of the commanders who have been dismally losing this war, but their replacements' battle plans would probably be little better. We know far too little about the threat without a name posed by the HIV/Aids epidemic. The intellectual struggle has barely begun. And we're not angry enough; not by far. ❑

Alex de Waal is the founding director of Justice Africa

'IT DOESN'T HAPPEN IN OUR SOCIETY'

NIMCO MAHAMUD-HASSAN

I was 17 years old when I first heard the word 'homosexuality'. That was 13 years ago. I was watching the one o'clock news. The English family I was living with were born-again Christians. Though I didn't speak much English I could tell that something bad was happening from their reactions.

The word 'homosexuality' confused me because I heard it as 'home sexuality', and could not understand why they were so against it. Home? Sex? Was that so bad? Now, I knew that Western people lived differently from the Somali Islamic tradition I was born into, but did they really go to special places to have sex? What was wrong with their homes?

Sue, the mother, who was sitting next to me, saw how bemused I looked and kindly explained what was going on. She spoke in that typical manner people use to talk to those with whom they do not share a common language: slowly, clearly and loudly. Not that she made it any easier to understand why a man would want to marry a man and a woman a woman.

I am certain my ignorance of homosexuality was not unique. Sex is not freely talked about in most African societies and especially in Somalia where almost everyone is Muslim. On those occasions when sex is mentioned it is mostly in the negative. Don't! The only form of sex that is acceptable is that between a man and woman who are married. Anything else is sinful; so sinful that some sexual acts such as homosexuality and adultery are punishable by death.

But the rape of a single young female or child abuse goes unpunished – because these things simply don't happen in our culture. Few Somalis would even admit that girls, and still less boys, are sexually abused in our society.

At the moral heart of Somali society are the Quran schools, the mosques and the individual sheikhs who go around on behalf of God, providing cures for every imaginable ailment from headache to heart disease, often using the same method. Quran teachers, mosque leaders and sheikhs are all men.

The Quran is written in Arabic, a language very few Somalis speak (including most of the sheikhs). This makes direct communication with God rather difficult, since all Muslims are required to pray in Arabic; and this is why Somalis often go to sheikhs and send their children to Quran schools for moral guidance. Our own language was not written until 1972, the year I was born. Almost all our parents were illiterate and therefore had no choice but to accept whatever way sheikhs and imams interpreted the Quran. This gave them power and influence wherever they went.

Some of these sheikhs, Quran teachers and imams were morally corrupt. But because society viewed them as God's messengers no one dared to question their authority. I remember when I was eight years old one of my Quran teachers came to see my parents at home. We called him teacher Ali. He was a tall and godly-looking man who always dressed well though he stank like hell. He told my parents what a wonderful student I was, patting my head, and that he was fond of me. If they had known just how fond they would have been appalled.

I hated him with passion. He did things to me and other kids, boys as well as girls, that made me feel bad and sad. Even the day he came to see my parents he masturbated in front of me, near our water tank, and when he ejaculated he told me to watch him as 'love was coming through him'. There was no way I could have told my parents. They would not have believed me.

Such things just do not happen in our society.

In Somali society, to be a proper woman you have to produce children. If a married woman cannot have children her husband has the legal right to divorce her under Islamic law. Where married couples are not able to have children it is automatically assumed to be a problem with the woman. Some of these women go to see sheikhs to find cures and save their marriages, even if it is the husband who is impotent. Some sheikhs rape these women under hypnosis, solving the problem of childlessness and saving the marriage. The more a sheikh 'cures' a woman, the more trusted he becomes.

My sister and I were joking the other day, wondering if this is the reason we Somalis look so alike. My sister added: 'Other people talk about their forefathers, as Somalis we can talk about our four fathers.'

My mother had six more children after I was born but it wasn't until I was 15 that I learned that my father had a part to play in their creation. That was when I received sex education in an English school. As children in Somalia we giggled over the idea of the couple next door having sex without having the faintest idea what sex was, except that it was naughty.

Aids has spread in Africa partly because of this culture of silence over sex.

If Aids has done one positive thing, it is to shine a light into those secret areas that we all knew about and all denied. A year ago, a UNICEF consultant investigating child sex abuse in Zambia and Zimbabwe found that many schoolgirls as young as 12 were trading sex for simple favours such as sweets and free rides to school. At even younger ages, both boys and girls 'played' at sex with a high level of realism. This isn't harmless experimentation. In some African towns, more than 20 per cent of 19-year-old girls are infected with HIV.

I was in Kampala, Uganda, earlier this year. One Saturday night I was invited out for a drink by a couple of Ugandan friends. We went to an area called Kabalagala, known for its nightlife. While chatting and drinking I noticed two attractive young men dancing together. I asked my friends if these guys were gay. My friends were shocked that I would ask such a question. It didn't happen in their culture either. After a few more drinks those guys sat near my friends and me. We started to chat and I eventually asked them if they were gay. Their answer shocked and disgusted my friends. One thing I can say about my Ugandan friends is that at least they were more tolerant than any East African I have ever met when it comes to homosexuality.

Two years ago, I met my first openly homosexual Somali male in a Brixton pub. We recognised each other as Somalis doing what we are not supposed to be doing: drinking alcohol. After chatting for a while he told me he was gay. He was amazed that I would continue to talk to him after he had confessed this. I asked him how the Somali community treated him. He rolled up his shirtsleeve, revealing a huge scar on his upper right arm, and said, 'This is how.'

There is a Somali saying: 'Ignorance is the enemy of love.' ❏

Nimco Mahanud-Hassan *is a Somali writer living in the UK*

Opposite: Somalia school, 2000: education breaks the culture of silence.
Credit: Rex Features

NO LAUGHING MATTER
PIETER-DIRK UYS

SOUTH AFRICA'S FOREMOST SATIRICAL
PERFORMANCE ARTIST TAKES A LOOK AT
THE SOUTH AFRICAN GOVERNMENT'S
TREATMENT OF AIDS

Is it patriotic to criticise a democratically elected government or does one censor one's anger and hope to pass the buck? The passion that surrounds HIV/Aids in Africa, and in particular the infuriating denials and confusions that emanate daily from Thabo Mbeki's government in South Africa, have resulted in much anger. Dangerous instinctive reactions, which have led to much ice cracking under the feet.

It started in a peak of fury after I spent four days in the South African hinterland doing 13 presentations of my Aids–awareness entertainment to over 20 schools and 9,000 learners, and realised how little hope there is for youth amid the present government paralysis with regard to information about HIV/Aids.

On Sunday 23 February 2003, I sent an email to whoever could take it further:

THE WEAPON OF MASS DESTRUCTION IS IN SOUTH AFRICA AND BEING HARBOURED BY THE SOUTH AFRICAN PRESIDENT AND HIS MINISTER OF HEALTH. IT IS HIV/Aids.

An investigative process should be put into place as soon as possible, with vigorous support in local South African and international legal and political circles. This process can result in President Thabo Mbeki and Minister Manto Tshabala-Msimang being summonsed to appear in The Hague at the International Court of Justice on counts of genocide. Rather this happen now than in ten years' time, when the world will no doubt look back at 2003 and the actions of the South African president and his minister of health, and

60m Africans have been affected by Aids: 30m are living with the virus; 15m have died; more than 11m have lost at least one parent | HIV/Aids in Africa infects over 30% of the population in four countries, and at least 10% in 12 countries |

realise that by acting sooner, millions of lives could have been saved from an unnecessary death from Aids.

THE SOUTH AFRICAN PEOPLE ARE DYING TODAY BECAUSE OF GOVERNMENT CARELESSNESS AND POLITICAL NEGLIGENCE.

The time to act is now. *Vuk'uzenzele!* (In Xhosa '*vuk'uzenzele*' means arise and act.)

I sent that email to many people, including President Mbeki, Minister Tshabala-Msimang and the speaker of parliament. The immediate reaction from government was the following:

Government has noted the email message being circulated by Pieter-Dirk Uys on the challenges of HIV/Aids facing our country.

South Africa is a free country and all citizens, including Uys, enjoy freedom of speech. While we are convinced that there are limits to satire, we do recognise Uys' right to overstate matters and respond flippantly to serious issues.

Government urges all South Africans to unite against HIV/Aids, in the campaign of hope and not despair. We would have thought that Pieter-Dirk Uys would realise from his own experiences in Aids prevention, as most South Africans do, that searching for scapegoats and instant solutions is not the correct response to the challenge of HIV/Aids.

Working with partners from all sectors of society, government will continue to implement the national comprehensive strategy on Aids, in all its elements, as the most rational approach to the pandemic.

(Issued by government communications Tuesday 25 February 2003)

There were many other reactions. My favourite email simply said:

'Pieter-Dirk Uys, are you mad?'

Yes. Mad as hell! But not as insane as those who think there are limits to satire.

1.7m young Africans are infected every year | 11m children have been orphaned | By 2010 there will be 20m HIV/Aids orphans: Nigeria over 2.6m; South Africa 1.7 million; Zimbabwe 1.1m; Cameroon 700,000; Côte d'Ivoire 600,000; Sudan

Genocide is a terrible accusation. It means the systematic, planned extermination of an entire national, racial, political or ethnic group. The word 'genocide' is mainly associated with the Nazi extermination of millions of Jews, gays, Gypsies and others during World War II. We watched more recent examples in Burundi and Rwanda on the TV news while eating supper. Kosovo and Serbia also had their share of planned murder. But does genocide always have to be at the end of a machine gun? Do we have to kill 6 million and ONE people to be worse than the Nazis?

When President Mbeki took over our democratic reins of power from Nelson Mandela, Comrade Thabo wore the red Aids ribbon. Many celebrated the proof that the new South African leadership would focus on what had without doubt become the most serious threat to our nation: the virus known as HIV and the resulting decline of health through the disease called Aids.

But in the four years that followed the 1999 election, the leadership of South Africa has virtually denied the existence of our present third-world war. At every opportunity the president, his advisers and especially his chosen minister of health have demeaned the seriousness of the pandemic and created havoc among those who seek help. It is leading to thousands of deaths. The national comprehensive strategy is starting to look like a systematic, planned extermination of an entire group of South Africans: those who are poor, unemployed, in prison, on the streets and hopeless. The new apartheid has already established itself. Black and white South Africans with money will live. Those without money will have no access to medicines and drugs. They will die.

Every one of us reading these words has heard of the pandemic. Many of us know people who are HIV-positive. Some of us have lost loved ones and friends to Aids. Countless of us have the virus. All of us now think it will inevitably lead to death. We're wrong. There is life after HIV, and there is a future with Aids. It is part of life, not death. There are treatments, medical regimes, disciplines and help available to everyone who needs it. But the first step is to acknowledge the existence of the disease. If the leadership ignores the symptoms of a national disaster all the people are left to suffer alone.

400,000 | In South Africa an estimated 17% of health workers are estimated to have HIV; nurses 50%, doctors 9% | WOMEN: women constitute 53% of all those infected; 59% of 15–49-year-olds | 10% of uninfected women in sub-Saharan

Pieter-Dirk Uys with
Mrs Evita Beguidenhout.
Credit: Pat Brownlow-Downing

How can Thabo Mbeki and Manto T-M be guilty of genocide? They're not firing guns as in Burundi, or turning up the gas ovens in Auschwitz. The unnecessary deaths of people who depend on government for leadership and don't get it is as criminal as firing machine guns into a crowd.

Happily, there is much goodwill in our land. We all have different experiences of the pandemic in South Africa. Anger and frustration find many ways to express themselves. The Treatment Action Campaign speaks with strong moral authority when it demands the right of medication for those who need anti-retroviral drugs. Judge Edwin Cameron and thousands of others live with Aids as an example of survival and courage. Patricia de Lille, leader of the newly established Independent Democrats, has risen above party politics to embrace the struggle against HIV/Aids as a new chapter in her commitment to defend democracy against corrupt laziness.

Africa become infected every year | In Zambia 65% of households where a mother died were dissolved | An estimated 60–80% of African women have sexual intercourse solely with their husbands | Fewer than 25% of Zambian

To ignore the terrible danger we are faced with is to show contempt for life. All the facts and statistics point to the loss of up to half the population of Africa in ten years. If 40 per cent of the workforce is HIV-positive, investment will not happen. Over 60 per cent of the armed forces are carriers of the virus. Twenty-five per cent of first-year students at universities have tested positive.

And still the minister of health, whose professional and sacred duty it is to protect us, chooses to scoff at the facts. She chooses to add crazy soundbites that would be the pride of any comedian. She proves there are no limits to satire! First came: South Africa can't afford the cost of treatment as submarines must be built to fight a US invasion. Most recently: why should Aids be regarded as more important than asthma? Do her words represent the thoughts of her president?

The last two years have taken me round 250 schools and I have met 500,000 young South Africans. I have entertained them with the need to laugh at fear and make that fear less fearful. And because Aids happens through sex, some words such as 'fuck' and 'naai' (Afrikaans for 'bonk') get used to describe where the minefield is. Some parents have complained, a few teachers have been offended, churches have frowned and government is silent. But the children are not. They are inspired and empowered with hope. And they want to talk.

'I appreciated how you did not treat us like stupid kids, but as equals,' wrote a girl in Grade 11, one reaction out of hundreds. 'Your show was brilliant and seriously did make people think twice. You showed us the reality, but didn't scare us. Instead you made us more aware, brave and determined to go out there and make it.'

If we can keep our youth alive, we will have the greatest country in the world. But that means keeping them alive now. Talking to them. Encouraging them to ask questions!

The depressing side is that because the subject of sex is so controversial, no one feels free to talk. And because the president won't be drawn into the debate, the focus falls away. Imagine if once a week, our president talked on television to people who are frightened of HIV/Aids and the stigma attached to it. Imagine how together they could confront their fears and

women agreed that a woman could refuse to have sex with her husband, even if he was known to have HIV | In Ghana almost 50% of women and 43% of men agreed that a woman deserved to be beaten if she used contraception without

help everyone realise that life is possible. He could be the Father of the Nation and embrace us with humanity.

Don't forget we survived apartheid, the first virus. We were told: democracy is too good to share with just anyone. And so we went through 40 years in the political wilderness because we believed our leaders. They were wrong: democracy is the only solution. And thanks to the freedoms we all enjoy, we all can make our voices heard. Today we have violence, crime, corruption, arrogance and denial – all the things that have made us a successful third-world African democracy. But we also have the vote. This we often forget in the rush to complain.

It's easy and important to criticise a democratically elected government. That's part of the deal between politics and society. And what a gift the present government with its Mbekivellian policies is to a satirist – from ANC MP Tony Yengeni pleading poverty from a new Mercedes sports car to Mama Winnie Madikizela-Mandela offering to go to Baghdad to catch US cruise missiles in her teeth. It's unfair to say that the present government is more corrupt than the previous apartheid regime. They're just better at it. That's not genocide. That's tatty politics and they'll always get away with it, if the people don't say STOP.

But Aids is not politics. It's health. In this case, safe sex is not about morality; it's about hygiene. It's like brushing teeth. If we don't protect ourselves, we will get sick. And the only way we will take control of our lives is by talking about our fear. By focusing on surviving a virus. Not denying its existence.

Do I want to put the entire South African government in the dock at The Hague? Of course not. We are only here today thanks to the generosity of the so-called former enemies of South Africa. These men and women came out of their prison cells and exile to allow us all a second chance to live in this great land. There are excellent professionals in government, especially in the Department of Health. But without leadership and inspiration, they cannot catch up with the needs of the people.

The anger in South Africa is growing on every level, from business to suburb. But it's always where the ground has been freshly dug and the crosses crowd into small cemeteries where the reality strikes home. Mothers

telling her husband | Prevalence rates among Nigerian sex workers are estimated at 36% | In Uganda, the number of unmarried 15–25-year-old females reporting sexual activity fell from 35% to 22% | ECONOMY: 80% of Africans

are losing children to a disease that has only stigma and no name or recognition. Sons and daughters have lost their parents. Politicians are dying of 'backache' and 'lung problems'. If Rock Hudson and Freddy Mercury had been members of the ANC they too would have died of 'natural causes'.

This denial at the highest level, that HIV/Aids is the most serious assault on our future, has led to more deaths. The president's version of what he regards as the reasons for Aids – poverty, TB, racism, yellow flowers and sticky biscuits – are being religiously repeated so often and given so much credence that the fear and suspicions lead to the rape of babies and the killing of suspected sufferers of the 'thinning sickness'. And when a two-month-old baby is raped by a man who thinks it will cure him, does the president say anything?

No.

He flies around the globe in his expensive new aeroplane like Supermouse, trying to solve the problems of the first world, while auditioning for the part of Kofi Annan. He pops into South Africa occasionally on a state visit and shows how much he dislikes us by ignoring us. He confuses us even more with details of an African Renaissance, an African Union and a New Partnership for Africa's Development, diverting attention away from the battlefields of fear.

But let us be fair to this consummate politician with such grand ambitions. Let Thabo off the hook. Let him and Manto run the United Nations and let's find a president who cares for us, a minister of health who heals and embraces us. And together we can all realise that HIV/Aids as a weapon of mass destruction can be disarmed without fear. By confronting it with information and knowledge. By allowing us our humanity, compassion and humour.

And there is always that final solution. Not the International Court in The Hague. It'll be the ballot box on Election Day 2004. South Africans can decide who they want to be in charge. Vote!

Vuk'uzenzele!

Mid-September 2003, after months of bullshit from the highest office in the land – and still anti-retroviral drugs are not being made available to the people who need them – Thabo Mbeki drops another hint of his true

depend on small-scale, subsistence agriculture for their livelihood | Between 1985 and 2000 7m African agricultural workers died from HIV/Aids in the 25 most affected countries; 16m agricultural workers are expected to die in the

colours in an interview with the *Washington Post*. He says he knows no one with HIV. He knows no one who has died of Aids.

The ice cracks again.

A letter to the editors of South African newspapers went off on Friday 26 September – and was published by most – hours after the news of Mbeki's words filtered through the barrage of sports details and soap opera synopses:

> When the president of South Africa speaks, he represents a democracy where 5 million citizens have HIV; where more than 600 people die each day from Aids-related diseases; where 250 babies are born every 24 hours with the virus.
>
> Yet our President Thabo Mbeki says to the US-based *Washington Post*: 'I don't know anyone with HIV. . . Personally, I don't know anybody who has died of Aids.'
>
> He lies and so condemns his nation to death.
>
> It is time to replace this man with a leader who cares about his people!
>
> Not only does Thabo Mbeki spend most of his time outside South Africa, speaking at international political jamborees, but he has now shown himself totally out of touch with his own country.
>
> We are a young democracy, in which this man is but a chosen leader and not the member of a royal dynasty. The African National Congress deserves to celebrate the 2004 tenth anniversary of our young democracy. The ANC is a former liberation movement, now a successful political party, committed to the issues of human rights and freedom. But this party of liberation will soon be remembered by history only as an accomplice to the genocidal Mbekivellian policies of its present leader.
>
> Replace this failed leader with a comrade of compassion.
>
> There are many politicians in the ruling party, and on the fringes of power. Men and women of compassion and care, of focus and commitment. They are needed now. Replace this failed civil servant in denial with a citizen who can heal and help, a leader who

next 20 years | In Zambia farming families with a chronically ill household member planted 53% fewer crops than those without one member chronically ill | The average income of Côte d'Ivorien households living with HIV/Aids drops by

confronts the problems of our people and embraces our needs and aspirations.

No more Thabo Mbeki.

We need leadership to inspire confidence and optimism in our time of national fear and need.

We need to inspire an impatient world to invest in us and believe in our future.

With 40 per cent of our workforce HIV-positive, no one will invest in South Africa.

And yet our president knows no one with HIV?

While everyone in our country has buried, nurtured, cared for, said farewell to, wept for and remembered a loved one who has died of this virus that has no cure, our elected president is confused and innocent of the pain and the tears.

Like when Steve Biko died, the then apartheid Minister of Justice Jimmy Kruger famously said: 'It leaves me cold.'

South Africa leaves Thabo Mbeki cold.

There is no time for party politics here.

Replace this man now with a committed leader and let him, or her, lead and help us to live!

Pieter-Dirk Uys

The president's Rasputin was quick to react. From the office of the president, his minister for the presidency Dr Essop Pahad reacted to my letter with the following observations:

GOVERNMENT-LED EFFORTS AGAINST HIV/AIDS ARE NO LAUGHING MATTER

HIV/Aids is a serious subject which engages the attention of the nation as never before. For instance, the report of the National Task team, charged with preparing an operational plan on public sector anti-retroviral therapy, is now with the Department of Health, having met the end-September deadline. It is to be discussed by cabinet in the coming days.

Against this serious background the antics of Pieter-Dirk Uys

40–60% | In Botswana the poorest households are expected to be 13% worse off financially as a result of the impact of HIV/Aids | By 2010 South Africa's GDP will be 17% lower than it would have been without the epidemic | Zambia pays

over HIV/Aids – curiously afforded serious treatment in sections of the media – are a complicating irritant of minor scale. But some damage is undoubtedly being done to South Africa's campaign against the scourge in terms of influencing public opinion, particularly the youth, against government-led efforts and, particularly, against President Thabo Mbeki.

These government-led efforts are widely acknowledged as the biggest and most comprehensive campaign against HIV/Aids in Africa, which is presumably news to Uys.

Only last week, the Secretary-General of the UN, Kofi Annan, praised South Africa for tripling its HIV/Aids budget since the last summit of the UN on this issue.

House clowns in any democracy have some, mainly amusement, value. British society through the years would not have been itself without the lampooning of *Private Eye* and *Spitting Image*, and the Americans even go further.

Uys's satire did have a useful influence on enlightenment in the days when there was a total absence of democracy in South Africa, and his lampooning had something to do with helping to change attitudes away from apartheid and repression. But his recent statements on the government's programme against HIV/Aids can, if taken too seriously, hinder and confuse the national will to do something about the pandemic.

There is a need for all South Africans to remain resolute in the face of the grave challenge which the government and all sectors are dealing with responsibly and caringly. We should not be swayed by sideshows and contrived controversies.

Unfortunately, Uys undermines what most of us took as a sincere and well-meant effort to spread awareness of the dangers of HIV infection, especially in schools.

Something seems to go wrong and he confuses satire and serious policy pronouncements. Or is this the problem of the editors who choose to air some of his bizarre views in presumably serious columns?

---

cUS$125m a year interest on its national debt – more than 66% of the amount it spends on health, education and welfare combined | In 2001 the cost of a month's supply of anti-retroviral treatment fell from US$700 to US$125 | Some African

In his latest assault on Mbeki, Uys latched on to third-hand conclusions drawn from what the president said to the *Washington Post* about whether he knew people in his own family or among his close associates who had died of Aids, or were infected with HIV.

The president gave an honest answer. He was speaking about his limited circle of family or close friends. And need we be reminded that, even among those people, as many of us well know, no one is obliged to declare their status; nor is a doctor obliged to reveal direct or indirect causes of death to anyone, including a president.

Yet it was grist to the mill for Uys and used to make the fanciful call for a personal attack on the president. This, at the very moment when the government is finalising the last element of our comprehensive strategy, ARV treatment.

The government can endure the barbs flung by Uys. We do even enjoy him at times. He was aptly described in one paper that ran his letter as 'a comedian'. Indeed.

Surely the media should not dignify his twaddle by publishing it in serious columns. Unless of course we are wrong to assume that these are indeed serious columns.

(Published in the *Cape Times*, 2 October 2003)

And so here we are in the minefield of fear, denial, death and horror. Too frightened to confront the reality of the virus and too polite to tread where racists aim to go. White criticism of a black government can too easily be seen as racist. Criticism of bad governance must try to rise above petty ethnic bitchery. It is not a crime to point out carelessness. It is a crime to censor the anger and let it slide. It has been said: A patriot is someone who protects his country from its government.

So, as we say in one of our 11 official languages: *Vuk'uzenzele!*

Stand up and do something! ❏

Pieter-Dirk Uys is South Africa's best-known satirical performance artist whose one-man shows, many of them dealing with Aids, have been seen in many countries. In his persona as Evita Beguidenhout he is known as 'the most famous white woman in South Africa'

countries impose therapy import duties of up to 45% on ARV drugs | Zimbabwe has imposed a 3% surtax on personal and corporate income to fund grass-roots projects combating HIV/Aids | EDUCATION: in Mozambique, where both parents

TAKING ON THE GOVERNMENT

ZACKIE ACHMAT

A SOUTH AFRICAN AIDS ACTIVIST
CHALLENGES HIS GOVERNMENT'S
AIDS POLICY AND MAKES A STAND
FOR DEMOCRACY IN THE PROCESS

It is abundantly clear that HIV/Aids has created a crisis of governance in South Africa: our political leaders have closed their eyes to the issue. Despite the fact that we have the evidence of 13 years' systematic study of HIV prevalence and a good base for understanding what's happening with the epidemic in our country, no one has taken this epidemic seriously. Either they are in denial or they fear the costs of dealing with it.

When we first started our campaign, the anti-retroviral drugs I need would have cost about 4,500 rand (US$750) per month, and I would have had to take 19 pills every day instead of the two that I take today. At that point, we wouldn't push our government into risking bankruptcy by demanding the full package for people living with HIV. It would have been irresponsible and morally wrong.

When our president became an HIV-denialist in 1999, when he denied the scientific connection between HIV and Aids, it represented the worst moment in the crisis of governance. At that point, a critical piece of legislation was to be enacted in parliament: the Prohibition of Unfair Discrimination and Equality Act. For all intents and purposes, the Act covers people living with HIV, but there was a debate as to whether HIV should be explicitly included. Since the president didn't want to give HIV/Aids the symbolism of being mentioned separately in the Act, he stopped both the Justice Committee, and parliament itself, from including HIV.

Notwithstanding the fact that South Africa has one of the best legal frameworks for dealing with the epidemic – you can't lose your job, you can't lose your house, you can't lose this, you can't lose that – unless people claim rights, no legal framework matters.

are alive, 58% of children go to schools; where only one parent is alive this figure drops to 24% | In South Africa and Zimbabwe 50% of 15-year-olds are expected to die of HIV/Aids | Between 1996 and 1998 HIV/AIDS killed 5 teachers each

The crisis of governance has touched many of our institutions. One example is the South African Human Rights Commission. Having first supported our court case to compel the government to provide drugs for the prevention of mother-to-child transmission of HIV, it later withdrew.

Another instance is the Medicines Control Council. There's never been such a saga as the registration of Nevirapine in the history of medicine registration in our country. Nevirapine is registered for combination use in therapy for adults for life. I have to use it for life. But one woman, wanting to use it just once in her pregnancy, was denied it on the grounds that it was not 'safe'. That wasn't the action of the MCC: that was the government.

Just a year before the Nevirapine scandal, there'd been a saga in which the MCC had resisted registering a product called Viradene, on the valid grounds that it had not been adequately tested or been through clinical trials. At this point, the government removed the chair of the MCC. As a result of this experience, the MCC equivocated and did not register Nevirapine for 18 months for fear they might lose their jobs.

What happened next? One of South Africa's most eminent institutions is the Medical Research Council, headed by South Africa's best scientist, William Magoba, a well-respected immunologist. And until he told the president that his views on Aids were wrong, he was a good friend of the president. Under Magoba's leadership, the MRC produced a report on what had happened to mortality rates in South Africa. It concluded there had been a dramatic increase in the deaths of women aged between 24 and 40, and a significant increase in the same age group for men – and that Aids had become the leading cause of death among adults.

For two years, the government stopped the MRC from releasing its report. Enormous pressure, both personal and economic, was brought on all the scientists who participated in the study not to release it. Eventually, when it became clear that it was going to be released, our president's office leaked a letter to *Business Day*, intending to take the sting out of the MRC report. It claimed that the leading causes of death in South Africa were violence, TB and a few others, and recommended that we should look at reprioritising our spending. After the report's release, William Magoba was forced to leave the MRC; his colleagues no longer work for the government.

week in Côte d'Ivoire | 1,300 teachers died in the first ten months of 1998 in Zambia | 1m African children have lost a teacher to HIV/Aids | LIFE EXPECTANCY: South African life expectancy at birth is expected to hit a low

The government also enlisted one of our best independent bodies, Stat South Africa, to argue its case. Stat South Africa fudged the issue; but when it did finally produce its 'official statistics report on deaths in South Africa' – when we were all asleep over Christmas and journalists had gone home – it largely confirmed the findings of the MRC report. But no one in the media picked it up.

Parliament was one of the places that several times allowed us a voice to give evidence. We were able to use it as a platform to reach many people in communities and to gain allies among the parliamentarians. We joined our government in the legal case against the drug companies and, at that time, the minister of health, parliamentarians and civil society organisations all sat together.

When the court ordered that the government should provide drugs to pregnant mothers to prevent their children contracting HIV, our case on mother-to-child transmission nearly became a test of democracy itself. Our health minister announced that she wasn't going to let any judge tell her what medicines to give and refused to obey a court order. At which point, our minister of justice stepped into the breach and it became a test of whether our constitutional court would be obeyed. In a most unusual step, a unanimous judgement, with the full weight of the entire court behind it, was explicitly handed down in the name of the court and she was forced to come to heel.

It's important to be adversarial when it's necessary. It has been necessary for us to march and petition. And because we have a tradition of anti-apartheid struggle, we've been able to use that tradition in an effective way. ❏

Zackie Achmat is the director of Treatment Action Campaign

Excerpted from a speech at the launch of the African Civil Society Governance and Aids Initiative in October 2003

of 45.6 years by 2010, 22 years less than it would have been in the absence of HIV/Aids | By 2020, the total population of South Africa is expected to be 23% smaller than it would be without Aids | *Sources: UNAIDS, WHO, World Bank*

WHAT FUTURE DEMOCRACY?

AZIZ RANA

THE THREAT POSED BY AIDS TO THE
DEVELOPMENT OF DEMOCRACY IN AFRICA
PLAYS NO PART IN CURRENT DISCUSSIONS
OF THE IMPACT OF THE DISEASE

The HIV/Aids epidemic in Africa is assailing the foundations of democracy
on the continent. By killing people of working age, it is haemorrhaging
human resources from the institutions necessary to keep societies functioning. The epidemic is a long-wave event that will need sustained public
health programmes over decades, demanding resources vastly in excess of
what the continent can mobilise internally. For years, it will throw Africa on
the mercies of the rich world. But at the same time as the advent of life-
sustaining treatment brings life-and-death choices to the centre of politics,
we have to ask if liberal constitutionalism is best suited to resolving such
fundamental public policy dilemmas.

Hopes for democracy in Africa rest on three pillars – material progress,
independence from external control and the functioning of constitutional
procedures. All three are jeopardised by Aids.

Public opinion polls in South Africa suggest that most black South
Africans view democracy in terms of material progress rather than constitutional procedures. The public associates democracy with access to the basic
necessities of life: food, water, shelter and education. Africa's most recent
initiative for democracy and prosperity – the New Partnership for Africa's
Development (NEPAD), the brainchild of South African President Thabo
Mbeki – twins the promise of 'good governance' with the achievement of
7 per cent growth per annum – enough, it is estimated, to reduce poverty
by half by 2015.

In recent years, however, Africa's continental economy has scored
between 3 and 4 per cent, barely enough to keep ahead of an expanding
population. The HIV/Aids epidemic is cutting an estimated 1 per cent off
that growth each year, and the shackle is getting heavier. Africa's prospects
for reducing poverty are evaporating. By undermining economic development, Aids is placing fragile democracies in jeopardy. An economic crisis is
often a political crisis as well.

Soweto, South Africa, 1994: making a mark for the first time.
Credit: Carlos Reyes-Manzo / Andes Press Agency

In Africa, given the history of colonial rule, any vision of democracy requires that African publics rather than international powers must control political and economic decision-making.

For many on the African left, it is on the axis of autonomy that HIV/Aids enters the political landscape. Today, the sovereignty of sub-Saharan African states is under enormous pressure. Real economic control increasingly lies in the nexus between international aid donors, multinational investors, particularly oil and arms companies, and the Bretton Woods institutions. In the 1980s, structural adjustment programmes imposed a vision of free-market orthodoxy, marked by privatisation and market liberalisation, on weak and dependent economies. Today, similar conditionalities determine whether African states qualify for Heavily Indebted Poor Countries (HIPC) debt relief. Donor governments such as the United States demand economic policies that focus on fiscal discipline and strengthen US trade and investment, giving African politicians no leeway in policymaking.

Africa has no prospects of mobilising the US$10 billion or so needed per annum to mount scaled-up anti-retroviral treatment to millions of people living with HIV and Aids. Those funds can only come from the developed world. More aid flows to stagnant or shrinking economies can mean only one thing: still greater economic dependence.

Domestically, democracy requires functioning institutions. The capacity of all institutions is undermined by Aids illness and death. The disease is devastating teachers, parliamentarians, university teachers, policemen: everybody. It reduces the number of government officials and policy-makers who have been at their jobs long enough to develop specialised skills. Greater turnover, less experienced civil servants and shortened time horizons will also increase the likelihood of corruption as shorter time spans increase the incentives for opportunistic behaviour. Judicial systems are grinding to a halt in some rural areas because of the shortages of judges and lawyers. HIV/Aids threatens electoral institutions, with voter lists needing more regular updating and the deaths of MPs necessitating frequent and expensive by-elections. Additionally, the state's control over violence is imperilled as Aids undermines the cohesion and readiness of armies and police forces.

Equally fundamentally, the HIV/Aids epidemic injects an element of permanent emergency into political life. Liberal constitutionalism rests on an empirical precondition: for publics to accept procedures as the basis for legitimating outcomes, citizens must not take disagreement too seriously. Even if we think a decision is wrong, we are still willing to accept the outcome as valid. For such partial agreement to hold, citizens must believe that their disagreements are not matters of life and death. If one truly thought that survival rested on the right outcome, the fact that a numerical majority of citizens or elected representatives voted the other way, or a judge reached a contradictory conclusion, would not legitimise the choice. In a sense, the entrenchment of liberal democracy requires a retreat of politics; citizens do not find the questions they debate in political life a matter, literally, of life or death.

The fragility of liberal democracy in Africa is linked to the lack of this empirical precondition. Marked by wars and famines, politics on the continent have been intricately bound up with issues of survival and economic necessity. Basic needs are at the heart of politics on the continent; this places great strain on the functioning of constitutionalism.

The Aids epidemic places questions of life and death at the very centre of politics. Anti-retrovirals can prolong the lives of people living with HIV, but no African government, even with donor assistance, can afford to buy and dispense them universally. Rationing will take place, either deliberately or by default. The need to prioritise treatment could undermine the legitimacy of democratic governments that find themselves forced to decide who lives and dies.

What is to be done? Up to now, the Aids discourse has been medical, technical and moral. There has been no meeting point between the framing of the agendas of democratisation and the transformation of the African state, and the demands of responding to HIV/Aids. The pandemic remains predominantly the domain of health specialists. In an important sense, international donors, including the Global Fund To Fight Aids, Tuberculosis and Malaria along with the international NGO community and domestic political elites, have shaped how the crisis itself is constructed, conceiving of HIV/Aids as a technical matter. Confronting the disease is seen as a matter of enhancing medical expertise and public health capacity – and more money. The aid-to-health approach has marginalised issues of political governance and democracy.

The international emphasis on technical skill insulates political authorities, both domestic and international, from any criticism save that 'they are not doing enough'. Citizens find themselves blocked from political entrance, unable to hold international donors and foreign governments accountable for their directives, and similarly unable to claim ownership over the decisions of national leaders. As long as the debate remains squarely one of expertise and institution building, political elites can simply deflect failure by referring to the ongoing need for more money.

The biomedical challenges of HIV have prompted the creation of a new branch of medical science; the social and political implications of the HIV/Aids epidemic also demand a new approach to democratic politics. There are no easy answers to the dilemmas of how to sustain democracy under the onslaught of HIV/Aids, but we can at least make a start by discussing the issue openly and frankly. ❏

Aziz Rana is a student at Yale Law School

OLD WINE IN NEW BARRELS

GAYLE SMITH

US AID TO AFRICA HAS LESS TO DO
WITH COMBATING AIDS THAN WITH
SECURING NEW AND SAFER
SUPPLIES OF OIL

During his campaign for president, George W Bush said that even though it was 'a country with many problems', Africa was not an area of strategic importance to the US. But Bush's recent actions have proved to speak much louder than his words. Late last year, his administration secured a dramatic increase in funding to fight the global HIV/Aids pandemic and establish a new, robust foreign aid fund targeted to the world's poorest countries. Much of this new aid funding will go to Africa. Contrary to Candidate Bush's previous assertions, the continent has assumed strategic importance as the focus of two of the Bush administration's primary policy goals – fulfilling the agenda of 'compassionate conservatism' and the pursuit of new supplies of oil.

Although Americans contribute to private charities at commendable levels, official foreign aid has never been popular in the US. Funds allocated by Congress to foreign aid programmes are commonly viewed as competing with domestic spending, and most Americans believe that the US spends far more on international development than is actually the case. The annual negotiations between the legislative and executive branches of government over the foreign operations budget do little to build public confidence, as they traditionally feature sharp attacks on the US Agency for International Development (USAID) and battles over the 'earmarks' that allow members of Congress to target aid to specific projects or constituencies. These battles reached fever pitch in the mid-1990s, when arch-conservative Senator Jesse Helms attacked the Clinton administration for pouring taxpayer dollars down 'foreign rat holes'.

There was initially little indication that the new Bush administration would move the ball forward. But midway through his term, President Bush dropped two surprise announcements. The first came at the March 2002 Conference on Financing Development in Monterrey, where he announced the 'Millennium Challenge Account', a US$5 billion-dollar fund designated for the developing world's poorest yet best economic and polit-ical 'performers'. In his State of the Union speech nine months later, Bush stunned critics and fans alike by following his take-no-prisoners stance on Iraq with the announcement that he would triple US spending on global Aids.

The president's announcement marked a significant departure from his administration's earlier stance. Six months before his State of the Union announcement, Bush had announced a three-year, US$500 million interna-tional Aids programme focused on mother-to-child transmission, thus undercutting a proposal by Senators John Kerry (Democrat) and Bill Frist (Republican) to provide US$2.1 billion in international Aids funding in fiscal year 2003 and US$2.5 billion the following year. Meanwhile, when it came time formally to request its newly proposed funds from Congress, the Bush administration undercut its own pledge, asking for less funding than had been forecast by the president's announcements.

Activism and advocacy by development and Aids organisations, Bono and key members of Congress brought the numbers up, and almost one year later Congress was set to approve a new foreign operations budget for 2004 and provide the administration with US$2.4 billion for HIV/Aids prog-rammes in 15 countries, most in Africa and the Caribbean, and US$1.3 billion to launch the Millennium Challenge Account.

No doubt, these are aid levels that set historic precedents, define George W Bush as a champion of foreign aid and mean more money for Africa. And given how hard it has been to increase US development spending since the end of the Cold War, the Bush administration deserves credit for doing what many had thought impossible. But consistent with his other grand gestures, Bush's new aid policies bear the trademark of his administration: the triumph of ideology over facts.

The conservative side of George W Bush's global compassion was evident from the first day of his administration, when he reinstated what is called the 'Mexico City' policy, less charitably referred to as the 'global gag rule'. Originally announced by President Ronald Reagan at the Second International Conference on Population in Mexico City in 1984, this provi-sion dictates that US aid for family planning cannot be provided to foreign non-governmental organisations that use funding from any source to provide abortions or abortion counselling, or which lobby to make abortion legal in their countries of residence. These restrictions remained in place throughout the Reagan and Bush Sr administrations, but were rescinded by

President Clinton. In 1998, leaders in the Republican-dominated House of Representatives conditioned the payment of US back dues to the United Nations on imposition of the global gag rule. Clinton vetoed the legislation, but caved in to congressional demands a year later in order to pay US$900 million in outstanding dues to the UN; he subsequently exercised his authority and waived the restrictions.

George W Bush went further than his father, however, and coupled the reinstatement of the global gag rule with the requirement that one-third of new US spending on international HIV/Aids programmes be allocated to abstinence programmes. The highly regarded American Medical Association and US National Institutes of Health have long backed comprehensive sex education. But supporters of abstinence from among conservative think tanks and the US radical right carry more weight with the Bush administration, and the weight they carry is substantial. Congress has allocated more than US$100 million to domestic abstinence programmes; the Centers for Disease Control has removed a page from its website that reviewed effective, comprehensive sex education programmes; US NGOs that do not advocate abstinence-only programmes, or have criticised the global gag rule, report an unusual number of audits by the federal government; the Bush administration has allied itself with Pakistan, Libya, Saudi Arabia and other non-democratic regimes to oppose references to 'gay men' or 'sex workers' in UN resolutions, and with members of Congress to ensure that USAID avoids the same references in its own public materials.

Bush's conservatism is fast trumping the effectiveness of his compassion, particularly in Africa. The gag rule has forced the closure of clinics in Kenya, curtailed community outreach programmes in Ethiopia, Zambia and Uganda, and forced established family planning organisations to close or reduce services. According to recent reports by the Center for Reproductive Rights and Population Action International, USAID – once the world's leading provider of condoms to the developing world – has terminated condom shipments to 16 developing countries whose family planning associations are affiliated with International Planned Parenthood and to another 13 countries whose main, but not only, family planning organisation will not sign on to the gag rule.

In August of 2003, Bush expanded the coverage of the gag rule to include, in addition to USAID funds, family-planning assistance provided by the State Department. Significantly, however, the administration has not imposed the gag rule on the new funding allocated under the president's new HIV/Aids programme which, in a marked departure from past practice, will be managed by the State Department rather than USAID. While this compromise has been heralded by critics of the gag rule, they point out that the rule still applies to other funds, and are concerned that the NGOs already rendered ineligible for USAID funding will be similarly avoided by the State Department as it implements the new HIV/Aids programme. And even if the new HIV/Aids programme operates free of the gag rule, the wisdom of shutting down health clinics with one aid programme while fighting an epidemic through another is questionable at best.

It is certain that the Bush administration will retain the gag rule as it applies to other development assistance, and possible that the State Department will opt for elective compliance with the gag rule as it allocates new Aids funding. One of the administration's core constituencies is the radical American right. According to the *New York Times*, 40 per cent of those casting their votes for Bush in the 2000 presidential elections hail from historically 'evangelical' denominations. In recent years, they have expanded their focus from a purely domestic agenda to the international arena. It was to this constituency that Bush directed his comment, in 2002, that new funding for mother-to-child transmission would help 'the innocent victims of HIV/Aids', and his references to sex trafficking in his 2003 speech before the UN General Assembly. Having struck common cause with traditionally liberal foreign aid advocates, conservative America has become a key actor in campaigns to increase Aids funding, particularly in Africa. The Bush administration enjoys the best of both worlds, receiving the praise of liberal advocates for increasing the quantity of foreign aid, and from conservative pundits for ensuring that its quality reflects their particular values.

If compassionate conservatism is one leg of the Bush administration's Africa strategy, then calculated consumption is the other. Early in its term, the Bush administration made clear its intent to diversify US oil supplies, and an administration task force, headed by Vice-President Dick Cheney and informed largely by the US oil industry, concluded in 2001 that Africa would soon emerge as a leading supplier to the US. Driven more by industry than by innovation, the Bush administration has given far less attention to alternative sources of energy or conservation than it has to securing these new oil supplies. And the need is urgent: the US burns an estimated 19 million barrels of oil per day and consumption is growing.

Angola 1993: government soldier guards US oil facilities during the war with Jonas Savimbi's UNITA. Credit: Getty Images

It is estimated that Africa today provides the US with between 12 and 14 per cent of its oil supplies; industry experts estimate that the continent could provide as much as 25 per cent within the next 15 years. (The Persian Gulf states today provide an estimated 26 per cent, with Canada and Mexico combined providing close to 30 per cent. Middle Eastern oil reserves, however, are estimated to be much larger than those in Africa.) US imports now draw heavily on Nigerian and Angolan oil supplies, but are slated to expand to a new generation of producers in West Africa including Chad, Congo-Brazzaville, Equatorial Guinea and São Tomé and Príncipe.

African oil is of particular appeal. Transportation of West African oil to the US takes just over two weeks, as compared to the six weeks it takes oil to move from the Middle East to US shores; major oil supplies in West Africa are within reach of US military forces positioned in the Atlantic; and, because much of Africa's oil is offshore, exploitation requires neither stability nor a highly visible industry presence. Finally, a majority of Africa's oil exporters are not members of OPEC, and are thus unconstrained by OPEC price controls and free to tie their revenues to the US dollar.

US interest in African oil is not new. While US support for Unita forces in the Angolan civil war was ostensibly rooted in the global fight against communism, it had at least as much to do with preventing the Soviet Union from monopolising that country's oil reserves. George Bush Sr facilitated introductions of African leaders to oil industry magnates in Texas. And the strong support by the Clinton administration for the democratic transition in Nigeria was not unrelated to consideration of Nigeria's prominence as a leading oil supplier.

What is new is the alliance between the White House and the oil industry. George W Bush was himself an oilman; Dick Cheney left a position as CEO of Halliburton to join the Bush administration; National Security Adviser Condoleeza Rice served on the board of Chevron before assuming her position; and a host of White House advisers earned the lion's share of their personal wealth from investments in the industry. Policy, therefore, gives due consideration to the industry's interests, and less to the administration's oft-stated desire to promote 'American values' around the world. The State Department recently opened a new embassy in Equatorial Guinea, not because that country has reformed but because it has begun to exploit significant reserves of oil. Angola has been given the equivalent of a political free pass despite its failure to pursue promised reforms following the death of Jonas Savimbi. Former Assistant Secretary of State for African affairs Walter Kansteiner made several visits to São Tomé while Secretary Colin Powell stopped off in Gabon. Neither state can be said to be among the 'good performers' that the Bush administration has identified as its priority.

The Bush administration has abandoned the Clinton administration's emphasis on a new US 'partnership' with Africa, making clear its disdain for a 'soft' policy that reeks of liberal hand-wringing and opting instead for a hard-headed policy rooted in the realities of a world it believes to be more cruel than collaborative. That this has allowed Africa to gain status as 'strategically important' is not all bad, for the fact of the matter is that the allocation of US attention and resources derives directly from its perception of strategic interests. But it is also a setback. Even if it does signal heightened US compassion, a family-planning strategy that delivers dollars but closes clinics is unlikely to bolster Africa's ability to fight HIV/Aids or future epidemics. And the Bush administration's reversion to the realpolitik of the Cold War, even if it is buttressed by a significant investment in the fight against HIV/Aids, means that the US need for oil will trump Africa's need for progress. ❑

Gayle Smith is an adviser to USAID and former senior director for African affairs at the National Security Council during the Clinton administration

THE SECRET EPIDEMIC

JACOB LEVENSON

FIFTY-FIVE PER CENT OF ALL NEW
HIV CASES IN THE US ARE AFRICAN-
AMERICANS AND THE NEW EPICENTRE
OF THE DISEASE HAS SHIFTED FROM
THE COASTS TO THE SOUTH

David deShazo is chain-smoking Marlboros as he drives north out of Mobile on a bright November morning, in 2000. A garbage bag stuffed with blankets, baby clothes and toys takes up most of the back seat of the Pontiac. The car is chilly because deShazo's heater is busted, and he doesn't have the 200 bucks it will cost to get it fixed. He's headed up to Choctaw County to find two sisters, Sara and Rebecca Jackson, who are infected with HIV. They live with their mother and their two baby sons down a dirt road somewhere outside of Gilbertown, near the Mississippi border. The girls haven't been heard from in seven months. He takes another draw off his cigarette, squints through his bug-smeared windshield at the two-lane highway and tries to resist a flickering current of anxiety.

DeShazo hadn't really known what to expect when he was hired to work in the poor counties of southern Alabama to search out people infected with HIV, to convince the at-risk to get tested and to warn community leaders about the threat of Aids. In the 18 months since he took the job, he's driven more than 60,000 miles talking about the virus to just about anyone who will listen. He's caught hateful stares at general stores and gas stations. A county commissioner over in Wilcox attacked him verbally at a church meeting for talking about Aids without permission. And he's heard comments that the 'niggers' and 'faggots' are just getting what they deserve. None of these things has really surprised deShazo. What's more unsettling is the silence that surrounds him in these towns. When he talks to people it often seems as though he is shouting across an unbridgeable chasm.

By December 2001 c362,827 people in the US were living with HIV/Aids: whites 42%; blacks 37%; Hispanics 20%; Asians 1%; Native Americans 1% | 282,250 men (of 13 years or older) were living with HIV/Aids: 57% had sex with men (MSM);

The Alabama that deShazo has been travelling for a year and a half ceased to exist in the minds of most Americans after the Civil Rights movement. Somehow it was never remade into the New South of Ted Turner, *Emeril Live* and urban sprawl. There remains an expansive, aching beauty to these counties. The countryside, with its forests of hickory, oak and pine, its cotton fields and tangles of green creeks and rivers, feels timeless. A procession of churches lines every road: NEW PROVIDENCE BAPTIST, JESUS IS LORD OLD ZION MISSIONARY, LITTLE ZION BAPTIST.

All of this lends the region a sense that it is somehow insulated from the perils of modern life. But now the greatest epidemic of recent times is spreading slowly and quietly through the black communities of rural Alabama. In the years since Aids hit the headlines, the disease has gradually become a black epidemic. In 2000, according to the Centers for Disease Control, 54 per cent of all new Aids cases were African-Americans. More than half of HIV infections are in people under 25. Aids is now among the top three causes of death for African-American men aged 25–54 and African-American women aged 35–44. What's perhaps even more surprising is that the South is the new epicentre of Aids in the United States. More people are living with Aids in this region than in any other part of the country. And while the disease is still concentrated in Southern cities, there are warning signs that it is creeping into the countryside.

DeShazo and his co-workers represent a thin line of defence against this brewing public health crisis. Impoverished patients have already overburdened Alabama's small network of Aids agencies. Mobile Aids Support Services (MASS), for which deShazo works, has five caseworkers for roughly 800 clients in Mobile and the surrounding six rural counties. Most of their patients don't have private insurance or Medicaid, the most direct avenues to the new drug cocktails. The caseworkers spend the bulk of their time just trying to get medicine for their clients. MASS needs to hire more staff, but as it is can only afford to pay people like deShazo a salary of US$23,000, plus a small allowance for every mile he drives.

As deShazo crosses Choctaw County, a couple of logging trucks stacked with trees rush by in the opposite direction. The last cotton plantations disappeared in the 1960s, and paper mills are the primary industry now. The

24% were intravenous drug users (IDUs); 9% were heterosexual | 59% of women with HIV/Aids were heterosexual; 38% were IDUs | African-Americans have accounted for 38% of Aids cases since the beginning of the epidemic; in 2001

county is home to 16,000 people, roughly half of whom are black, with 22 per cent of the population living in poverty. And there are no hospitals or infectious-disease doctors in Choctaw County.

DeShazo drives through Gilbertown – which isn't much more than a stop light, a cemetery, a grocery, a pharmacy and a dollar store – and makes a right turn down a narrow, unmarked dirt road. He saw the Jackson sisters once before, as a favour to the social worker in Selma who is supposed to be in charge of their case. A part of him is pissed off that they've dropped off the agency's radar since then. At the same time, he's not surprised, given the patchwork nature of Aids care in Alabama. As worried as he is about these girls, he seems charged up about the case, confident that he has the skills to work through the welfare system so that the sisters can get the medications, doctors and care that might save their lives. It's a sense of purpose that he has rarely felt in other social-work jobs, which mostly left him feeling weak and hopeless.

DeShazo pulls over in front of a trailer home, steps out, climbs three rickety steps and knocks. A female voice yells to come on in. He opens the door and feels a wave of heat. The first person he sees is Sara, who is sitting on a couch changing a two-year-old boy on her lap. She's wearing a Michael Jordan T-shirt and her hair is in long cornrows. He is relieved to see that she has full cheeks and looks healthy. Another child in blue pyjamas is giggling and waddling back and forth on the floor. Piles of clothes, empty soda cans and an overturned tricycle litter the living room. A raspy cough comes from the kitchen, where Sara's sister Rebecca is slumped over a chair facing an open oven, trying to keep warm. She must have fever chills because the trailer is stifling, almost too hot to breathe in. DeShazo sets his bag of clothes and toys down on the floor, and introduces himself.

Sara looks up from the couch and says hi. He had been worried about how they would receive him. White men who work for the government aren't always greeted warmly around here. But there is a loose confidence to Sara's smile, and the casual way she continues changing her son's diaper puts him at ease. David says that he's brought some supplies and then abruptly starts firing questions at Sara. How long has Rebecca been like that? What kind of medicine is she taking? Sara says that she's been running a fever for

they accounted for 50% of cases among adults | By December 2001 more than 168,000 African-Americans had died from HIV/Aids | African-American women accounted for 64% of cases among women in 2001 | African-American women

three days, and she's not sure about the medicines, but she could show him. David asks if Sara gets medication. She says she gets some while she's pregnant, but she's going to lose her insurance when she has the baby.

'You pregnant again, Sara?' David asks incredulously.

'Seven months,' she says, shaking her head, smiling, wondering how he didn't notice.

David asks if they are still seeing the doctors in Waynsboro, Mississippi. Sara says yes but that they don't have a car, and she's missed her last couple of appointments because she doesn't have any way to get there.

Rebecca coughs again – a coarse hack, heavy with phlegm – stands up, walks slowly past Sara and pushes through the screen door. Sara goes into the kitchen, opens a cabinet and hands David a plastic basket packed with prescription bottles, many still in sealed boxes. Rebecca takes some of them, Sara tells David, but there are so many that the regimen often becomes confusing.

Sara tells David that she'd been turned down for Medicaid before she got pregnant. Back then she'd been taking her sister's medications. Rebecca pushes through the screen door and collapses on the couch with a yellow blanket. David asks Sara if her boyfriend has been tested. He tested negative a year ago, she answers, but he hasn't been retested since she got pregnant again. And, as far as she knows, Rebecca's boyfriend hasn't been tested, either. Then Sara tells him that her boyfriend takes some of her medications just to be careful.

David starts into a series of questions about birth control and the children, but is interrupted by a visitor at the front door. Sara glances over. It is her aunt Jesse, who is visiting from Mississippi and has dropped by to help with the laundry. Sara introduces her. Jesse nods and makes her way to the back of the trailer.

'I don't want my aunt to know 'cause she talks too much,' Sara whispers.

As deShazo talks with Sara, Rebecca's son William laughs and teethes on a closed bottle of pills. He's fat, playful and, at a year and a half, completely unaware that his mother is gravely ill.

are 16 times more likely to be HIV-positive than white women of the same age | The rate of infection among African-American women is four times higher than among Latin American women of the same age | Aids is the leading cause of

THE CONDOM IN YOUR POCKET

At the very outset of the epidemic, it was perhaps inevitable that Aids would be viewed as a men's disease. The organised communities in which it was first detected were emphatically male: urban gay men and people with haemophilia, a blood disorder that for genetic reasons is found almost exclusively among men. Within a few months of the emergence of Aids in June 1981, however, the first cases had been diagnosed among women and the numbers have mounted steadily since. Yet in those first days, a persistent shroud of denial descended around the issue of women and Aids that continues to threaten the 20 million women suffering from the disease and the hundreds of millions more at risk globally.

'Even as women were becoming infected in the early 1980s, they were treated as anomalies,' says Dr Anke A Ehrhardt, a leading sexuality researcher and director of the HIV Center for Clinical and Behavioral Studies in New York City. Apart from cases involving prostitutes or the occasional blood transfusion, women's vulnerability to Aids was systematically discounted. Eager to avoid panicking the 'general population' while continuing to link Aids with such behaviour as anal sex and drug injection, public health authorities throughout the developed world took little interest in assessing women's risk factors.

In a similar way, between 1981 and 1993, the clinical definition of Aids, established by the US Centers for Disease Control and Prevention (CDC) and used throughout the world, was based on a fixed list of medical conditions and symptoms derived almost exclusively from reports on male patients. It excluded common HIV-related manifestations in women such as recurrent vaginal yeast infections and invasive cervical cancer. Women's risk was further blurred because female cases resulting from sex with male drug users were categorised as being attributable to the 'drug route' rather than heterosexual transmission.

This masking of the epidemiological data also contributed to a lower quality of health care for women. Many doctors failed to offer HIV tests to women patients or to diagnose the early symptoms of infection. Since comparatively few Aids cases were recorded among women, little effort was made to recruit women into clinical trials for anti-retroviral drugs or for treatments of opportunistic infections. As a result, new medications were developed almost exclusively on data from men.

Because the statistics showed women to be low-risk, minimal effort was put into tailoring gender-specific HIV prevention interventions. 'The early prevention messages were just lifted from men's campaigns,' Ehrhardt argues. 'It was "Don't go out without a condom in your pocketbook," the idea being that all women had to do was put on a condom – without any regard for the fact that women would not be the ones wearing the condom.'

It was not until after the first decade of the epidemic had passed that concerted efforts began seriously to address women's HIV-related needs. And, explains Dr Joyce Hunter, a long-time activist and co-chair of the Women's Caucus of the International Aids Society, when in 1993 the CDC finally did change the definition of Aids to include manifestations in women, 'then you saw the rate on the charts increase to such a point that all of a sudden there was an epidemic among women'.

This apparent increase in Aids cases contributed to a cascade of changes. Doctors became more aware of the signs and symptoms of HIV in women. The designers of drug trials began to enrol larger numbers of women. Social and behavioural researchers started to develop gender-specific prevention interventions. The search for female-controlled methods of HIV prevention and for the development of a vaginal microbicide that could be applied topically to kill HIV also began to gather steam. Political figures, in the US most notably Hillary Rodham Clinton and Health and Human Services secretary Donna Shalala, began to speak out publicly on the issue.

Progress on discovering a vaginal microbicide has been painfully slow. There have, however, been dramatic advances in the prevention of HIV transmission from mothers to infants through the use of anti-retroviral drugs during pregnancy and delivery, as well as through education about the risks of breastfeeding for HIV-positive women.

Mass denial about women's vulnerability to Aids seems largely a thing of the past, but 20 years into the epidemic and with many people mistakenly believing that Aids isn't a big deal in the era of anti-retrovirals, complacency about prevention has set in. As Hunter says, 'We still have a long way to go with regard to both prevention and treatment efforts for all women.' ❑

Raymond A Smith teaches political science at Columbia University and at New York University. He is editor of The Encyclopedia of Aids *and co-author of a forthcoming book on global Aids activism*

Alabama, which has always had a relatively low rate of Aids, now seems primed for a burgeoning epidemic. Crack – which often breeds a sex-for-drugs trade and seems inevitably to show up just ahead of Aids – has made its way into even the most rural counties. Already black women in the South are 26 times more likely than white women to have HIV. DeShazo is armed with these facts, but they seem somehow abstract in places like Gilbertown. The threat of Aids here feels deeply entwined with poverty and the lingering effects of segregation.

Every spring, Sara and Rebecca Jackson's high school holds a blood drive. It's always been a popular event with the students. Giving a pint of blood helps the sick, and it's an easy excuse to get out of afternoon classes. Sixteen-year-old Sara and her fourteen-year-old sister Rebecca volunteered to have their blood drawn.

Sara was the more rebellious of the two sisters. Always using her quick wit to get her way with her mother, she had declared her independence by moving in with her boyfriend. As soon as she graduated she planned to join the army. Rebecca, the baby of the family, was more sensitive and even as a youngster wanted to become a nurse. Their father – who had been in prison when the girls were young – worked as a logger and was making enough money to allow their mom to stay at home with Rebecca. On a warm afternoon after the blood drive, Sara came home for a visit and greeted her mother, who absently directed Sara to a letter from the county health department. Simple and straightforward, the letter thanked her for her donation but said that her blood was contaminated with HIV. Sara was stunned. She didn't know anything about the disease except that it was deadly.

A few days later an identical letter arrived for Rebecca.

Sara and Rebecca dropped out of high school. Sara's relationship didn't last, and the girls' father was soon back in prison. Their mother has tried to care for the girls and her grandsons as best she can but has avoided asking welfare workers or Aids agencies for help.

DeShazo is talking to Rebecca and Sara's aunt in the kitchen. He has been at the trailer for about an hour now. He is worried that he is not going to be able to keep these girls alive without help. He wants to enlist family

death among African-American women aged 25–34 and African-American men aged 35–44; and among the top three for African-American men aged 25–34 and African-American women aged 35–44 | A study in 11 US cities found African-

and neighbours who can drive Rebecca two hours to Mobile to see a specialist. That is going to be tough as long as the sisters keep their illness secret. When he comes back into the living room, he says to Sara, 'I know the doctors in Waynesboro have been good to you, but it may be time for you guys to see a specialist. How do you feel about that?'

'I'll do anything that'll keep me healthy like I am 'cause I don't want to leave my children like this,' Sara says. But when he asks if she would consider telling her grandparents or the host of cousins and in-laws who live in the area that she's infected with HIV, she is silent. All the MASS case-workers have heard stories about clients getting discriminated against at their jobs, frozen out by their churches and abandoned by their families. Occasionally, the social worker who handles the agency's rural cases must deliver medications to clients at 'secret' locations such as a grocery store parking lot.

Needing a break, deShazo offers to go down to the pharmacy in Gilbertown and pick up Rebecca's medication. Aids can move relatively quickly through a rural county. HIV spreads mainly through what epidemiologists call 'sexual networks', social groups in which people are sleeping together. On paper they can be traced like genealogical trees. When HIV is introduced into a small town where a significant number of people belong to a single tree, there is a real risk of a mini-epidemic.

After David returns from the pharmacy, he approaches Rebecca. 'Do you ever feel like there's no reason to live, Rebecca?' he asks.

William's head is buried in her breast, and she is rocking him back and forth. 'Sometimes,' she says and stares at the ground.

'Is there anybody you can go to when you feel like that?' he asks.

'There ain't nobody but myself,' she says and clenches her jaw. Her eyes fill with tears, but she stops herself just short of crying.

It is late afternoon, and deShazo prepares to leave. He has scheduled an appointment with the sisters for next week and has asked them to arrange for their mother to be there.

The job of getting Aids patients such as Rebecca and Sara Jackson the drug cocktails that have been popularly heralded as a panacea will ultimately fall on the shoulders of community-based organisations like MASS. In 2000, MASS, which operates on an annual budget of US$600,000, had to 'profes-

Americans were less likely than whites to receive ARV therapy | From 1996 to 1998 Aids incidence fell 38% among whites and 23% among African-Americans | Those infected with an STD are five times more likely to contract HIV/Aids |

sionally beg' pharmaceutical companies for US$1.8 million in medications for uninsured clients. The Alabama legislature has been unwilling fully to match federal funds to help all of the infected poor pay for expensive drugs.

The next Tuesday morning, deShazo drives out to see Rebecca and Sara. When he arrives at the Jacksons' trailer, there is no sign of anyone. A late-70s Chevrolet drives up the road. Sara is in the back seat with her son Benny. 'Where's Rebecca?' he asks. Sara says Rebecca collapsed on Saturday. Just stopped breathing. She's in the hospital in Waynesboro.

DeShazo shakes his head, smiles grimly, gets in his Pontiac, and pulls off in the direction of Waynesboro, talking as he drives. Rebecca's being in the hospital might be a good thing. A hospital stay will make it easier to get home health care. He's rationalising.

He finds Rebecca's door. Inside, she is in the foetal position facing a single window. She's alone. A movie is playing on a television bolted to the wall. Rebecca has her arms pulled up close to her face. An IV is hooked up to her right arm, and she's clinging to her blanket like a small child. DeShazo walks around to the side of her bed. He leans up against the radiator next to the window. 'How you feeling, Rebecca?' he asks. 'I'm going to have surgery tomorrow,' she says, her voice raspy.

'What for?' deShazo asks.

'My gallbladder,' she says, before being seized by a fit of heavy coughing.

'How old are you, Rebecca?' deShazo asks.

'Nineteen,' she answers.

'You know, Rebecca,' deShazo says, 'there's a lady in Mobile who does nothing but check on children whose parents are infected.'

'He ain't infected,' Rebecca says. This is the strongest statement she has ever made to him.

'I know,' he says, 'but it may be wise for William to see her anyway.'

'My mama's with him,' Rebecca says softly.

'Yeah, I know your mama's there doing a real good job.' Realising that there's nothing he can do or say at this moment to make the situation better, he decides to leave.

In the coming months deShazo will dedicate almost all of his time to this case. Rebecca's doctor will drop her for failing to make appointments.

African-Americans are 27 times more likely than whites to have gonorrhoea and 16 times more likely to have syphilis | *Sources: Centers for Disease Control and Prevention*

DeShazo will drive her to a specialist two hours away in Mobile, who will diagnose her with pneumonia, CMV (cytomegalovirus: generalised infection) and thrush. When he tries to get home health care for her, an anonymous caller will warn the Choctaw County health department not to send a nurse to the Jacksons' because Rebecca plans to bite and infect as many people as she can before she dies. Meanwhile, Sara will go into labour a month prematurely. The hospital in Waynesboro, saying they don't have the facilities to handle a premature birth, will refuse to admit her and opt instead to drive her to Mobile. Forty-eight hours after she gives birth, the hospital in Mobile, citing policy for mothers on public assistance, will attempt to discharge her with a bus ticket back to Gilbertown. DeShazo will get her another day in the hospital.

All of this is still in front of them, though. On the drive back from the hospital in Waynesboro, the harsh reality hits deShazo: keeping Rebecca alive with what few resources are available is unlikely. He passes a hand-painted sign for Pine Grove Cemetery on the corner of a dirt road leading into the forest. He is smoking another cigarette. Along the road, the trees have turned flaming orange and sunflower yellow. 'She's going to die,' he says. 'She's going to die, and there ain't one goddamn fucking thing I can do about it.' ❏

Jacob Levenson is a freelance journalist and a fellow with the Open Society Institute. His book, The Secret Epidemic: The Story of Aids and Black America, *a narrative that reaches across half a century, from the Great Migration to the North, to the boom of the post-war era and the subsequent urban decay, to the advent of heroin and crack, to the new South, will be published by Pantheon Books in February 2004*

WAGING WAR WITH DRUGS
AMY KAPCZYNSKI

AIDS IS FORCING A BREACH IN THE
ARMOURY OF THE PHARMACEUTICAL
MULTINATIONALS

In October 2003, former US President Bill Clinton made headlines by announcing that he had brokered a deal with four generic drug companies to cut the cheapest world price for anti-retroviral (ARV) therapy in half, to less than US$140 per year. No event could better mark the distance we've come in the past few years: ARV prices have come down a hundredfold, and Clinton – whose administration once threatened trade sanctions to prevent South Africa from using generic drugs – is making a post-presidency name by encouraging governments to provide generic ARVs to those of their people infected with HIV/Aids.

This free fall in price and the about-face in international political opinion vindicates the strategic decision of a group of Aids activists several years ago to define intellectual property (IP) rights as a key front in the fight against Aids. So are the days when patents took precedence over patients over?

Unfortunately not. First, a primer: patents are creatures of national law, but increasingly – at the behest of the US and major multinational companies – countries are signing bilateral and multilateral trade agreements that include strict IP provisions. The most prominent of these agreements is the World Trade Organisation's Agreement on Trade-Related Aspects of Intellectual Property (TRIPS).

TRIPS establishes minimum requirements for IP protection for all WTO members. It has a staggered timeline for adherence, but once countries are TRIPS-compliant, they will, among other things, have to offer 20-year patents on all technologies, including medicines; many countries have historically refused to allow medicines to be patented because of worries about public health. TRIPS also allows governments to override patents

In May 2000 five major Western pharmaceutical companies announced the Accelerating Access Initiative to make ARV drugs more available to the developing world | In 2000 the cost of a triple combination of ARVs was US$10,000–15,000

through a process known as 'compulsory licensing', as long as they follow certain procedures.

So why all the fuss about TRIPS? Perhaps because no developing country has yet successfully issued a compulsory licence in order to import or produce generics. Many countries, Brazil for instance, have not had to, either because they have not yet complied with TRIPS or have done so only recently. TRIPS demands certain procedures, steps that are administratively complex, time-consuming and expensive. Typically, countries must negotiate with patent-holding companies before overriding patents. They must also establish systems of review and remuneration, and give individualised determination to each patent in question. There are

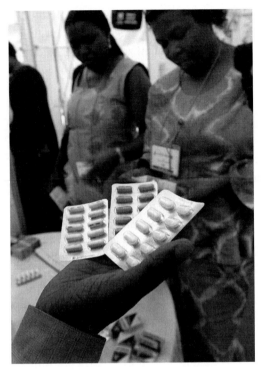

International Aids conference, Kenya 2003: drugs for sale – at a price. Credit: AFP

ways to streamline this process, but it has taken activists several years to figure out how to do this without violating TRIPS. It takes time, too, to put legislation in place to allow compulsory licences, and when countries like South Africa have tried to do so they have been rewarded with lawsuits and threatened trade sanctions.

The administrative friction created by TRIPS, particularly in the context of continued bilateral pressure from countries such as the US, has been enough to slow the effective use of generics in some countries by years and, perhaps, to make the system unusable for those countries that have the least bureaucratic capacity and may need generics the most.

per patient per year (ppy) | The entry of generic ARVs reduced the price from US$10,439 ppy to US$727 within three months | Brazil was the first country to manufacture 'generic' ARV drugs in the early 1990s | Brazil's triple-combination

Rather than address this fundamental conflict between TRIPS and public health, recent events at the WTO have simply made things worse. Consider the celebrated agreement, struck on 30 August 2003, to modify TRIPS to allow countries with insufficient manufacturing capacity to import generic drugs. The original TRIPS agreement stated that countries could only use compulsory licences to produce drugs 'predominantly for the supply of the domestic market'. That's fine for countries such as Brazil or the US that have the capacity to make their own drugs. But for countries without such capacity, it means nothing to have the right to use generics if other countries are denied the right to supply them.

At the Doha Ministerial Meeting in 2001, countries promised to resolve this issue, but the US and EU made quick work of the promise. Many months of bitter negotiations later, member countries, tired of wrangling over medicines and hoping to pave the way for success at Cancún in 2003, 'solved' the problem with 3,200 words' worth of Kafkaesque conditions. Now countries without manufacturing capacity can import generics, but only after issuing a compulsory licence, conducting an assessment of their capacity to produce generics, notifying the WTO, finding a supplier, getting that supplier to obtain their own compulsory licence and so forth. The list goes on.

The 30 August agreement is only temporary, but there is little reason to suspect that the permanent amendment, which will be negotiated soon, will be any better. And although the Canadians have recently pledged to make this wheezy contraption work by passing legislation to allow Canadian companies to export generics through it, this plan may well take years to realise. And it doesn't solve the basic problem: the labyrinthine structure of requirements that TRIPS interposes between people who need drugs and those drugs that can save their lives.

If we took these lives seriously, what we would be talking about would not be more procedures designed to protect the most profitable industry in the world. We would be talking about repealing TRIPS, or at least carving out an exception for drugs and medical technologies. As Jagdish Bhagwati recently pointed out in the *Financial Times*, there is nothing 'trade-related' about TRIPS. It's really just a poorly camouflaged scheme to use the WTO

therapy cost US$3,000 ppy | In February 2001 the Indian drugs firm Cipla announced that it would be selling ARV drugs for US$350 ppy | By April 2003 the price of Hetero, an Indian generic, was US$201 ppy | The price of ARVs

as a royalty-collection agency, dreamed up by companies who wanted to capture emerging markets but needed the muscle of the Office of the United States Trade Representative (USTR) to do it. The argument that TRIPS is essential to development and that IP is necessary to fund research is a canard: as the Final Report by the UK Commission on Intellectual Property Rights points out, rich countries long used weak IP protection as a development tool, excluding entire sectors, such as medicines, from protection. Poor countries should also have the power to adapt IP policies to meet local needs – particularly since there is no evidence that IP protection plays any role in stimulating research in diseases of the poor.

Unfortunately, we're worlds away from getting rid of TRIPS: trade agreements that impose intellectual property restrictions are proliferating. The US is increasingly bypassing the harsh spotlight of the WTO and negotiating even more restrictive IP provisions through bilateral and regional trade agreements. We're a long way away – and getting further – from a simple system that guarantees that countries will be able to make use of generic drugs when public health needs demand it.

However, at least where Aids is concerned, those in a position to act are finally getting the relationship the right way round: life before patents, and patients' rights before patent rights. Local NGOs are increasingly using generics and daring drug companies to stop them. International NGOs are following their lead. The Clinton Foundation didn't worry about patent barriers to their new generic drug deal – they just secured the best price they could and assumed that any patent problems could be resolved later. Similarly, the WHO is on the verge of recommending the use of three-in-one ARV pills. These are the best option for simple first-line treatments but, because of patent barriers, are only available from generic manufacturers.

The scandal is that this consensus is only just developing and that the time it has taken to emerge is measured not in days but in lives. ❏

Amy Kapczynski is a treatment-access activist and recent graduate of Yale Law School

must drop to US$50–100 ppy to be effective in tackling the epidemic | *Source*: *Médecins Sans Frontières*

THE CASE FOR THE CONDOM

MJ KELLY

FACED WITH THE DEPREDATIONS OF HIV/AIDS
IN AFRICA, THE CATHOLIC CHURCH FALLS
BACK ON TRADITIONAL MORAL THEOLOGY
TO JUSTIFY THE USE OF CONDOMS

A comprehensive response to HIV/Aids must give attention to prevention, support, care and impact-mitigation. The response of the Catholic Church to the epidemic in Africa has manifested itself strongly in each of these areas.

Concern that transmissions be prevented has been a hallmark of the Church response, though many express dissatisfaction with the form that response has taken. Together with others from the faith-based communities, the Catholic Church has been remarkable in the consistency and the force of its messages propounding abstinence and the mutual fidelity of partners in a monogamous marriage. The insistence of the Catholic Church and other faith-based organisations on these approaches has helped to keep them prominent in international thinking, even though many programmes and projects tend to downplay them as placing unrealistic ideals before the majority of men and women.

Such defeatist attitudes overlook the fact that even in the countries most severely affected by HIV, three-quarters and more of the people are not infected, implying the possibility that a very large percentage do, in fact, abstain from risky sexual activity and/or live in mutual fidelity in the safe union of a marriage where neither partner is infected with HIV. Attitudes that suggest that it is excessively idealistic to consider promoting pre- or extra-marital abstinence, and fidelity in marriage, also ignore the evidence that the dramatic reduction in Uganda's HIV prevalence rates was due primarily to increased fidelity and, to a lesser extent, abstinence, with condom use taking what was quite clearly the third place. Fidelity and abstinence have the merit that they represent substantive behaviour changes – or the maintenance of intrinsically valuable human behaviours – and hence are more likely to be sustained than the superficial behaviour change involved in condom use.

The strength and effectiveness of this Church emphasis on abstinence and fidelity has been overshadowed in public discussions about the safer-sex approach, especially in so far as condom use is part of this approach. While condom use may be key to approaches that deal with very specific activities or groups, such as commercial sex work or men who have sex with men, there is no compelling evidence that it is central to successful approaches for the general population.

However, this is not to deny the importance of condom use as an important component of general HIV prevention approaches. It is not the only element, neither is it the most important element. But it can make a significant contribution to reducing the likelihood of HIV transmission.

While abstinence and marital fidelity, within a framework of a proper understanding of sexuality, constitute the safest and most human preventive approach against HIV transmission, Catholic teaching also allows for the application of traditional guiding moral principles that manifest a robust sense of reality and responsibility in response to a wide variety of ethically challenging situations, HIV transmission among them.

One such principle is that of the lesser of two evils. This principle states that if an activity implies the violation of two moral principles, it is lawful to modify the behaviour – or to recommend its modification – in such a way that it leads to the violation of only one such principle, since this reduces the potential moral harm.

Pre- or extra-marital sexual activity violates the moral stance on abstinence and/or fidelity within marriage. But within the context of HIV/Aids, such activity also violates the moral principle that one should avoid doing harm to another, especially the potentially life-threatening harm of HIV transmission. In order to avoid such harm, it is permissible for an individual who is determined to proceed with pre- or extra-marital sexual activity to use a condom, since this removes the major potentially harmful outcome of HIV transmission.

It is worth noting that the application of this same principle of the lesser of two evils makes it permissible to advocate less harmful ways of drug use, such as providing clean needles to injecting drug users or enabling such individuals to change from injectable drugs to those that can be taken orally.

A second long-standing Catholic moral principle, the principle of double effect, legitimates the use of condoms by a discordant married couple. The principle states that if an action has two outcomes – one regrettable, the other desirable or neutral – it is permissible to place the action, and thereby allow the occurrence of the undesirable outcome, provided the undesirable outcome is not itself the route that leads to the desirable and there is good reason for tolerating the undesirable outcome.

A discordant couple may wish to show their love and support for one another, above all in the very difficult circumstances that one of them is HIV-positive, through lovemaking and sexual activity. Their lovemaking and sexual activities are intensely human and at the same time deeply sacred. So that the possibility of transmitting HIV may not contaminate the achievement of this great good, the principle of double effect allows for the use of any means that will prevent the possible transmission of the virus. This centuries-old principle reassures the couple, and those who advise them, that in these circumstances the use of a condom is permissible.

Catholic principles can go even further. The most basic principle of morality is the protection of life. Guided by this fundamental principle and the judicious application of the principles of the lesser of two evils and the double effect, the growing consensus of Catholic moral teachers is that condom use is not only lawful in certain circumstances, but that it may also be the morally preferable course of action. In addition to being permissible, condom use may actually be the required moral option.

This position suggests that the time has come to put the condom debate to rest. People will be better served, and more lives will be saved, if their energy is directed, instead, to making a consistent, universally accepted response to the epidemic.

In the areas of care, support and impact-mitigation, the Catholic Church has responded vigorously, wholeheartedly and compassionately to the epidemic. More than one-quarter of the support provided worldwide for those who have been touched by HIV/Aids comes from the Catholic Church or its organisations, to say nothing of the care and support that come from individual Catholics. The Church has pioneered the provision of home-based care in many parts of sub-Saharan Africa. The dedication of religious groupings, especially sisters and other religious women, to the provision of direct support and care to the sick and to orphans is widely acknowledged. In the absence of such commitment, the response to HIV/Aids throughout sub-Saharan Africa would be very much weaker.

But Church members remain human beings. Hence, although the Church response to the epidemic is powerful, pervasive and very responsible, there is more that can be done. Church leaders and members alike need to:
• acknowledge more clearly the existence of HIV/Aids in their midst, conceding that there are HIV-infected priests, sisters and Church members;

- adamantly reject every utterance, pronouncement or practice that carries any connotation of stigma or discrimination, including the practice of requiring HIV testing in candidates seeking admission to priestly training or the religious life;
- acclaim the wonder and goodness of human sexuality as a firm basis for endorsing the complete A-B-C message (abstinence, fidelity, condom use) within the framework of traditional moral principles, for the prevention of HIV transmission;
- recognise even more clearly the dimensions of the orphans' challenge and mobilise their communities for a massive response to it in humane and practical ways;
- pour their enormous human resources into the major tasks of eliminating poverty and ending the subjugation of women while recognising the sea change this will mean for many internal structures and practices;
- work in cooperation and harmony with the representatives of other faith-based organisations and local cultures, civic personnel and local, national and international leaders;
- maintain a multidimensional response to HIV/Aids at the top of their agenda and as an integral element in their seminary and other training programmes;
- galvanise their members into action for the reduction of HIV transmission, the provision of care and support for those infected or affected, and the mitigation of the impacts of the disease and epidemic.

Finally, the response to the epidemic would be greatly strengthened if the Church went out of its way to identify in a public, caring and dynamic way with those infected or affected by the epidemic. People need to be reassured that throughout this epidemic God is more than ever with his people, irrespective of their faith or religious affiliation. The Church's basic belief is that God entered most deeply into the condition of humankind when Jesus Christ died in appalling suffering. It can give hope to people and a world with HIV/Aids that God continues to enter deeply into their condition, in a mysterious way experiences their sufferings with them and challenges every person to play a part in ending the tyranny of the epidemic. In a time of HIV/Aids, individuals and the world need hope. The Church is uniquely equipped and strongly challenged to respond to this need. ❑

MJ Kelly SJ is a professor at the University of Zambia and has written widely on Aids and education

SEX AND THE HOLY CITY

IN COUNTRIES WHERE CATHOLIC BELIEF
COUNTS, THE VATICAN'S TEACHING CAN BE A
MATTER OF LIFE AND DEATH — PARTICULARLY
WHERE IT ENCOUNTERS HIV/AIDS

STEVE BRADSHAW (BBC *Panorama*) The Pope [is engaged in] a war
against the permissive society and for a Christian ideal of love, the
family and motherhood. Millions have listened to his message in person
as he's travelled to over 120 countries. Even after an attempt on his life,
John Paul took his message to the streets and on to the world's political
stage. At the United Nations in New York the Vatican has special
permanent observer status because the Holy City in Rome is officially
a state. No other religious leader is so privileged. The Vatican status has
given the Pope the chance to influence the world's population and
development policy, working with some unexpected allies to the
irritation of liberal Catholics.

FRANCES KISSLING (Catholics for a Free Choice) When I go to the UN
and watch the Vatican representatives operate right on the floor, I see
them going up to Libya, to the Sudan, to Oman, to Muslim countries
that have similar conservative views on women and reproduction, and
wheeling and dealing just like every other government official in the
world.

SB Since the early days of Pope John Paul's reign, the world has been
facing a new and terrible crisis. It is in Africa that the Aids pandemic has
struck hardest, and it's also where the Church is ignoring widely agreed
scientific evidence on Aids. In Kenya, someone dies of Aids every
couple of minutes. It's thought up to one-fifth of Kenyans have the HIV
virus that causes Aids; and in Nairobi, when your loved one dies, this is
where you come. There are 16 coffin makers in the Street of Coffins.
A decade ago there were just three. The World Health Organisation
says the best way to prevent Aids is abstinence, or monogamy with
an uninfected partner; it also recommends condoms, which it says
significantly cut the risk of HIV transmission. But the coffin makers
know condoms are unpopular.

COFFIN MAKER Many young people don't trust condoms, they argue that dying of Aids is like being killed in an accident. People think condoms are not 100 per cent secure and they treat it as a similar risk to a car crash so they don't like using them for those reasons.

SB About one-third of Kenyans are Catholic and many clinics, hospitals and schools are Catholic-run. But while the Church does promote abstinence and fidelity to prevent Aids, it does not promote condoms. Vatican doctrine is opposed to condoms, claiming they break the link between love and procreation. Some priests get round this: they say it's a matter for the conscience. But not the Archbishop of Nairobi.

RAPHAEL NDINGI MWANA A'NZEKI (Archbishop of Nairobi) The Catholic Church does not advocate use of condoms under any circumstances. HIV/Aids is going so fast because of the availability of condoms.

SB You think condoms are causing Aids?

A'NZEKI Yes. I'll explain. You give a young Kenyan a condom; for him or for her it's a licence for sexuality. They think they're protected and they're not protected. Understand? . . . We don't use any produced condom; they should not be made at all.

SB Nobody should use them? Even people who are not Catholics?

A'NZEKI Anybody for that matter. The laws of God affect everybody.

SB Catholic bishops in Kenya produced this pamphlet which claims: 'Latex rubber from which condoms are made has pores through which viral-sized particles can squeeze during intercourse.' This is scientific nonsense, isn't it?

A'NZEKI That is true. First we have defective ones.

SB It doesn't say anything about defective condoms. It says: 'Latex rubber from which condoms are made has pores through which viral-sized particles . . .'

A'NZEKI It means they are not proof . . . complete 100 per cent proof.

SB But it says latex rubber, it says that viruses can pass through latex rubber. That's nonsense.

A'NZEKI You go and get the scientists to look at it.

SB Archbishop, with the greatest respect, what I'm suggesting is that you're peddling superstition and ignorance.

A'NZEKI We are not peddling ignorance. We shall be proved the only people who have been right in this matter in the long run.

SB The most authoritative recent report by the US National Institute of Health concluded: 'Intact condoms are essentially impermeable to the smallest sexually transmitted virus . . . the consistent use of male condoms protects against HIV/Aids transmission.' The WHO insists it is imperative to continue promoting condoms for HIV prevention.
  In 1996, Cardinal Otunga, who is the highest-ranking Catholic in Kenya, led a symbolic burning of condoms and safe-sex literature. In Africa. millions face death from Aids, yet here the Church is burning condoms. The bonfire was attended by a top Catholic gynaecologist.

STEPHEN KARANJA (Catholic gynaecologist) It was a condom bonfire. We had more than 5–10,000 people, young people, old people, simple men from the streets. I was there. I have to be there. I lead by example. We had discussions about the condom. We had scientific presentations, we had social presentations, then we had . . . How do you want to call it? We had a symbolic burning of the evil that is the condom.

SB But does anyone take any notice of the Catholic attack on condoms? A day's drive from Nairobi we've come to Lwak, by the shores of Lake Victoria. With no national health service or welfare state in Kenya, the Catholic Church plays a vital role in curing, caring and educating, just as it does across the world. Sister Victorine Akoth runs the Catholic clinic and, like other nuns here, she has her own painful experience of the Aids epidemic: she's lost a brother and a sister to the virus. Girls are particularly affected here, as many as four out of ten, thought to be the highest infection rate in the world. But the Church's anti-condom stance has a strong grip in Lwak.
  Attached to the medical clinic is an HIV testing centre and the man running it has to take notice of what the Catholics who run the church say about condoms.

GORDON WAMBI (HIV counsellor) What I tell people about condoms is that when condoms are used properly they prevent the spread of HIV/Aids.

SB Do you hand them out?

WAMBI I don't hand them out because I don't stock them here. Because we are on Catholic premises and the Catholics do not, maybe, encourage the use of condoms.

SB They don't allow it, in fact.

WAMBI Yes.

SB How do you feel about that?

WAMBI Well, it is something that is not good but there is nothing we can do about it.

SB So what did the nuns say about condoms to those who have already got the virus? Sister Victorine invited us to go and see one of her patients. Sister, just explain where we're going and who we're going to see.

SISTER VICTORINE AKOTH (St Elizabeth Health Clinic) We are going to see a man who has been having Aids for quite a long time, it is now already six years.

Honduras: last rites for Aids patient. Credit: Bill Stephenson / Panos

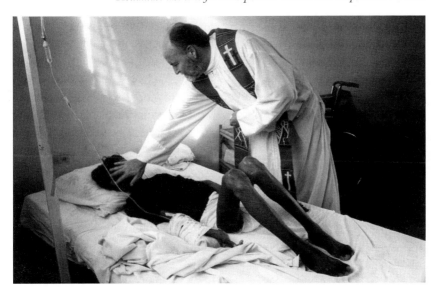

SB The patient with Aids was Mathias, a choirmaster and helper of the church clinic. Inside, he suggested we start with a prayer. Ill for six years and barely able to afford the medicines that keep him alive, Mathias hopes that his wife, Emadine, has so far managed to escape infection. I first asked Mathias whether his drugs were helping.

MATHIAS OTIENDO (choirmaster) Yes, so they're working, it is responding in me. It is expensive but I'm just trying as much as I can.

SB Sister, what's your advice to Mathias and his wife?

SISTER AKOTH My advice to him is only that they may keep praying because now there is nothing they can do about it. He is already sick. If the wife has accepted the situation then they may live, continue to love each other, be faithful to one another until the day . . . their last day on earth.

SB Tell me, Mathias, how this has affected your marriage. It must be difficult for you and your wife.

MATHIAS It's difficult but we have to control now because if you don't control we know the risk. I know that we have so many things, we have things like condom and me I can't use condom.

SB Tell me why not.

MATHIAS The Church tells us that it's not 100 per cent safe that we are . . . that there's some holes in it . . . in the condoms.

SB Sister, what are we to make of Mathias's story?

SISTER AKOTH They aren't 100 per cent useful because they can rupture, they're just made of rubber, they can rupture and, as you see, there is some pores in the condom that the virus can pass through. That is very true. So I seriously side with him that the option he has taken not to be with the wife, he will have to control himself, is very good.

SB Is there a place for condoms if they are used properly? If they work and they're used properly, is there ever a reason to use condoms?

SISTER AKOTH I don't see a reason of using them.

SB What's really heartbreaking is that the sisters here seem kind, they seem intelligent, they're hard-working and they could be the front line in the war against Aids, and yet what they're doing is peddling rumour and superstition, and the question is, really, who has made them believe it? We've come across what the WHO calls 'the dangerous allegation that condoms let HIV through' before. The Archbishop of Nairobi put his name to a pamphlet making the claim, and we'd heard the story from Catholics in two other continents, from the Head of the Pro-Life Clinics in Manila City . . .

ANNA DAHILIG (anti-contraception campaigner, Manila) What's wrong with condoms? You see condoms they are made of rubber, so even the Aids virus can pass through the pores of the condom.

SB . . . and we'd heard the same claim from the Cardinal in Nicaragua.

CARDINAL MIGUEL OBANDO Y BRAVO (Archbishop of Managua, Nicaragua) Now studying genetics we were told that Aids can be transmitted through the doctor's surgical glove which is less porous than a condom.

SB Clearly these extraordinary claims are being made by influential Catholics across the world, so we asked the Pope's spokesman on the family whether they are also the official view of the Vatican.
  Is it the position of the Vatican that the virus, the HIV virus, can pass through the condom?

CARDINAL ALFONSO LOPEZ TRUJILLO (Pontifical Council for the Family) Yes, yes, because this is something which the scientific community accepts, and doctors know what we are saying. You cannot talk about safe sex. One should speak of the human value, about the family, and about fidelity.

SB But I have spoken to the WHO and they say it is simply not true that the HIV virus can pass through latex from which condoms are made.

TRUJILLO Well, they are wrong about that, no dialogue is possible at that level, scientifically speaking, because this is an easily recognisable fact.

SB In Kenya, the Vatican's unyielding rejection of condoms is affecting real lives. Here in Kisumu, Irene already has Aids. She's telling a group of unwed mothers in a community project what it's like.

IRENE Take it seriously, it's hell. My dear sisters, it's hell.

SB This isn't a Catholic project so condoms are available, though with the propaganda against them there's been a local backlash.

JOAB OTHATCHER (Teenage Mothers' Association of Kenya) We need people who are working especially with teenage mothers and child prostitutes, people who are already engaging in sex are actually being seen as promoting promiscuity because we are telling them if you cannot . . . if you haven't reached a point where you are strong enough to abstain, then you'd better protect yourself rather than getting exposed.

SB Some of the women who work here say Catholic propaganda against condoms is partly to blame for their HIV-positive status.

EUNIC ATOGO ATIENO When I engaged in sex I didn't use a condom. I can remember my headmaster one day was trying to tell us about the condom but when we went to church I heard something the priest was saying that condom is not good for people, and in my life I say that if I could have had enough information on the condom use, I couldn't have contracted the virus.

OTHATCHER I think that the Pope perhaps is not in touch with the real problem. I know, working with young girls in this programme, I know how bad HIV/Aids has hit our adolescent girls, and I feel it. It is not so easy for someone sitting in Rome to know what happens on the ground. Most of the girls that we have here are girls from the Catholic background, and yet they are infected, they are HIV-positive. If they used a condom one time it would have saved their lives. Yet they cry and say it is too late. And we know it is too late because they are already infected, and that's my appeal to the Pope. You can do something. You can say something that will come down to the Church and the young people of the world will be saved. We are losing a generation of young people. ❑

Excerpted from 'Sex and the Holy City', broadcast by the BBC programme Panorama, *12 October 2003*

SEX, LIES AND HIV

ABDELSALAM HASSAN

ISLAMIC ATTITUDES TO AIDS COMBINE
A CASTIGATION OF 'MODERN WESTERN
VALUES' WITH DENIAL AND CENSORSHIP
IN MUSLIM SOCIETIES

When an Arab male appeared on international TV channels wearing the Arabic *augal* while watching the tennis at Wimbledon in the early 1990s, the well-known Egyptian columnist Mahmoud al-Sa'adani suggested that this man should be given an Arabic public honour. The ever-provocative columnist wrote in *Al-Hayat* that he had, by his presence, proved that rich Arab tourists in Europe could also be pictured, for a change, in decent and prestigious places like Wimbledon, not just in nightclubs, striptease shows and gambling joints.

These all too familiar images of rich Gulf tourists, police statistics in Islamic and Arabic countries on what are called crimes against public decency or honour, the number of abandoned newborn babies and so on are usually ignored by Middle Eastern and Islamic apologists when making their comparisons between the so-called 'decadence' of the West and the supposed 'chastity' of the Muslim world.

The challenge of HIV/Aids was met with the same logic. Early statistics showed a significantly lower rate of infection in the region and this was used as confirmation of the superiority of its morally committed societies and their impregnability in the face of this 'dirty disease'. However, statistics in subsequent years told a very different story and the dangerous process of silence and denial began.

The censorship of information about HIV/Aids was initially undertaken at the behest of both state agencies and individuals infected with the virus. It has since proved to be for the benefit of everybody. Governments can avoid facing the difficult and expensive responsibilities the spread of HIV/Aids brings and the embarrassing implication that public morality has deteriorated under their rule; infected individuals can live what remains of their lives without the social stigma against them and their families. The only draw-back was that silence and the no-action policy was the vehicle that brought about the high statistics.

On 5 March this year, key arts and media personalities gathered in Cairo with the aim of 'breaking the silence' on HIV/Aids. With over 500,000 people known to be living with HIV/Aids in Arab countries, the United Nations Development Programme (UNDP) convened this gathering to help create the awareness needed to keep prevalence rates down and prevent the further spread of the disease.

Attitudes are indeed changing, with countries such as Iran allowing sex education and safe-sex propaganda, and some North African countries calling officially for international help. Sudan has also lately joined the call for foreign assistance to combat the pandemic. But the campaign for the prevention of Aids will continue to suffer from the deep-rooted mentality of this particular type of silence, denial and censorship.

Let me attempt to trace the origin of this trend of thought among modern Islamic fundamentalists: the Islamists. The Islamists' discourse not only enjoys wide public support, it has been co-opted by many governments in the region to combat the political threat of the Islamists themselves or to win public support. Almost all of them have used a form of Islamist discourse; the only difference is the degree to which different governments have exploited it.

An excellent model of the Islamists' approach to the global Aids epidemic is Malik Badri's book *The Aids Crisis: An Islamic Socio-Cultural Perspective*. The author is not only a professor of psychology, he is an intellectual with a profound knowledge of many current cultural, scientific and philosophical matters. Yet his conclusions about the Aids crisis do not differ in essence from the conclusions of any half-educated imam in any remote village in the Islamic world.

Badri sees the current HIV/Aids crisis as divine retribution against the West's current abandon – homosexuality, promiscuity, drug and alcohol abuse – itself the result of modern society's lax attitudes towards these vices. He focuses his attack on what he calls 'modernity's sexual revolution', his preferred term for liberal attitudes towards sexuality. The author goes on to attack the current Western model of Aids prevention based on the concept of safe sex, concluding that it has failed to address the real problems. Because even 'if a cure or a vaccine for Aids is discovered, a new gene mutation [in HIV] cannot be avoided if the sexual revolution and modernity's attitude to drug intake are not changed'.

The author clearly does not see Aids as a sexually transmitted disease and, in his zeal to prove that point, subscribes to the theory that Aids is not the direct result of the HIV virus. He even claims that an 'HIV-positive person who has been infected by a blood transfusion will not catch Aids' provided he has a 'healthy immune system and a morally clean lifestyle' – in other words, if he refrained from consuming alcohol or drugs and from 'un-Islamic' sexual activities.

Although Malik devotes a good deal of his book to detailing the sexual abandon supposedly brought about by modernity's total rejection of any revealed morality, he also comments: 'It is also true to state that most Westerners, who constitute the "silent majority", do not subscribe to the extreme views of the protagonists of the sexual revolution, nor to the odd practices of liberated gays.' One is left wondering what happened to the author's theory of retribution if, as he argues, the majority of Westerners do not commit what caused God's retribution in the first place. And in the Islamic world 'it is true to say that many Muslims do not strongly follow their religion, otherwise Aids would not have been a problem'.

So what response should the Islamist make to Aids that is different from that of the West if he is to avoid God's retribution and Badri's anger? The answer: 'What such a prevention programme hopes to achieve is to put Islamically unsanctioned sexual practice back into the darkness of the "closet" and not, as modernity does, to take out one shocking offence after another.' Furthermore, his commitment to censorship in the Aids context is total: 'In my view, the scissors of censorship in many Muslim countries have become too blunt. They need sharpening.' ❏

Abdelsalam Hassan *is a Sudanese lawyer living in London*

WHEN AIDS COMES HOME
KIIZA NGONZI

A PERSONAL STORY FROM UGANDA

I have come to the conclusion that HIV/Aids is not entirely about death. People die and will continue to die for one reason or the other. Aids is also about the living.

I am Ugandan so I have been around Aids all my adult life. I have watched my friends die; schoolmates wither and disappear for some concocted reason; my friends' parents fall sick, become incapacitated, die and be buried. I have played my role in fighting Aids, worked with organisations with strong HIV/Aids policies and community HIV/Aids intervention programmes. I have attended HIV/Aids seminars, workshops on Aids, listened to the most moving experiences by victims and activists.

Yet in spite of all this preparation, there is nothing that prepares you when Aids comes home. All I can say is that there's an aura of hopelessness that settles around your entire being. You know that no matter what you do and will try to do, the certainty of losing this person 'soon' is written in stone.

I was born Sarah Nightingale to Elizabeth Miriam Najjuma on 24 December some years ago. I had to wait eight years for my father and his people to give me a name as is customary in our society. Indeed, I did not see him until I was eight when he came from Kenya to check on his illegitimate daughter. My father went to the extent of ensuring that none of his children had English names nor carried his name as a surname, so when I entered his household as an eight-year-old, I became another: Kiiza Ngonzi. Ngonzi means love and Kiiza is a name given to the child born after twins.

I straddle two families – my father's fourth child; my mother's twelfth and last-born – but am their only child. My father is a dental surgeon, the first professional in his family or village. He is the only African I know whose qualifications overflowed his business card. He had spent 32 years, many of them in exile from Idi Amin's attacks on doctors, in England amassing these. By the time he moved back to Kenya, he had become head of the dental department at Guy's Hospital in London; in Nairobi, he took charge of the university dental school and lectured in the university itself.

My mother, on the other hand, was a simple but remarkable woman. She was a midwife in Mulago Hospital in Kampala, Uganda. By the time I was conceived, she was the single mother of eight children, three boys and five girls with whom she had fled from her husband's homestead to Kampala. As the story goes, my mother had been given at 16 years old by her stepbrother to a local chief. In 20 years, she bore him 11 children, two of whom died at birth.

In my father's house, I learned to use forks and knives, to speak English and my father's language. I met TV for the first time and my teacher-stepmother introduced me to the world of books. It was the childhood of my dreams.

After my father returned to Uganda and the country was liberated, I went to boarding school near Kampala where I excelled; then to Makerere University where I studied physics, chemistry and geology, and, finally, to do my MSc in the Netherlands.

Since then, I have lost five members of my family within the space of five years: siblings aged between 30 and 45 who have left behind 12 orphans between them and a series of financial disasters in their wake. To top it all, our mother, having gone through the worst nightmare of any parent – that of burying her own children before her – died of it too. If I did not know better, I would think it is in the family genes.

By the time my mother died, she had lost five children and left behind 27 grandchildren and great-grandchildren, of whom 12 are orphans between the ages of six and 21. The orphans have been divided among us remaining four girls: I have no biological children of my own yet, but I have a teenage 'daughter' and a 'son' for whom I am financially responsible.

In the process of her dying, I spent my entire savings financing my mother's and my sister's recovery for that one year I was home. I could not plan ahead because every need was immediate; and even though they were at one time in a private hospital, one of us had to be there to nurse, wash and feed them, and ensure that we were on top of their treatment. I became so broke that when my sister became worse after Mother's death,

I could not keep her in a private hospital and opted for a government one. She was reacting so badly to the ARV cocktail she was put on that she was losing a huge amount of blood: literally drying up because of the medicine.

The government hospital told us their blood supply had run out and, because I didn't know the ropes, I dragged all the family members I could to go and donate blood. Later, after I had managed to squeeze 230ml from myself, I discovered that all I had to do was grease someone's palm to get the blood I needed.

She died four months later, leaving four very distraught children who could not understand how their mother had deteriorated so fast. They have, of course, been absorbed by the family

I am comforted by the fact that I was able to look after my mother and make sure she got all the care she needed. My sister, on the other hand, did not fare so well. By the time we had buried Mother, caught up with the funeral and hospital bills, I was too broke to keep up the payment for her medicine and had to leave Uganda to get work to be able to send money back to help out. Sadly, by the time I got the money she was in a coma and died three days later. The money went on the funeral and the accumulated hospital bills.

As I said in the beginning, it is not so much about the victim's imminent death or the emotional anguish you go through as you watch them slowly but surely physically and emotionally waning from the time of discovery to full–blown Aids.

It is about the impact on the family individuals who care for them with the knowledge that they will not recover, and who want to give up but are duty-bound.

It is about the financial consequences of access to quality treatment.

It is about the inability to plan and save for the future, the liquidation of family assets so that you can meet payments and other matters that arise.

It is about the frustration of seeing money poured into a bottomless pit and getting nothing for it.

Most important, it is about the children, the next generation, who are moved from relative to relative, usually separated to ensure that the responsibilities are spread evenly throughout the family. It is about their upbringing amid the chaos and neglect; it is about equipping them with survival skills; it is about their growing up before time.

I have become exhausted and despairing: nothing seems to shift. I cannot affect the lives of the teenagers in my care because I am not there.

'They that can give up essential liberty to obtain a little temporary safety deserve neither liberty nor safety' Benjamin Franklin

NOAM CHOMSKY ON
ROGUE STATES

EDWARD SAID ON
IRAQI SANCTIONS

LYNNE SEGAL ON
PORNOGRAPHY

... all in

SUBSCRIBE & SAVE

UK and overseas

○ **Yes! I want to subscribe to _Index_.**

❒ 1 year (4 issues)	£32	Save 16%
❒ 2 years (8 issues)	£60	Save 21%
❒ 3 years (12 issues)	£84	**You save 26%**

Name _____

Address _____

_____ B0B5

£ _____ enclosed. ❒ Cheque (£) ❒ Visa/MC ❒ Am Ex ❒ Bill me
(_Outside of the UK, add £10 a year for foreign postage_)

Card No. _____

Expiry _____ Signature _____

❒ I do not wish to receive mail from other companies.

INDEX

✉ Freepost: INDEX, 33 Islington High Street, London N1 9BR
☎ (44) 171 278 2313   Fax: (44) 171 278 1878
🖥 tony@indexoncensorship.org

SUBSCRIBE & SAVE

North America

○ **Yes! I want to subscribe to _Index_.**

❒ 1 year (4 issues)	$48	Save 12%
❒ 2 years (8 issues)	$88	Save 19%
❒ 3 years (12 issues)	$120	**You save 26%**

Name _____

Address _____

_____ B0B5

$ _____ enclosed. ❒ Cheque ($) ❒ Visa/MC ❒ Am Ex ❒ Bill me

Card No. _____

Expiry _____ Signature _____

❒ I do not wish to receive mail from other companies.

✉ Freepost: INDEX, 708 Third Avenue, 8th Floor, New York, NY 1001
☎ (44) 171 278 2313   Fax: (44) 171 278 1878
🖥 tony@indexoncensorship.org

They, in turn, are not interested in school and the times I have gone home and talked to them about the importance of education they look as though it is going in one ear and out the other. Often I want to give up and tell myself they are not my children and if they cannot understand their lot in life then too bad!

Then I remember that their mothers and fathers contributed to ensuring that I, at least, made it. I feel caught in a quagmire of gratitude and responsibility and do not know which to choose. Life is hard and the good schools are very expensive and we cannot afford to put 12 orphans in them plus our own children and so we have opted to put them in schools that we could afford so that they can all get an education.

We ask them to study hard and we are honest with them about the reason why their parents died and ask them to be careful. Most of the younger ones are still in school but the teenagers have opted out; and to date my 14-year-old 'daughter' is out of school after running away several times. And I am out of the country.

So when anyone asks me how I feel about this epidemic and how my experience has strengthened my resolve to continue fighting against it, the only thing I can say is that if I can feel this exhausted, this worn out, this desperate, hopeless and at times helpless during and after the Aids visit into my home, how badly do those who are far worse off than me feel, and who is there to help them? ❏

Kiiza Ngonzi works for Justice Africa in London

STRIP SEARCH by Martin Rowson

1 WELCOME, WELCOME EVERYONE TO THIS OUR ANNUAL GENERAL MEETING AFTER YET ANOTHER FANTASTICALLY SUCCESSFUL YEAR OF **EXPANSION** AND **GROWTH!**

POLITE APPLAUSE

C.E.O

3 SO HOW HAVE WE — HAVE **YOU**, AS PART OF THIS MAGNIFICENT TEAM — GOT TO WHERE WE ARE TODAY? IN NO SMALL PART IT's THANKS TO THE **VISION** AND SIMPLE **HARD WORK** OF ALL YOU **WONDERFUL** GUYS IN OUR **FRANCHISING DIVISION!!**

SUSTAINED APPLAUSE!

YEAH! RIGHT! **RIGHT ON!** BUT SERIOUSLY, IT's OUR COMMITMENT TO **MEETING LOCAL CHALLENGES** WITH **LOCAL ANSWERS**, MATCHING **LOCAL CONDITIONS** WITH **LOCAL SOLUTIONS** THAT HAVE MADE THIS **PHENOMENAL** SUCCESS STORY A **REALITY!!**

C.E.O

5 SNORK!! SNIFF!!! SORRY, I JUST **LOVE** ALL THOSE GUYS! SNURF! NO, PLEASE... SERIOUSLY NOW, YOU AND I KNOW THAT A **HELL** OF A **LOT** OF OUR **SO-CALLED RIVALS** ARE JUST **DYING** TO KNOW THE SECRET OF OUR **SUCCESS**. AND YOU KNOW WHAT? **THERE AIN'T NO SECRET!** IT's SIMPLE AS **CATCHING A COLD**, BECAUSE WHAT **WE** DO IS QUITE SIMPLY **LINK** IN WITH

WHAT... PEOPLE... DO. DON'T GIVE ME ANY OF THAT CRAP ABOUT "EXPLOITATION" AND DOING ALL THIS POLITICALLY CORRECT BULLSHIT ABOUT "HEALTH RISKS". AS LONG AS **PEOPLE** ARE **PEOPLE**, WE'RE GONNA BE **RIGHT UP THERE ALONGSIDE THEM!**

C.E.O

THE ECONOMICS OF AIDS
BOB SUTCLIFFE

THE LONG-TERM ECONOMIC
CONSEQUENCES OF AIDS ARE LARGELY
UNDERESTIMATED — OR IGNORED

Where illness is, denial is never far away: not only the denial of people living with or in danger from the disease or that of negligent authorities in whose territory it occurs but also a more pervasive intellectual refusal to believe that it can overturn long-held assumptions about social and economic laws. HIV/Aids has been treated more as a personal and a medical problem than a social or political one and least of all as an economic one.

Economists have developed a kind of orthodoxy which argues that, even in the countries most affected, the worst the epidemic can do to the economy is reduce the growth rate of income per head by a relatively small amount because of the loss of some skills, a possible decline in incentives and an increase in costs of health care. But on this theory, the damage can mostly be made good by ever more vigorous pursuit of the 'right' policies, which are the protection of private property and the free market. They won't make HIV/Aids go away but they will allow the economy to surmount the problems it creates.

A *Financial Times* supplement on South Africa published in September 2003 was filled with glowing prospects for investors; an overview mentioned HIV/Aids briefly in passing, although one article did explain that some companies (less sanguine than the economists), fearing major impacts on their workforce, were encouraging in-house health care and treatment. In the same month, the World Bank's annual *Global Economic Prospects* was only expressing widely shared thinking when it predicted that Aids in Africa would result in a reduction in the growth rate of approximately one percentage point. Some economists have even speculated that by relieving population pressure on land and capital, the epidemic might actually enhance productivity, just as many historians say the Black Death did in the fourteenth century. Botswana, whose HIV infection rate for adults aged 15 to 49 was estimated at the end of 2001 at 39 per cent, and which is one of the most unequal countries on earth, is regarded by some influential economists as a special kind of success story, a model for other developing countries to follow. Botswana's great virtue, they claim, is to have established good institutions – an innocent-sounding code word, it turns out, for those 'right' free-market policies again. Behind all these ideas is a widely held notion that health and demography do not have much effect on economics, but that economics has a lot of effect on health and demography. Even recent theories of economic growth that emphasise the importance of 'human capital' see more education as more productive than better health.

It is not hard to see how these views have taken hold. More people are living with HIV and Aids in South Africa than in any other country, yet the national income per head has not yet fallen significantly during the years since the formal end of apartheid. And in the period in which 39 per cent of Botswana's young adult population was becoming infected with HIV, the national income was growing faster than in almost any other country.

A number of things have begun to cause a belated reassessment of this economic denial. In South Africa, for instance, it is increasingly appreciated that the prospect of up to 7 million Aids-related deaths in the present decade and the creation of up to 5 million orphans by the middle of the next decade is an unprecedented disaster from which the economy cannot be shielded. Recent analyses that predict the economic impact of major Aids epidemics are reaching increasingly pessimistic conclusions because they are taking into account the specific epidemiological character of HIV/Aids, particularly the concentration of illness and deaths among young adults. The World Bank, a very recent convert to this less sanguine view, recently published a new research study which, in effect, predicts that if there are no major policy changes, and if the growing numbers of orphans fail to receive adequate education, the epidemic could destroy a large part of the country's human capital and reduce it to extreme poverty over the next 80 years. More than a decade after the rapid growth of the infection began, Aids is being increasingly seen as a problem that transcends even the health of millions of people and has become a problem of the survival of society.

This changing perspective is fortified by the growing gravity of the statistics published by national governments, WHO, UNAIDS and others. According to WHO's estimates, during 2001 about 56.5 million people died (about 9.5 per 1,000 of the world's population). In Western Europe, of all the deaths that take place, less than 1 per cent are of people under 15 years old; and as many as 73 per cent are of people over 70. Yet in Africa, WHO has estimated that 24 per cent (much more in the poorest countries) of deaths are of children under 15. The death rates of infants and children

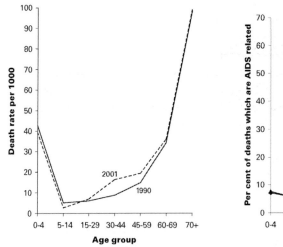
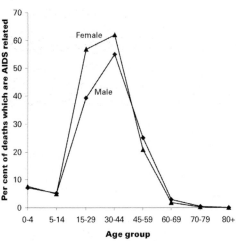

Left, graph 1: sub-Saharan Africa, death rates by age group, 1990 and 2001.
Right, graph 2: sub-Saharan Africa, percentage of deaths due to Aids-related causes,
by age group, 2001. Source: World Health Organisation World Health Report *2002*

under five remain shockingly different between the North and the South. And because so many people die so young, the expectancy of life for a newly born person is severely reduced. Statistically, there has for decades been a very close correlation between infant and child mortality and life expectancy (a figure calculated from age-specific death rates). The differences between North and South in life expectancy for ten-year-olds are still very significant but they are much less than they are for the newly born.

In most places and for many decades, child mortality rates have been falling, even in Africa, and life expectancies have been slowly extending. The HIV/Aids epidemic is changing that profoundly. In the first place it has changed age-specific death rates, as can be seen by comparing 1990 and 2001 in Graph 1. Aids kills an alarming number of young children (nearly 200,000 under-15s globally in 2001). But, as Graph 2 shows in more detail, it is more especially a killer of young adults. In Africa in 2001, WHO attributes almost 21 per cent of deaths to Aids – 19 per cent of male and 22 per cent of female deaths. The age profile is very uneven: 7 per cent of deaths of children under five years old, 5 per cent of those between five and 15, then rising rapidly to reach a peak of around 60 per cent of deaths in the 30–44 age group before declining again. Graph 2 also shows the often remarked fact that Aids is taking an even greater toll of women than of men (p106). In most other parts of the world, still less affected by Aids, male death rates are higher than female at all ages and especially in the young adult age group.

The HIV/Aids epidemic in South Africa is not only one of the most severe, but it is also one of the best documented. Well-researched figures estimate that at the present time almost 12 per cent of the population (over 20 per cent of the adult population) are living with HIV or Aids and that life expectancy at birth has already fallen from 63 to 47 years. Whether the number of new infections has now peaked (a polemical issue), the total number of cases will not reach its expected maximum of perhaps 8 million – almost 20 per cent of the population – until the end of this decade. Since HIV normally takes some years to become fatal, the number of deaths, in the absence of wide use of anti-retrovirals, will not peak until several years later, by which time it is projected that over 6 million people will have died. The peak in the number of orphaned children will not come until towards the end of the next decade and the worst of the economic impact would come even later.

Such projections as these are far from new but seem suddenly in the latter part of 2003 to have broken some of the layers of public denial. After many years of ambiguity, the South African government – stung by a serious loss of political prestige at the Durban conference on HIV/Aids in July 2000 – shifted into a higher gear and has been announcing programmes of state-aided anti-retroviral treatment. This is one of the conditions for mitigating the worst of the scenarios set out by recent demographic and economic research.

Changes in the pattern of illness and mortality can have huge effects on economic development. But economic realities also play a leading role in the present epidemiology of the disease. It is indeed true that poverty causes HIV infection and Aids, not in the sense that it is an alternative to the virus but in the sense that it creates the economic and social conditions that permit the virus to spread. Aids in South Africa, as in most other places, is above all a disease of the poor, and in South Africa that means the black part of the population. Health indicators have always shown stark differences between blacks and whites: white life expectancy in 1997 was about 70 years for men and 77 for women. The black figures were 52 and 55 and the colour gap has grown since then. Sample surveys indicate that the incidence of the disease closely reflects position in the class and colour hierarchies. About 50 per cent of black unskilled workers are living with HIV, compared

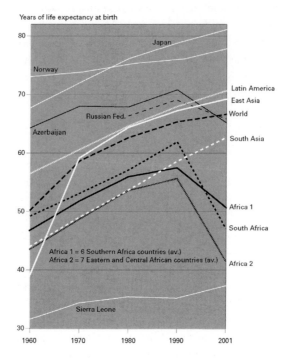

LIFE EXPECTANCY IN THE WORLD 1960–2001

Years of life expectancy at birth

Africa 1 = 6 Southern Africa countries (av.)
Africa 2 = 7 Eastern and Central African countries (av.)

The graph shows some data about the evolution of life expectancies in the world from 1960 to 2001. The country that at present has the longest life expectancy is Japan, the shortest Sierra Leone; they are shown on the graph as the limiting cases. During the three decades after 1960 there is a strong upward movement in all countries and areas because of public health improvements, inoculation and in some cases better diets. After 1990, longevity fell sharply in two areas: first in the former Soviet Union as a result of the effects of the traumatic transition to market capitalism, and then in African countries largely due to Aids-related deaths. In seven East and Central African countries (Africa 2), life expectancy has now fallen to only slightly above the country with the world's lowest level. South Africans lost more life expectancy in ten years than they had gained in the previous 30.

Source: World Bank World Development Indicators 2003 (CD-ROM version)

with 17 per cent of white unskilled workers. For skilled workers the figures are 40 and 9 per cent and among junior managers 23 and 8 per cent. Low pay, job insecurity and an enormous rate of unemployment among black South Africans are crucial determinants of the patterns of social and sexual contacts in which the virus spreads. Black working-class women are the least able to avoid infection as the figures already quoted show. The arrival of cheaper drugs should produce a welcome reduction in mortality and its consequences (such as the number of orphans) but it won't solve poverty and inequality. Since the end of apartheid the poorest South Africans have got poorer. Only the richest blacks, benefiting from 'black economic empowerment', have made significant income gains.

There is no simple end in sight to the HIV/Aids epidemic in South Africa and other African countries. It will continue to be horribly destructive of life and welfare. But the projections of demographers and economists are not inevitable. There are many possible interventions that can mitigate the worst possibilities they envisage. But the 'right' economic policies will not do any of the things that have to be done if the harm is to be limited. They will not end taboos on discussing the issue, strengthen the position of working-class women, reduce the marginalisation of the gay population, eliminate unemployment, promote greater equality, encourage the use of condoms, buy, distribute and administer anti-retroviral treatments, or provide other needed medical care. All of those are mainly tasks for public authorities and popular organisations, not the market.

Many other countries have not yet begun to prepare themselves to resist an HIV/Aids epidemic. They may look on at the plight of southern Africa and blithely think they do not have a problem. They should be reminded that in 1990 the estimated rate of HIV infection of adults in South Africa was 0.5 per cent. ❏

Bob Sutliffe *is an economist specialising in development and migration who teaches at the University of the Basque Country in Bilbao*

SEX IS A LETHAL WEAPON

STEPHEN LEWIS

At the UN Special Session on Aids in 2001, the Declaration of Commitment contained the toughest articles on the rights and protection of women that had yet appeared anywhere. It was truly memorable. Why then do I put it in the past tense? Because before the ink was dry, the words shrivelled on the page. There is very little evidence, in the aftermath of the Special Session, of governments taking seriously the commitment to women. It was one thing to recognise, rhetorically, that women were overwhelmingly at risk, it was quite another to act on the rhetoric. And it would appear that yet again, as ever, with indifference aforethought, the women are betrayed. The women are always betrayed.

Just look at the current figures. Of the 28 million people in sub-Saharan Africa living with Aids, aged 15 to 49, 15 million are women. That's 58 per cent. Of the 8,600,000 in the age group 15 to 24, 67 per cent are young women and girls. How is that possible?

We're just beginning to understand that where Aids is concerned, gender inequality is lethal. It requires a campaign, across the continent and the world, to enshrine gender equality in the family, in the laws, in the institutions and in the apparatus of the state. We've never faced anything like this. There's a passing comment in the US National Intelligence Council's 'Next Wave' study, pointing out that in a country such as China – but China is merely an example – 'as Aids moves more into the general population, past experiences in other countries suggest it will exacerbate an already existing gender imbalance because of the practice of female infanticide'. What is happening is a kind of Darwinian nightmare, where the survival of the fittest results in the annihilation of women. There will be, down the road, in many communities, in many countries, a demographic skewing of gender, such that the voices of women will no longer be heard in the land.

The world has to be made to understand that Aids has brought into brutal relief the predatory sexual behaviour of adult males, and the terrible consequences of intergenerational sex, and the equally terrible vulnerability of women who have neither sexual power nor sexual autonomy. More, we are just beginning to understand that the levels of sexual violence, the levels of rape, inexorably transmit the virus. Whether it's the violence of conflict, or the violence of a domestic household, women are the targets. It's a part of the human condition that cries out for study and desperate, immediate response.

Tanzania: these young women are two to three times more likely to become HIV-positive than their boyfriends. Credit: Panos

All my adult life I've believed that gender is the toughest issue to deal with. Tougher even than race. And I don't really know how we cope with what is happening except to reverse the pattern through a massive, international, single-minded initiative.

Just two weeks ago, I was meeting in Arusha, Tanzania, with a group of women living with Aids. I asked them, as I always do, to tell me what they most needed and wanted, and as always the same replies came back: food, because everyone is hungry, especially the children; money for school fees, and some kind of guarantee to keep their kids in school, because when they die they want their children to be assured of an education. And drugs. Anti-retroviral drugs to prolong life, so as not to leave their children so prematurely orphaned. To be quite honest, I never know what to say in such a situation. I'm strangled by the double standard between developed and developing countries. I'm haunted by the monies available for the war on terrorism, and the war in Iraq, but somehow never available for the human imperative.

I believe that all the things those women asked for could be provided, or at least provided in large measure, if we had the money. And I know that if the 'Next Wave' is to escape the wretched fate of the last wave, then the world and its governments will have to come to their senses. ❏

Stephen Lewis *is UN special envoy for HIV/Aids in Africa*

Excerpt from speech to Conference on the 'Next Wave' of HIV/Aids (affecting China, India, Russia, Ethiopia and Nigeria), 4 October 2003

PREVENTION IS BETTER THAN CURE
SALIL TRIPATHI

WITH MONEY IN SHORT SUPPLY FOR
COMPREHENSIVE AIDS TREATMENT,
INDIA MAY BE FORCED TO EXERCISE A
FORM OF TRIAGE IF IT IS TO STAND ANY
CHANCE OF CONTROLLING THE EPIDEMIC

The first news story was short, as if describing a road accident. A three-paragraph piece in the *Indian Express*, filed by a news agency, saying that doctors believed six sex workers in Madras were infected with the HIV virus. This was in early 1986. I was a freelance writer in Bombay at that time and, commissioned by *Imprint* magazine, I flew to Madras and then to the hospital where Dr Sunithi Solomon had been treating the six patients.

The women were skinny, looking weak and undernourished. They were obviously poor, and sex workers in India are exposed to a whole host of infections from their clients. But Dr Solomon was convinced that Aids had reached Indian shores. Another doctor in Madras, whom I met later, insisted that the sex workers were actually suffering from TB, or any of the many other diseases common in India. It was not Aids; it could not be Aids. 'It is a publicity gimmick,' he said, 'to attract funds.'

A week later, in New Delhi, I met Dr V Ramalingaswamy, the director of the Indian Council for Medical Research, who had stunned the establishment and defied government protocol by writing directly to the then prime minister, Rajiv Gandhi. He warned him that a major catastrophe awaited India and urgent steps had to be taken. Gandhi took him seriously. He asked his bureaucrats to form a national council.

Given the loquacious democracy that India is, immediately there were counter-arguments, some valid, some puritanical. The arguments that appeared valid at that time included the claim that Aids was not an easy disease to get if one took precautionary measures; and that India's public

There are officially 4m people with HIV/Aids in India | Adult prevalence rate (15–49 years) is 0.8% of the population; in six Indian states the prevalence rate is over 1%; in Maharashtra/Mumbai and Manipur the rate is 1.75% | 39% – c1.5m – of

health system had many other priorities, from cholera, typhoid, malaria, filaria, leprosy and tuberculosis to diarrhoea, to say nothing of other sexually transmitted diseases. The puritanical arguments included the claim that Indians simply did not indulge in the kind of promiscuous behaviour that, it was then believed, was the sole cause of the transmission of the virus. In the nearly 4,000-word article I wrote at that time, I concluded that India's health budget was going to face a severe strain unless further resources were made available. Since the disease is likely to spread exponentially, I urged, India will need to take urgent steps, as well as seek international assistance, without taking its eye off the ball represented by other equally important diseases. Easier said than done, of course.

Today, India has about 4 million people infected with HIV, set to rise to 20–25 million by 2010 (a projection many Indian officials dispute). Only some of them are sex workers, sexually promiscuous or gay. There are patients from virtually every community, religion, caste and language group. Some 250,000 of them are in Bombay, India's commercial capital. According to US intelligence estimates, India is one of five countries (the others are China, Russia, Nigeria and Ethiopia) that will see an explosion of the disease.

The Aids crisis is indeed global. Twenty-two million people have died and 40 million continue to live with the infection, many of them from poor countries. Some 14,000–16,000 new cases are being reported worldwide daily. In countries such as Botswana, one-quarter of the population is infected. Nigeria and Ethiopia will see a similar spread in the next two decades. Ninety-five per cent of those infected with HIV live in less developed countries, home to 80 per cent of the world's population. At a global level there is a statistically significant relationship between low income and HIV prevalence rates: that is, the poorer the country the greater the HIV prevalence. There is a similar relation between income distribution and HIV prevalence, meaning countries with greater income inequality face a more serious epidemic. Absolute poverty rates, defined as income below US$1 a day, are strongly associated with HIV prevalence rates, as are low rankings on the UN Development Programme's Human Poverty Index, which takes into account mortality, literacy, malnutrition and access to water, sanitation

those infected are women; 170,000 are children | 50,000–100,000 may already have died from Aids | In Manipur 1% of women attending antenatal clinics are infected with HIV | In Mumbai HIV prevalence has reached 50% in sex workers,

and health services. Only 5 per cent of the 5.5 million people in developing countries who need anti-retroviral treatment currently receive it.

While infection rates are stabilising in sub-Saharan Africa (although they remain at a very high level), the epidemic is still growing in Asia and Eastern Europe. The lack of an imminent vaccine or cure means that many more deaths are inevitable. Over a hundred companies around the world have forged a coalition to use their expertise – in marketing, educating, distributing, researching and producing – to combat HIV. That's a good start, but it still remains in its infancy compared with what businesses can potentially do. Rajat Gupta, managing director at McKinsey & Co, the management consulting firm, wrote recently in the *McKinsey Quarterly*:

> Any multinational corporation that can't see how it is directly affected by the global disease epidemic is dangerously myopic. The causes of the problem may be complex and its solutions vexing, but its implications are startlingly clear: Companies that seek to benefit from globalisation also have a vested interest in helping to manage the global health crisis – indeed, a moral, strategic and financial responsibility to do so.

The problem for a country such as India is the sheer overwhelming nature of the disease. Significant steps have been taken, both by the government and the private sector. Private companies sponsor advertisement campaigns about the virus. Non-governmental organisations are active in educating particularly susceptible groups – sex workers, truck drivers, intravenous drug users – and charities are providing medication cheap, and in some cases, free. An Indian company, Cipla, has challenged global orthodoxy and conscience by offering Aids treatment at US$350 a year – the same cocktail costs US$15,000 a year in the developed world. Cipla is able to do this because India does not recognise product patents, but process patents: this means a company can only patent the way it makes a particular product, not the product itself, allowing alternate ways in which the same product can be made. Needless to say, such an approach is controversial, and Western pharmaceutical companies say Indian pharmaceutical companies are stealing ideas.

36% in STD patients and 2.5% in women attending antenatal clinics | In 1995 50% of blood transfusions were not screened for HIV | India has an estimated 98–118,000 intravenous drug users (IDUs) | The HIV/Aids prevalence among

Bombay, India: Aids education by a former prostitute in the city's red-light district.
Credit: Jan Banning / Panos

Without getting into the debate about intellectual property rights, there is a point in what Cipla's CEO Yusuf Hamied says: that he is doing this because he wants treatment to be offered at the price the poor can afford. He told journalist Michael Specter in December 2001: 'Aids is the worst tragedy this country could ever experience – with the possible exception of a nuclear war – and it is a completely foreseen tragedy. Why are we doing nothing about this great plague? I decided right then that, if I had to, I would do it by myself. People think this is all about Africa, but it's not. For me, it's about my own home.'

IDUs in Manipur rose from undetectable levels in 1988 to 70% in four years |
Indian women are infected by husbands belonging to high-risk 'bridge
populations' – men who also have sex with men, sex workers and IDUs |

BLIND PREJUDICE

Throughout the nineteenth century, commercial sex was seen as an important public health issue. While concern about it declined in the twentieth century as a result of improved management of sexually transmitted diseases and unwanted pregnancies, the HIV/Aids epidemic has refuelled concern. Public health once again dominates the way most societies deal with commercial sex. Legislation, public policy and widespread societal attitudes permeated by moral outrage fail to recognise that there are complex dynamics at play that call for complex solutions. We need to listen to those most affected: the women in prostitution themselves. As activist Durga Pujari from Veshya Aids Muquabla Parishad (VAMP), a collective of women in prostitution from Sangli, puts it: 'Over the years, from "common prostitutes" we have become "commercial sex workers", debates are held about us and we are discussed in documents, covenants and declarations. The problem, however, is that when we try to inform the arguments our stories are disbelieved and we are treated as if we cannot comprehend our own lives. Thus we are either romanticised, victimised or worse, and our reality gets buried and distorted.'

The inability to accept that the movement for prostitutes' rights can be informed by the women in prostitution and sex workers themselves is as much a denial of their human rights as is discrimination against mainstream women on the basis of caste, class, race or religion. The same attitude ensures that the women are officially denied a role in dealing with the disease that is threatening their lives.

In a report prepared by India's National Commission for Women, women in prostitution and sex work from as far afield as West Bengal, Orissa, Andhra Pradesh, Karnataka, Maharashtra, Tamil Nadu, Kerala and the Union Territories of Goa and Pondicherry testify that accessing health care is a major concern for them. While the 'immoral whore' image makes it difficult to get good medical treatment, illiteracy, ignorance and fear of the medical establishment render them open to exploitation and extortion. They report that medical and paramedical staff at government hospitals have a callous, indifferent and often humiliating attitude; irrelevant and embarrassing questions about sexual positions etc. are often asked; forced free sex with doctors and social workers is commonplace; doctors often refuse treatment and admit women to hospital claiming that they are Aids carriers; in many centres, doctors make the *peons* (servants) and attendants conduct the physical examination and only then treat the women.

The HIV/Aids epidemic has singled out people in prostitution and sex work as 'carriers and vectors of the spread of HIV'. Apart from the stigma already attached to their work, society has further marginalised them as core transmitters of HIV infection. It fails to recognise that they are only links in the broad networks of heterosexual transmission of HIV. Women in prostitution and sex work constitute a community that bears and will continue to bear the greatest impact of the HIV epidemic in India, suffering high levels of infection and re-infection. Propagating the myth that they are core transmitters of HIV reinforces the moral and judgemental prejudice that Aids is an 'impure' disease that afflicts immoral and evil persons. The net result is further to target the women by increasing public and police violence against them; reducing their ability to assert themselves; allowing customers to force unsafe sex on them, increasing the rate of HIV among women, customers and the families of the customers; and denying them access to health-care services.

Women who have been trafficked and are working in prostitution are even more vulnerable to the risk of contracting HIV. As illegal migrants engaged in an illegal trade, they are frequently subjected to sexual abuse at the hands of the authorities, including immigration and police officials, whose systematic involvement in the trafficking trade is well known and documented. Forcible detention, lack of access to redress, police corruption and invisibility ensure that women can be violated, controlled and abused. The trafficked person who fears repatriation is unlikely to access treatment and services for HIV.

Though it is now widely acknowledged that they are the best educators of their male clients, the role in HIV/Aids prevention of women in prostitution and sex work is little recognised. As a result, programmes that view women in sex work as a means to reaching the sexually active male population rather than the sex workers themselves remain a dream.

Meanwhile, short-term project-oriented interventions in the control of governments in the region are proving to be an alienating process that continues to blame marginalised communities rather than empower them to combat HIV. ❏

Meena Saraswathi Seshu is the founder of Sangram, an NGO working with sex workers and rural women in India

Hamied's act has energised other companies to do more. Western firms have since withdrawn from a threat to sue the South African government over potential intellectual property (IP) rights violations. Countries have agreed at the World Trade Organisation to waive the IP rights which would prevent poor countries from importing alternate anti-HIV medication from other suppliers. At the Genoa G8 summit, leaders agreed to commit US$12 billion towards fighting Aids. US President George W Bush has committed funds of US$15 billion over the next decade. The Global Fund To Fight Aids, Tuberculosis and Malaria has committed US$2.1 billion. Economists estimate that currently some US$7–10 billion is needed annually to combat Aids, a figure set to rise to US$21 billion a year by 2015. The World Bank has issued US$1.7 billion since 1986.

In early 2001, a group of Harvard professors said it was no longer morally permissible for the West to deny patients in the world's poorest countries Aids drugs that could extend their lives. The Bill and Melinda Gates Foundation has committed millions of dollars (from its asset base of nearly US$18 billion) to anti-Aids efforts. Former US President Bill Clinton is now leading another initiative, to make anti-HIV medicines affordable to poor countries. Even South Africa – whose president, Thabo Mbeki, questioned the very existence of the disease, and whose health minister argued that traditional African remedies, such as sweet potato, could be experimented with to find a cure for Aids – has backtracked somewhat. Giant sophisticated billboards in major South African cities now carry Aids-awareness messages near townships, often poignantly above matter-of-fact advertisements for funeral services.

While the disease has begun to command a huge share of Indian – and global – resources, few public health officials are willing to say publicly what they believe in private: that it is more sensible to prevent HIV than to focus on treatment. The drugs, it is accepted, are not easy to administer. Some require the patient to drink eight glasses of water – and in many poor countries little clean potable water is available. Other drugs have to be stored in refrigerators – again, in many poor countries, either there are no refrigerators, or there is no guarantee of uninterrupted power supplies to service those refrigerators.

90% of the men who visit male sex workers are married | A sampling of 400 women in Pune showed 13% were HIV-positive; 91% reported having sex only with their husbands | c3–4% of people in some rural populations have a

Maharashtra, India: truck drivers take a lesson in safe sex.
Credit: Alex Majoli / Magnum Photos

Beyond that, there is a cruel-sounding, but necessary, economic argument: there are finite resources and infinite demands, and politicians must make rational choices allocating those resources. The demand for resources can overwhelm any nation. India's health budget is about US$11 billion, which sounds generous, but works out at US$10 per person annually. Can the country really afford to offer treatment which, even with Cipla's generosity, would work out at US$350 a year per patient, even if there are only 4 million patients at present? Where would the resources come from to treat the 1.1 million cases of malaria, the 2 million new cases of TB (which kills a thousand people daily) and other diseases such as hepatitis B, which could be prevented with simple shots of immunisation or injection?

sexually transmitted disease | HIV/Aids is spread to rural areas through migrant workers and truck drivers; up to 10% of truck drivers are infected | There are 2m women in sex work in India; 30% are minors | 5–10,000 girls and women

Calcutta, India: Aids education for local community volunteers.
Credit: Peter Barker / Panos

Indians also believe that their social conservatism might help them. Surveys cited in the *New Yorker* say that once Indian men marry, they are more likely to remain faithful to their wives than men from many other cultures. Some half of Indian women marry before they are 18, and more than 90 per cent have not had sexual experience prior to their marriage.

But that's only part of the story: Indian highways are busy with smoke-belching trucks, and there are over 100,000 drivers. Some avant-garde Indian films have gradually revealed their unconventional lives: in the 1960s Satyajit Ray film *Abhijan*, there were only hints of a romance between a truck driver and a woman in another village; in the 1970s, in Mani Kaul's *Uski Roti*, such a relationship was explored further. And in the 1980s, Rabindra Dharmaraj's *Chakra* had an in-your-face woman, who lived in a slum, in relationships with at least two men, one of whom suffered from a sexually transmitted disease. Who will educate them? One truck driver told Specter that he had sex only once a week on the road, and he made sure of

are trafficked to India annually from Nepal | The prevalence rate among sex workers in Nepal rose from less than 2% in 1990 to 20% today | Tuberculosis is the presenting symptom of Aids in over 60% of cases | In Bombay 10% of

having a bath with lime water after that, imagining that that was sufficient to prevent him from being infected, or infecting someone else. It is hard to estimate the number of sex workers in India, but reports claim there are at least 250,000. And, as in China, tens of millions of workers come to large cities for jobs for part of the year.

An oft-cited US intelligence report claims that heterosexual transmission in India is the driver of infections, except in two regions, Nagaland and Manipur, where intravenous drug use is a serious problem. Thirty to 60 per cent of prostitutes and up to 15 per cent of all truck drivers are infected with HIV/Aids. But many who receive treatment don't take it seriously. Of 200 HIV-positive patients referred to a specialist centre in India because of poor response to anti retroviral treatment, it was found that only 10 per cent had adhered to treatment, 50 per cent had stopped taking the drugs on the advice of traditional healers, and 80 per cent had been receiving incorrect doses.

Specter notes the contrast in approaches to HIV in two Asian countries, India and Thailand. Under the leadership of former health minister Meechai Veerawaidya, Thailand has aggressively spread education about sex and disease. Meechai had no inhibition about being called 'Dr Condom'; in India, family-planning advertisements continue to remain coy. Thailand spends more than US60c per person on HIV; India's expenditure is less than one-tenth of that. India's total anti-HIV budget is US$60 million, twice that of Thailand, but its population is 16 times the size of Thailand.

Either because of the stigma attached to Aids, or because of the fear of being confounded by the crisis, many Indian officials underrate the impact. While their denial is not as firm as Mbeki's, senior leaders, including the health minister Sushma Swaraj, have criticised Western newspapers and governments for focusing too much on Aids in India. When Bill Gates, for example, announced a particularly generous donation for anti-Aids efforts in India, former movie actor and later health minister Shatrughan Sinha dismissed the concerns, saying India did not need the money or attention. Gates still made the donation, with the comment:

India cannot face the challenge of Aids alone. Wealthy nations, businesses and the philanthropic world must contribute to efforts to contain India's Aids crisis before it expands. Far greater resources and

tuberculosis patients are HIV-positive | An Indian household affected by HIV/ Aids spends 49% of income on treatment in the early stages of the disease; the proportion increases to 81% in the later stages | The average decline in

expertise must be devoted to prevention programmes, training health-care workers and supporting research into new medical advancements. The choice now is clear and stark: India can either be the home of the world's largest and most devastating Aids epidemic or, with the support of the rest of the world, it can become the best example of how this virus can be defeated.

Indian reluctance to address this does stem from conservatism, but that conservatism is not restricted to the Hindu nationalist Bharatiya Janata Party that leads the governing coalition. *Ganashakti*, the newspaper of the Communist Party of India (Marxists) called homosexuality, which it blamed for spreading HIV, a Western import in India – as is Marxism itself, an irony *Ganashakti*'s editors did not appear to notice.

The reluctance to address the issue, based on the assumption that Indian culture would somehow withstand the crisis, is a stumbling block. Many Indian doctors argue that it is wrong to assume there is a cure for Aids. If you offer that alternative, goes the argument, promiscuous Indians – and even if they are an exception, as the late Nirad Chaudhuri noted once, in India exceptions run into millions – will continue to have sex, like those truck drivers, without condoms, hoping ablutions in lime water will protect them. Improper use of drugs, too, would be harmful. Solomon told Specter in 2001: 'We have to get more training. Food. Clean water. Give us condoms, for God's sake. Teach women to read. But keep your drugs. They really won't help us now.'

The really difficult question, for India and for the world, is this: is the emphasis on providing affordable treatment to Aids patients taking health dollars away from preventive mechanisms or investment in research towards a vaccine? In his article, Specter notes that more than five times as much money is spent treating sick people as is spent keeping them healthy in the first place. And, he adds chillingly, much of that money is spent on people who are on the verge of death. 'Can that be fair?' he asks.

Ruth Levine of the Center for Global Development in Washington thinks economists are already losing the argument. She wrote recently:

It is now no longer a question of whether Aids treatments will be provided to people in poor countries, but only when, how and in

monthly income due to loss of work is Rs3,000 (US$61) this falls to Rs750 (US$15) after six months' treatment | Before attending a South Indian HIV/Aids treatment centre 46% of clients reported a loss of income; after six months'

what volume. [A huge amount of] money from taxpayers in rich countries is now flowing toward the purchase of Aids drugs. Insistence on the economic logic of choosing prevention over treatment – making those difficult trade-offs – has become a decidedly unpopular minority view. It appears that economics has taken a distant backseat to compassion.

But then she asks:

Are we now compassionate about all health problems in developing countries, regardless of cost, or are we compassionate only about Aids? If our previous understanding that there is a fixed amount of money to transfer from rich countries to poor ones for health is wrong – and, at least for Aids, that has clearly been shown to be the case – what is the basis for deciding how much will be transferred, and how those funds will be used?

Clearly, the argument is not specific to India: it applies to the US as well, where millions of dollars are spent on prevention but over US$6 billion is spent on treatment. There are many people around the world who can't afford the medication. Should the world then be compassionate only towards the patients in Africa and India?

In a world of infinite resources, the issue of fairness wouldn't matter. But we live in a world of finite health budgets. Economist Jeffrey Sachs claims that for US$10 a year per American, the US can spend enough to protect Africa from the Aids crisis. Others have argued that the cost of educating every truck driver and sex worker in India would cost much the same, but might have a far greater preventive value in the longer run.

The issue is not simply about dividing the budget between those already infected and protecting those who may get infected, it is also about looking after and curing the millions of others who contract diseases because of the poor quality of water they drink, because of the mosquitoes that bite them, because of the air they breathe. Their health needs also matter. Ignoring them is the true, hidden cost of the Aids crisis. ❏

Salil Tripathi *is a writer and freelance journalist*

treatment the figure had dropped to 31% | *Sources: International AIDS Economic Network,* Wall Street Journal, *WHO, UNAIDS*

INDEX ON CENSORSHIP 1 2004   119

REAPING THE WHIRLWIND

JASPER BECKER

CHINESE COMMUNIST PARTY PROPAGANDA
CLAIMS AIDS IS THE ULTIMATE SYMBOL OF
WESTERN DECADENCE. TODAY THERE MAY BE
2 MILLION INFECTED CHINESE — BUT THERE
COULD BE 30 MILLION DEAD WITHIN FIVE
YEARS IF THE GOVERNMENT REFUSES TO ACT

The first senior politician publicly to shake hands with a Chinese Aids patient was ex-President Bill Clinton. He came to China in November 2003 to take part in an international conference called as a last chance to prevent the epidemic there spiralling out of control. Clinton, who is co-chairman of the International Aids Trust, shook hands with 21-year-old Song Pengfei, who has had the HIV virus since a botched operation in a small hospital in Shanxi Province.

China's leaders have preferred to tout the success of China's first man in space, a costly but useless technological feat, rather than boost China's underfunded health services or research medical solutions to the looming Aids pandemic. The Aids crisis, like the Sars virus panic in the summer of 2003, has cruelly exposed the shortcomings in China's lopsided economic reforms.

The state is directing vast amounts of money into building up the country's physical infrastructure, which is helping to power the economy as cities are rebuilt and new roads, bridges, airports, telephone systems appear at an impressive rate, but is spending very little on health care, education or sanitation. What it does spend is concentrated on a small minority in the cities who work directly for the state or the Communist Party. The billion-plus rural population is largely ignored by the central government; so while China has the highest number of CAT-scanning machines, its per capita spending on health is among the world's lowest.

At the end of 2002 there were thought to be 2m people with HIV/Aids in China | On some estimates China will have 10–15m HIV/Aids cases, 2% of the adult population, by 2010 | Since 1998 the number of reported cases has increased

So far, China's HIV/Aids epidemic is largely limited to two groups and has yet to spread to the general population. The total number of victims is now thought to be around 2 million, though no one is really sure, many of whom are among the country's 6 million intravenous drug addicts and concentrated in ethnic-minority areas where the drugs are produced or transported. The second and larger group is among the very poor peasants in inland provinces like Henan. The peasants contracted the disease after selling blood via local government-run, profit-making schemes in a country where blood donation is a social taboo. Multiple donors would be hooked up to the same blood plasma machines and the virus spread from one infected patient to many others.

Aids experts have been warning that if the virus jumps into the general population through prostitution or, as with Song, via hospital blood transfusions, it will rapidly turn into a pandemic: within five years there could be 15 to 30 million people living with HIV and Aids. US demographer Nicholas Eberstadt has estimated that a mild epidemic could lead to 19 million deaths in China between 2000 and 2025 and, in the worst-case scenario, the death toll could rise to 40 million.

For many years, Communist Party propaganda presented Aids as a symbol of Western decadence and linked it to a breakdown in Western morals. It generated such hysteria that every foreigner coming to live in the country had to submit to an Aids test. Those people who contracted the HIV virus were shunned and discriminated against to the extent that they received no treatment nor any government help. The complacency around the issue was bolstered with regular reports that China did not need to import expensive Western drugs because Chinese traditional medicine offered cheap alternative cures. When reports of the disease began to surface in rural China, local officials went to extreme lengths to deny the existence of the disease and to punish or silence those brave individuals who sought to draw attention to the growing threat and the plight of the poverty-stricken victims.

The same pattern of behaviour was cruelly exposed in 2003 during the Sars virus when the Beijing municipal government had shamefully and belatedly to admit that it had misled the world about the number of

by c30% yearly | By 2010 China could have 260,000 orphans | Heterosexual unsafe sex accounts for 7.3% of China's HIV infections | A 2001 law in one Chinese province prohibits HIV-infected persons from marrying | A 2001 survey

reported cases (*Index* 2/2003, Diary from Beijing). Once the problem had been recognised at the highest levels, and it was realised that the health crisis was blocking economic growth, the government responded with great efficiency and thoroughness. The attempt to cover up the Sars virus epidemic in Beijing only came to light when one retired doctor, 72-year-old Dr Jiang Yanyong of the People's Liberation Army Hospital 301, raised the alarm. After failing with the official channels, he broke the story to the Western press.

A similar sequence of events has taken place with Aids. The crisis in Henan Province has been exposed through the brave actions of a handful of individuals. One of them is 77-year-old retired paediatrician Gao Yaojie, who persisted with her efforts to publicise an Aids outbreak that started in the early 1990s despite a continuing and orchestrated campaign of intimidation.

She started by leading two Shanghai journalists to a village where blood sales continued even after a government ban, and continued to speak out despite every effort to silence her. Chinese and foreign journalists who went to the villages to interview the Aids sufferers found themselves arrested and their film seized. In one incident, the villagers detained a French journalist and threatened to infect the police who had come to arrest the reporter. Local government officials prevented Dr Gao from travelling abroad this summer to receive the Magsaysay Award, Asia's version of the Nobel Prize, by refusing her a passport; she was also prevented from meeting President Clinton when he came to Beijing.

She fared better than some. A health official, Ma Shiwen, the deputy director of the Henan Centre for Disease Control, was arrested briefly for providing information about the epidemic in the province to Aids activist Wan Yanhai. Wan, who had founded China's first Aids hotline, was arrested and accused of leaking state secrets after he posted the documents on his group's website. He has since been released.

Meanwhile, Liu Quanxi, who headed the Henan health department and ran the region's blood business during the 1990s, was promoted in February to be deputy director of the Chinese Communist Party's health committee. Chen Kaiyuan, head of the Henan Communist Party, who blocked all media access to the Aids-plagued villages and arrested locals who gave infor-

found that 20% of respondents had never heard of HIV/Aids; 60% did not know how the disease spreads | Estimates in 2001 indicated that cUS$400m would be needed by 2005 for prevention | China's spending on HIV/Aids is approximately

Aids victim Wang Cuizhi shows her blood sales record book. Illegal blood sales contributed massively to the HIV/Aids explosion in China. Credit: SQ Lai (SPX) / Rex Features

mation to foreign reporters, was recently named President of the Chinese Academy of Social Sciences

In the last two years, the central government's attitude to Aids has slowly begun to shift, following a spate of reports warning that an Aids epidemic could slow economic growth. The authorities have used Aids Awareness Day to change public attitudes to Aids patients, prostitution and drug abuse, and are encouraging students to publicise the dangers of the disease. They have also lifted restrictions on the advertising of condoms and the installation of condom machines in public places. But the central government has allocated no more than token funds to help the families of Aids victims, treat the patients or prevent the spread of the disease. The underlying assumption remains: patients have only themselves to blame for contracting the disease.

Foreign charities offering help run foul of official distrust of NGOs; Ministry of Health negotiations with the Bill and Melinda Gates Foundation

half the overall need | 68% of HIV cases in China are intravenous drugs users (IDUs) who share needles | Up to 80% of IDUs in Yunnan Province, Guangxi Zhuang Autonomous Region and Xinjiang Uyghur Autonomous Region are HIV-

came to nothing. The Global Fund to Fight Aids, Tuberculosis and Malaria was prepared to offer China US$98 million but withheld the funds when the Ministry of Health insisted on retaining half the funds to pay for the cost of distributing free medicines to poor families. Like many other forms of international aid, the Global Fund grant obliges the recipient country to encourage public participation and consultation, in particular that of NGOs. In fact, over the past ten, even 20 years, most organisations – including the World Bank – have flouted these conditions as the price for operating in China. It now seems that the Global Fund has reached some sort of undisclosed agreement with the Chinese authorities that once again waives the rules. The health ministry will create its own government-organised non-government organisations, commonly known as GONGOs, and thus qualify for funding.

China's economic reforms forced every branch of the state, including the military, to become self-sufficient. Most diversified into a range of business activities that ranged from growing vegetables, to borrowing, to investing in speculative real estate projects to raise money to cover even their most basic costs such as wages. The health system, especially the rural health system, was badly hit. It was now dependent on local government. Those districts that prospered in their new business ventures could afford good hospitals, those whose ventures failed could not. It was this funding shortage that drove local governments in the poorest parts of rural Henan to pile into the blood plasma trade as a way of financing their medical services. Once in the business, officials were reluctant to abandon such a lucrative source of revenue, even when the trade was banned. The neglect of health spending has also contributed to a sharp rise in other infectious diseases such as tuberculosis.

Sars, which spread out of southern China and killed 774 people around the world, prompted the central government to find some extras funds to inject into the national health system, especially by improving the national system for the monitoring, control and prevention of infectious disease. Helping local governments in rural China became a priority. In November 2003, deputy health minister Gao Qiang announced that the central and local governments now planned to spend some US$850 million to improve

positive | 9.7% known HIV/Aids infections are due to unsafe commercial blood donation practices in the 1990s | In December 2002 23 provinces, autonomous regions and municipalities were still practising unhygienic blood collection |

and expand prevention and control programmes in the provinces. A further US$272 million would be spent on upgrading blood-testing stations in central and western China. During Clinton's visit, Gao also implied that the government was now prepared to spend money to help poor rural Aids victims. In his speech announcing the launch of free treatment for Aids patients, Gao said US$24 million would be spent yearly on a special fund for HIV/Aids prevention, care and treatment. He said 40,000 people would receive free treatment between now and the year 2008, and 5,000 poor patients would receive free treatment this year.

China itself has allocated only US$2 million to help the rural Aids victims in Henan, and Gao omitted to refer to the agreement with the Global Fund, whose programme is to focus on impoverished farmers who contracted HIV by selling blood at state clinics. It remains unclear exactly who will qualify for free government-distributed drugs.

Compared to the government's spending on prestige projects such as a US$1 billion magnetic levitation train between Shanghai and a second airport at Pudong, or the US$2 billion annual expenditure on the space programme, the sums dedicated to Aids are puny. Yet few dare to challenge the state's priorities. One who does is the economist Hu Angang. 'Beijing should stop neglecting health and welfare in favour of economic growth,' he said. 'The government has to make the transition from a developmental government to a public service government.'

There is still a great deal of confusion about the government's assessment of the gravity of the crisis. China's Ministry of Health claims that only 45,000 HIV/Aids cases have registered with the authorities and envisages free treatment for 40,000 people by 2008. However, on the basis of its own national survey, the government has been claiming that the number of HIV infections is rising by 30 per cent a year, resulting in something like 840,000 HIV carriers, including 80,000 Aids cases.

Meanwhile, in October, the state media suddenly announced that the number of Aids patients in the first half of 2003 had jumped by 140 per cent compared to the same period a year earlier. The *Beijing Youth Daily* quoted Wang Xinlun, director of the health education office of the China Epidemic Prevention Centre, but did not explain why there had been such a sudden

Tainted blood transfusions are estimated to have infected over 1m victims in Henan Province alone | In January 2002 80% of Houyang village residents were HIV-positive; 90% of its adults had participated in illegal blood donations | The

increase. 'It means there would be nearly 800,000 unidentified HIV carriers and Aids patients in China, continuing their high-risk activities without awareness,' argues Jing Jun, a professor from Qinghua University who attended an Aids and Sars symposium in Beijing.

Aids activists claim there are 1 million peasants suffering from Aids in Henan alone, and more in other provinces where the same blood trade was practised. And when one member of a family falls sick, it is the whole family who suffers: it can neither feed itself nor send the children to school. In some Henan counties, entire adult village populations are dying, health workers say, because they can't afford the treatment needed to keep them alive. Even the domestically manufactured drugs, available at around US$600 for a year's supply, are way beyond the means of most peasants. Henan also has in the region of 10,000 children who have been abandoned or orphaned by the epidemic, all in need of help. The authorities have become increasingly alarmed that, left unchecked, an epidemic could trigger large-scale protests in some parts of the countryside.

Discrimination against those with HIV/Aids is widespread: many hospitals are reluctant to admit HIV-positive patients, and activists are concerned that the social stigma attached to Aids prevents many patients from coming forward and receiving the treatment. 'Draconian crackdowns against people at high risk of HIV will only drive them underground and make it less likely that they will come forward for testing and treatment,' says Brian Adams, executive director of Human Rights Watch. 'China urgently needs a national law barring discrimination against people with HIV/Aids, and should establish a mechanism through which victims of discrimination can file complaints. How will the Chinese government give out medicine if the patients can't even get into the hospital?' ❑

Jasper Becker is a freelance journalist and writer working in Beijing

prevalence rate among commercial blood donors in rural eastern China was 12.5% | 100m rural migrants relocate to cities to find work, increasing sexual contact between migrant men and prostitutes | Only 30% of prostitutes in Hainan used a condom | Prostitutes in Yunnan do not use condoms with boyfriends or husbands | *Sources: National Intelligence Council, UNAIDS*

INDEX
for free expression

After more than 30 years tracking and challenging abuses of freedom of expression through its pages, *Index on Censorship* magazine is getting closer to the story with a programme that takes its team to the front lines of the fight to defend free speech.

Already the world's principal focal point for reports on free-expression issues, the magazine can now be found working directly with free-speech champions in their own countries.

'*The magazine was originally created as an outlet for banned writing and monitoring violations of free speech,*' says *Index on Censorship*'s editor-in-chief Ursula Owen. '*So it's a natural step to find new ways of using our publishing skills, our contacts and our historical knowledge of the problem by standing side by side with the people who write for us at such risk.*'

With the Iraqi media training project very much in full swing, the *Index* team is expanding the scope of the project to cover Central Asia. *Index* will support the monitoring, reporting, training and publication activities of key free-expression groups in Uzbekistan, Tajikistan and Kyrgyzstan, and build links with the print media in all three countries. Parallel to this, *Index* will direct a trio of training programmes to support wider media development in radio, on the internet and through greater commercial sustainability.

'Index on Censorship *needs to do more than just report the process,*' adds Ursula Owen. '*It can play a direct part, too. And if it can, it should.*'

IF YOU WOULD LIKE MORE INFORMATION ABOUT
INDEX ON CENSORSHIP
OR WOULD LIKE TO SUPPORT OUR WORK
**PLEASE CONTACT HUGO GRIEVE, DEVELOPMENT MANAGER,
ON 020 7278 2313**
OR EMAIL HUGO@INDEXONCENSORSHIP.ORG
WWW.INDEXONLINE.ORG

WHO KILLED JESUS CHRIST?

ERIC J GREENBERG

AN AMERICAN JEWISH COMMITTEE SCHOLAR WHO
REVIEWED TALMUDIC PASSAGES REFERRING TO
JESUS CHRIST FELL INTO THE ROW SURROUNDING
FILM STAR MEL GIBSON'S CONTROVERSIAL FILM
ACCOUNT OF CHRIST'S FINAL DAYS

The controversy over Mel Gibson's upcoming film about the death of Jesus has spurred painful exchanges between Jews and Christians and progressive and traditional Catholics in recent weeks.

To date, the debates have centred on the 'proper' interpretation of the role of Jews in Jesus's Crucifixion, as presented in the four New Testament Gospels. But Gibson's US$25 million biblical epic, which the director insists is about love and forgiveness, has triggered a new squabble – among Jewish scholars.

The texts in question are not New Testament but rather passages about Jesus from the Talmud long censored by Christian authorities. The Talmud is the encyclopaedia of Jewish law and tradition considered sacred by traditional Jews.

Raising the issue is an article by Steven Bayme, the national director of Contemporary Jewish Life for the American Jewish Committee (AJC), which declares that Jews must face up to the fact that the Talmudic narrative 'does clearly demonstrate . . . fourth-century rabbinic willingness to take responsibility for the execution of Jesus'.

'Jewish apologetics that "we could not have done it" because of Roman sovereignty ring hollow when one examines the Talmudic account,' Bayme said. He contends that Jewish inter-faith representatives are not being honest in dialogue if they ignore the explicit Talmudic references to Jesus.

His article was posted on the AJC's website in late September 2003, then removed after media enquiries. Ken Bandler, a spokesman for the AJC, said the article was taken down to 'avoid confusion' over whether it represented the organisation's official position. AJC officials now refer to the article as 'an internal document'.

Some Jewish scholars and inter-faith officials were upset by the article, questioning either Bayme's scholarship or his timing – saying this was a particularly delicate time to call attention to Jews' role in Jesus's death – or both. But Bayme was unswayed.

Citing the continuing controversy over Gibson's film *The Passion*, which has reignited concern over Christianity's ancient charge against Jews as 'Christ-killers', he wrote that it is also important 'that Jews confront their own tradition and ask how Jewish sources treated the Jesus narrative'.

Bayme cites a passage from the Talmud, Sanhedrin 43a, which relates the fate of a man called Jesus who is hanged on the eve of Passover for practising sorcery and leading the people of Israel astray. When no one comes forward to defend the accused sorcerer during a 40 day reprieve, Jewish authorities put him to death, despite Jesus's 'connections with the government'.

The Talmud cites this incident during a discussion of due process and capital punishment in Jewish law. Bayme acknowledges that the passage was written by Talmudic scholars in Babylon, who lived about 400 years after Jesus. 'To be sure, historians cannot accept such a text uncritically,' Bayme wrote.

But he says the passage is significant because the Talmudic text 'indicates rabbinic willingness to acknowledge, at least in principle, that in a Jewish court and in a Jewish land, a real-life Jesus would indeed have been executed. No effort is made to pin his death upon the Romans,' Bayme said. 'Pointedly, Jews did not argue that crucifixion was a Roman punishment and therefore no Jewish court could have advocated it.' Bayme said he wrote the piece for two reasons: to educate Jews and to promote honest dialogue with Christians.

He cited the Catholic Church's 1965 statement that Jesus's death 'cannot be blamed upon all Jews then living, without distinction, nor upon the Jews of today'. Bayme said Gibson's movie 'has alienated many Jewish leaders who correctly worry whether the movie's graphic description of the Crucifixion and its alleged overtones of a Jewish conspiracy to kill Jesus may ignite long-dormant Christian hostilities to Jews'.

That's why the Gospel and its association with anti-Semitism need to be confronted as well as Jewish sources, he said. But Bayme stressed that he is not suggesting a moral equivalency between problematic anti-Semitic Gospel passages 'which have caused the death of Jews' and the Talmudic Jesus references.

Indeed, the Catholic Church, which burned copies of the Talmud in the Middle Ages, officially censored the Talmud's Jesus references in the thirteenth century. Even today the standard Vilna edition of the Talmud omits any discussion about 'Yeshu', Jesus in Hebrew. The Jesus omissions began to be restored in the last century, Bayme said.

And the passages 'are now included in most of the new printings of the Talmud', said Yisrael Shaw of Daf Yomi Discussions, an online Talmud service. 'If you do an internet search for Sanhedrin 43a, you will find that it is one of the favourite sources of the Christians to use as proof of the Jewish murder and hatred of their god,' Shaw said.

But Bayme is concerned that Jews know nothing about the censored texts. 'Whenever I talked about the origins of Christianity with fellow Jews, I discovered massive ignorance of Jewish narratives concerning the death of Jesus. It's something I thought Jews ought to confront fairly,' he said.

Bayme contends the Talmudic text resonates with the Gospel accounts for several reasons. He said the Talmudic charge of practising sorcery and seducing Israel into apostasy, a biblical capital crime, matches recently discovered 'hidden Gospels' that 'a historical Jesus was indeed a first-century sorcerer'.

'A mature relationship between two faiths should allow for each faith to . . . uncover these texts and view them critically,' Bayme said. But some disagreed with Bayme's analysis and policy suggestion. His own organisation pulled the piece only a couple of days after it was posted.

Rabbi David Rosen, the group's director of inter-religious affairs, said Bayme's views were not the 'official AJC position' concerning the trial of Jesus. He called the Talmudic text historically 'dubious' and questioned Bayme's connecting the text with the Gospel stories, noting the actual charge against Jesus and the nature of the court 'is in conflict'.

Some outside specialists also refuted Bayme's article. Brooklyn College history professor Rabbi David Berger, a specialist in Christian–Jewish issues, said it would be a mistake and a diversion to bring the Talmudic texts into the inter-faith dialogue.

'The Second Vatican Council properly rejected collective Jewish guilt for the Crucifixion, even though it affirmed that some Jews were involved,' he said. 'Consequently, raising the question of the historical involvement of Jews, with or without reference to Talmudic texts, diverts us from the key issue, which is the denial of contemporary Jewish culpability for these events.'

He noted that in the Middle Ages, 'most Jews assumed that Jews executed Jesus of Nazareth based on these Talmudic passages, though some asserted that the Jesus of Talmud is not the same as the Jesus of Christianity'. Rabbi Adin Steinsaltz, whose Talmud edition has been translated into English, Russian and Spanish, said he believed the Talmudic Jesus is probably not the Christian Jesus.

'It could very well be somebody else', who lived 100 or 200 years earlier, because the stories do not match the Gospel account, he said. Rabbi Steinsaltz noted that the Hebrew name Yeshu was popular then and that 'stories about the resurrection of dead leaders are a dime a dozen, before Jesus and after him. This is not a historical issue.'

In any case, Rabbi Steinsaltz said Christians would do best to avoid these texts because there is nothing politically or theologically significant to them in Jewish tradition. Ellis Rivkin, professor emeritus of Jewish history at Hebrew Union College and author of the seminal book *What Crucified Jesus*, said dragging in the Talmud text is 'dangerous, utterly meaningless and irrelevant'.

But Dr David Kraemer, professor of Talmud and rabbinics at the Jewish Theological Seminary, supported Bayme's call for honesty about Jewish texts and Jesus. 'I think it's very relevant to bring up evidence of the difficulty of our relationship with Christianity,' he said, contending that it is indeed Jesus of Nazareth in the text.

Kraemer believes the text was written at a time of fierce competition between the early rabbis and Christian leaders in the early centuries of the Common Era. 'The attitudes expressed [in the Talmud] can be pretty hateful attitudes,' he said. 'It's not about comparing them [with the anti-Semitic Gospel passages]. Just because you can't equate them doesn't mean you can't raise the issues.' ❏

Eric J Greenberg is a staff writer at The Jewish Week *newspaper in New York, where a version of this article first appeared*

A censorship chronicle incorporating information from Agence France-Press (AFP), Alliance of Independent Journalists (AJI), Amnesty International (AI), Article 19 (A19), Association des Cinéastes Documentaristes, Libération, Association of Independent Electronic Media (ANEM), the BBC Monitoring Service Summary of World Broadcasts (SWB), Centre for Human Rights and Democratic Studies (CEHURDES), Centre for Journalism in Extreme Situations (CJES), the Committee to Protect Journalists (CPJ), Canadian Journalists for Free Expression (CJFE), Democratic Journalists' League (JuHI), Digital Freedom Network (DFN), Glasnost Defence Foundation (GDF), Human Rights Watch (HRW), Indymedia, Information Centre of Human Rights & Democracy Movements in China (ICHR DMC), Institute for War & Peace Reporting (IWPR), Instituto de Prensa y Sociedad (IPYS), the United Nations Integrated Regional Information Network (IRIN), the Inter-American Press Association (IAPA), the International Federation of Journalists (IFJ/FIP), Media Foundation for West Africa, the Media Institute of Southern Africa (MISA), Network for the Defence of Independent Media in Africa (NDIMA), International PEN (PEN), Open Media Research Institute (OMRI), Pacific Islands News Association (PINA), Radio Free Europe/Radio Liberty (RFE/RL), Reporters Sans Frontières (RSF), The Southeast Asian Press Alliance (SEAPA), Statewatch, Transitions Online (TOL), the

World Association of Community Broadcasters (AMARC), World Association of Newspapers (WAN), World Organisation Against Torture (OMCT), Writers in Prison Committee (WiPC) and other sources including members of the International Freedom of Expression eXchange (IFEX)

AFGHANISTAN

On 17 September, Chief Justice Mawlawi Fazl Hadi Shinwari announced the founding of a Council of Ulama of Afghanistan, tasked to counter 'enemy propaganda and preach Islam'. The council will send 80 clerics to each province to challenge anti-government Islamist radicals who call for jihad against the US-backed government in Kabul. (RFE/RL)

Shah Zaman Warez-Stanakzai, Information and Culture Ministry publications chief and publisher of the political journal *Palwasha*, received death threats in September. He accused mujahedin warlords still powerful in Afghanistan of destroying Kabul during their 1992–6 internecine war and plundering the country's wealth. (RFE/RL)

Another critic of the warlords, journalist **Abdul Samay Hamed**, was named as one of four winners of the 2003 International Press Freedom Awards by the Canadian Journalists for Free Expression. Hamed, who was

attacked by warlord supporters in April, founded the Association for the Defence of Afghan Writers' Rights and the magazine *Telaya*. (Reuters)

On 19 October, the 2002 film *Osama* by Afghan director **Siddiq Barmak** was awarded the top prize at Montreal's New Movie and New Media Festival. The work is one of the first major feature films produced in Afghanistan since the fall of the Taliban. (Reuters, RFE/RL)

ALGERIA

Doctor and human rights activist **Salaheddine Sidhoum**, who went into hiding in 1994 until recently, had his 20-year jail sentence for 'acts of terrorism or subversion' quashed on 16 October after turning himself in to the courts on 29 September. He had spent years documenting human rights abuses by the security forces and their allies. (AI)

Fouad Boughanem, editor of *Le Soir d'Algérie*, was arrested on 16 September. Fellow editors who went in support to the police station where Boughanem was being held were also arrested, including senior editor **Malika Boussouf** and executive editor **Badr-Edine Manaa**, as well as **Rabah Abdelah**, secretary-general of Algeria's National Union of Journalists. (AFP)

Six major daily newspapers led a 'day without the press' on 22 September in protest at increased state harassment. *Liberté, Le Matin, L'Expression, Le Soir d'Algérie, El Khabar* and *Er-Rai* halted printing for a day. All were among newspapers forced to suspend publication in August (*Index* 4/03), officially for defaulting on debts to state printers. (AFP)

On 6 November, journalist **Hassan Bourras** was jailed for two years and banned from journalism for five more for libelling, among others, the wife of the local district attorney. He is also the representative of the Algerian Human Rights League in the town of El Bayadh. (RSF)

ARGENTINA

On 5 October, **Clara Britos** (*Index* 4/03), owner and editor of the monthly *La Tapa*, was seized by a group of men in a passing car and again threatened, apparently in connection with her reports on alleged local government corruption in the city of Guernica, in Buenos Aires province. (WiPC)

On 14 October, journalist **Gustavo Corvalán** of *El Liberal* newspaper in Santiago del Estero province, was threatened as he was covering a protest by unemployed individuals who were making demands for food at the province's Health and Social Action Ministry. (*Periodistas*)

AUSTRALIA

On 6 November, the International Federation of Journalists called on the government to withdraw its plans to ease Australia's media ownership laws. They presently prevent one company from controlling a daily newspaper and TV station in the same city and restrict foreign ownership. Rupert Murdoch's News Corporation controls nearly 70 per cent of metropolitan newspapers by circulation and the rival Fairfax group controls virtually all the rest. (IFJ)

AZERBAIJAN

On 7 September, Reporters Sans Frontières complained to the Uzbek government about the blocking of the opposition news website **Ozod Ovoz** (www.ozod ovoz.org), set up in April. It has been inaccessible from inside Uzbekistan since 2 September. (RSF, RFE/ RL)

On 7 October, the *Yeni Nesil* journalists' union revealed the results of its survey of campaign coverage ahead of the 16 October elections. It found that the candidate backed by outgoing President Heidar Aliev – his son and current prime minister, Ilham Aliev – got 1,000 per cent more TV coverage than either of the two main opposition candidates. (Article 19, CJES)

Meanwhile, Reporters Sans Frontières reported that up to 25 local and foreign journalists had been beaten or detained by security forces at an eve-of-poll protest in Baku, including **Azer Hasret**, secretary-general of the Azerbaijan Journalists Confederation. Several were hospitalised and one, *Avropa* editor **Azer Garachenli**, was later jailed for 15 days on unspecified charges. He was freed pending appeal on 22 October. Ilham Aliev won the election. (RSF, JuHI, IPI)

Six popular dailies, *Azadliq, Yeni Musavat, Baki xabar, Hurriyyet, Yeni Zaman*, and the Russian-language *Novoye Vremya*, were barred from the state-owned printing press and closed on 15 November. Private printing houses have been warned off working with private media and the price of newsprint has been forced up by state intervention as part of the strategy. (IPI)

BANGLADESH

Reporters Sans Frontières raised concerns on 12 September over changes the government proposes for the 2001 Bangladesh Telecommunications Act to deal with alleged security threats. RSF say the amendments, if approved, would tighten control over email traffic, legalise invasion of privacy and undermine free expression. (RSF)

Hiramon Mondol (*Index* 4/03), a correspondent for the daily *Dainik Prabarttan*, was released from jail in Khulna and exonerated of charges of extortion on 20 September after the police failed to make a case against him. (CPJ)

The Bangladeshi feminist writer **Taslima Nasreen** was sentenced *in absentia* on 13 October to a year in jail on a charge of writing 'derogatory comments' about Islam in her books. This is the first sentence against the writer who was forced to flee Bangladesh in 1994 after receiving death threats from Muslim extremists. Nasreen, who now lives in Sweden, told the BBC she had no idea that a case had been filed against her, or that a trial was taking place. (BBC)

On 10 November, **Selim Jahangir**, a photographer for the national daily Bengali-language *Janakantha*, was freed from a jail in the north-west after ten days. He had been arrested and charged with obstructing and threatening the life of a police officer on 1 November. He denies the charges. (CPJ)

Also on 10 November, a bomb was thrown at five journalists in the town of Feni. **Bakhtiar Islam Munna**, correspondent for the daily *Ittefaq* and the wire service United News of Bangladesh, was the likely target; he is scheduled to give evidence in the trial of the men accused of the 2001 assault on journalist **Tipu Sultan** (*Index* 2/01, 3/01, 4/02, 3/03, 4/03). The other journalists were **Osman Harun Mahmud Dulal** of the daily *Janakantha*, **Shahjalal Ratan** of the

daily *Jugantor*, **Muhamed Jalal Uddin** of the daily *Manabzamin* and **Asaduzzaman Dara** of the daily *Bhorer Kagoj*. No one was injured. (CPJ)

BELARUS

On 19 September, the Belarus Association of Journalists staged a one-day 'no work' protest at recent closures of independent newspapers. (RSF, IFEX)

On 23 September, a Minsk court ordered the closure of the daily newspaper *Mestnoye Vremya Press* after the Tax Ministry claimed that it had failed to notify them of a change of address. It is the sixth independent newspaper to have been closed this year. (WAN, IFEX)

BOLIVIA

In October, journalists found themselves the target of systematic intimidation as they covered Bolivia's social and political crises. Among the threatened: staff at **Radio Fides**, **Canal 2** and **Canal 39** TV, and staff at **Pachamama**, **Celestial** and **Erbol** radio. Journalist **Juan Yupanqui**, of the daily *El Diario*, was beaten up by security police on 7 October as he followed demonstrators walking from El Alto to La Paz. (PFC)

Seven journalists at state-run TV resigned on 12 October, charging the government with trying to block news of clashes between demonstrators and security forces in the city of

El Alto. On 15 October, all issues of the daily *El Diario* and the weekly *Pulso* were seized by security forces and in Oruro, south of the capital La Paz, a bomb destroyed the transmitters of **Radio Pio XII**, a Catholic radio station, and **Televisión Universitaria** TV. Government officials had previously criticised the station for its coverage of the crackdown. (PFC)

In October, **Walter Chávez**, editor of the Bolivian edition of the French monthly *Le Monde Diplomatique* and the bimonthly *El Juguete Rabioso*, accused intelligence agents of harassing him in La Paz and of forcing him to suspend a special issue on the case for the president's resignation.

BOTSWANA

On 6 September, Batawana tribal chief Tawani Moremi smashed the camera of **Booster Galesekegwe** of the weekly *Mmegi* as he worked on a story about South African DJ Phat Joe. When Galesekegwe's colleague **Kagiso Sekokonyane** arrived to help, the chief attacked him too. The trouble continued at a nearby police station. Charges have been filed against the chief, but he has since disappeared. (MISA)

BURMA

Burma's military government released five top opposition National League for Democracy (NLD) figures from house arrest on

23–4 November, but left NLD leader **Aung San Suu Kyi** in detention. The five – **Than Tun, Nyunt Wei, Soe Myint, Hla Pe** and **Lun Tin**, all in their 70s and 80s – were freed two weeks after United Nations human rights envoy Paulo Sergio Pinheiro visited Burma and called for the release of political detainees. The Nobel prizewinner was detained on 30 May, following clashes between her supporters and a government-backed mob. (BBC)

BURUNDI

Burundi's minister of communications ordered a one-week ban on privately owned **Radio Isanganiro** on 13 September, accusing it of defaming the government's peace efforts. The station had defied a state ban on broadcasts by spokesmen for the Hutu rebel National Liberation Forces (FNL). On 16 September, the minister struck again, permanently closing **Radio Publique Africain** after it interviewed FNL spokesman Pasteur Habimana. (RSF)

CAMBODIA

Chuor Chetharith, deputy editor-in-chief of royalist Cambodian opposition radio station Ta Prum, was shot dead in front of its Phnom Penh studios on 18 October. Prime Minister Hun Sen had warned the station four days earlier to 'better monitor its programmes' after it criticised him. The king commented

on his website that the killing was 'politically motivated' and complained that 'in 99 per cent of cases, those responsible are not found and go unpunished'. (RSF)

CAMEROON

Radio Veritas, founded by Catholic Cardinal Christian Tumi, has been banned for reportedly failing to meet licensing requirements. President Paul Biya allegedly hopes to stifle media criticism in the run-up to 2004 presidential elections, which Tumi is rumoured to plan to contest. Meanwhile, legal action to reopen Freedom FM, closed by government order in May 2003 on alleged licensing grounds, is being challenged by the Communications Ministry. (RSF, IRIN)

CHAD

Community radio station **FM-Liberté** was accused of 'illegal and deviant behaviour' and closed by the Public Security Ministry on 21 October. It had compared President Idriss Deby with the country's former dictator Hissene Habre, and allegedly accused him of allowing foreigners to threaten the country's economy and its citizens. (RSF)

CHILE

On 3 September. *El Mercurio* journalist **Ximena Marré** and editor **Mario Ovalle** were summonsed by Supreme Court magis-

trate Domingo Kokisch and told to reveal the source of a story about thefts of confidential financial information. When they refused, Kokisch ejected them both from the court. Alberto Luengo, director of *La Nación* newspaper, has since alleged that Kokisch assaulted journalist **Luis Narváez** in January in an incident not reported at the time. (PFC)

CHINA

Chinese officials banned a song by one of the country's top-selling stars because it refers to opium. **Faye Wong**'s song 'In the Name of Love', which includes the lyrics 'opium is warm and sweet', will be removed from her upcoming album. The Xinhua News Agency reported it was banned on 30 October because 'the lyrics were too decadent and will influence the health of young people'. (BBC)

A Chinese publishing house claimed in September that it 'did not have time' to get agreement to cut passages critical of China's human rights record from its published translation of former US First Lady **Hillary Clinton**'s memoirs. An example of the changes made was a reference to Chinese dissident **Harry Wu**, a human rights activist who spent 19 years in Chinese work camps. In the Chinese translation, Wu is not named and simply described as 'a person wanted for espionage and detained awaiting trial'.

Internet essayist **Du Daobin** was arrested on 28 October. His wife Huang Chunrong was told by police in Yingcheng, Hubei Province: 'We have spoken to Du Daobin several times, but he did not listen. He has already crossed the line.' They also warned her not to inform the foreign media about her husband's arrest. (CPJ)

Web journalist **Huang Qi**, jailed for the last three years for starting a website for notices about missing people in China, has been beaten in jail, says his wife, Zeng Li. She told a French journalist that 'yes, he was beaten. He has a long scar on his forehead and he has lost a tooth.' (RSF)

Ma Shiwen, deputy director for Disease Control at the Henan Provincial Health Department, was released from custody in October. He was arrested in August for allegedly leaking a state document blaming state blood collection centres for Henan's Aids crisis. (*China Aids Survey*, *The Peking Duck*, HRW)

Culture Ministry official Lui Qiang said that a shortlist of fewer than 100 major companies, equipped with monitoring software, will be allowed to open internet café chains and that while cafés outside the big chains will not be banned the culture minister will 'encourage mergers and acquisitions'. (RSF)

Psychology student **Lui Di** was released on bail by the Chinese authorities after a year in detention for posting web messages under the pseudonym 'Stainless Steel Mouse' that called for web users to 'ignore the Chinese regime's propaganda' and to 'live in full freedom'. Two other web dissidents, **Wu Yiran** and **Li Yibin**, were released at the same time – three days before German Chancellor Gerhard Schroeder's visit to China, and a week before the visit of Chinese Prime Minister Wen Jiabao to the United States. (RSF)

COLOMBIA

A broadcast relay tower was destroyed on 23 September, allegedly by the Revolutionary Armed Forces of Colombia (FARC). The bombing caused some US$5 million damage and may cut off public TV broadcasts to municipalities in Valle, Cauca and Nariño departments for up to six months. (FLIP)

Radio announcer **José Nel Muñoz** was killed on 5 October near Puerto Libertad in southern Colombia, where he had been working for Latina Estéreo radio station for more than a year, hosting music and community information programmes. He also occasionally covered news about the armed conflict and political issues. The killing has been ascribed to FARC. (FLIP)

Journalist **Zully Esther Codina** was assassinated on 11 November in the city of Santa Marta, in Magdalena department. The 49-year-old journalist hosted the *Entérese* opinion programme, broadcast every Saturday on Radio Rodadero Todelar. She was also working at the Julio Méndez Barreneche central hospital in Santa Marta. (IPYS)

Two journalists in Barrancabermeja in north-east Colombia received death threats. On 15 October, journalist **Pedro Javier Galvis**, an editor for the weekly *La Noticia*, was told to leave the city by two armed individuals on a motorcycle. He did so five days later. Then journalist **Yaneth Montoya Martínez** of the daily *Vanguardia Liberal* received several death threats. Montoya usually reports on security matters and the activities of community groups. (FLIP)

On 6 November, a proposed anti-terrorism statute was approved by Colombia's House of Representatives on its sixth reading. The statute would allow the army to carry out searches, tap telephones and intercept private correspondence without a warrant, during a 72-hour period, in cases involving individuals suspected of having terrorist links. If applied to journalists, these provisions could threaten confidentiality of sources. (RSF)

COMOROS

French journalist **Morad Ait-Habbouche** was arrested in Moroni on 22 September. He was caught in a sweep against French-Comoran opposition leader **Said Larifou**, accused of plotting a coup against President Colonel Azali Assoumani. Ait-Habbouche was freed after a few days and left the country. (AFP, RSF)

DEMOCRATIC REPUBLIC OF CONGO

The editor of the Kinshasa-based satirical newspaper *Pot-Pourri*, **Guy Kasongo Kilembwe**, was taken to the Kinshasa Public Prosecutor's office on 29 August where he was reportedly interrogated by Pius Mwabilu, publisher of the pro-government daily *L'Avenir*. Mwabilu then allegedly threatened **Tshivis Tshivuadi** of the media rights group Journalistes en Danger (JED) before publishing an article in *L' Avenir* accusing JED of support of 'enemy newspapers'. (JED)

Police confiscated most newspapers and magazines on sale in Kinshasa on 26 September and arrested more than a dozen newspaper vendors. No official explanation was given for the operation. (JED)

The director-general of Radiotélévision Lumière, **Augustin Lubukayi**, was detained for a night on 3 October by National Intelligence Agency Officers two days after one of his TV show hosts, **Illunga Mwenyapale**, had commented on a pastor who charged his congregation US$100 a blessing – but never actually gave it. (JED)

On 29 October, **Symplice Kalunga wa Kalunga**, a political journalist for private CMB TV, was forcibly taken to the public prosecutor's office and interrogated about his 23 October interview with **Kundura Kasongo**, president of the Front for Social Integration (FIS) and a critic of the government. Kalunga was released after Kasongo turned himself in and took full responsibility for his statements. (JED)

CÔTE D'IVOIRE

Côte d'Ivoire rebels and opposition parties were banned from street demonstrations on the eve of a planned 18 October march to call on President Laurent Gbagbo to respect the terms of a current peace deal for the troubled country. The measure followed violent demonstrations in Abidjan by pro-government groups. (BBC)

Radio France Internationale correspondent **Jean Hélène Gbagbo** was shot dead on 11 October at point-blank range by policeman Sergeant Dago Theodore. Gbagbo's supporters have accused the French press of supporting rebels in the north of the country. Theodore has confessed and faces 20 years in jail. (IFJ, RSF, IRIN)

Gangs of youths launched a series of attacks on newspaper vans belonging to the country's only distributor, Edipresse, removing and destroying opposition titles as Gbagbo's supporters grew ever more angry at rebel activity. (IRIN)

CUBA

Detained journalists **Manuel Vázquez Portal**, **Juan Carlos Herrera Acosta** and **Normando Hernández González** were moved from Boniatico Jail to an unnamed prison after going on hunger strike on 31 August to protest against 'unfair' and 'inhumane' treatment. (RSF)

Deputy editor **Claudia Márquez Linares** of the banned magazine *De Cuba* and wife of jailed dissident **Osvaldo Alfo** was arrested on 29 October and threatened with jail by state security personnel. (IAPA, IFEX)

On 29 October, **Abel Escobar Ramírez**, a correspondent for the independent news agency Cuba Press, was detained and questioned by police for three days before being released. (RSF)

CYPRUS

Basharan Duzgun of the daily *Kibris*, editor-in-chief **Suleyman Erguclu** and editorial writer **Hasan Hasturer**, along with **Hasan Kahvecioglu** and editor-in-chief **Mehmet Davulcu** of the daily *Ortam* in Turkish-run northern Cyprus, faced prosecution in November for allegedly 'insulting the army'. The military objected to reports of a demonstration in the village of Doganci in March 2002 that was violently broken up by paramilitary police. The five face sentences of between ten and 44 years in prison. (RSF)

Murat Kanatli, editor of the opposition weekly *Yeni Cag*, was beaten up on 17 October by members of the far-right Grey Wolves nationalist group after seeking to interview their leader. The police made no arrests, despite calls from the South-East Europe Media Organisation for action after the Grey Wolves had threatened two other journalists on 30 September. (SEEMO, AFP)

ECUADOR

In September, the so-called Legión Blanca death squad contacted *El Comercio* newspaper and told it to pass on threats against journalist **Kintto Lucas**, editor of the alternative newspaper *Tintají* and a correspondent for Inter Press Service; **Pablo Dávalos**, a political analyst for several radio stations and papers; **Marlon Carrión** of the alternative news agency Pachacámac and others. (CEDHU, PFC)

On 19 September, columnist **Rodrigo Fierro** of *El Comercio* was jailed for six months and ordered to pay US$1,000 compensation after being found guilty of libelling a former president by linking him to Ecuadorian bank failures. The journalist has appealed against the sentence. (RSF, IPYS)

On 14 November, President Lucio Gutiérrez demanded that *El Comercio* reveal its sources for a story about an alleged donation to the president's electoral campaign by an individual implicated in drug trafficking. Gutiérrez warned he would resort to legal measures to obtain the names from *El Comercio* if the paper failed to reveal its sources. (PFC)

EGYPT

Sixty-two men were reportedly rounded up on 28 August by Cairo police, who used police wagons to block either end of a Nile bridge reputed to be a meeting place for homosexuals. The men were held for three days, then freed on bail after being charged with the 'habitual practice of debauchery'. (HRW)

A collection of poetry by renowned writer **Ahmad al-Shahawi** called *Commandments of Love for Women* was returned to the shelves on 13 September despite the condemnation of Cairo clerics and the views of an Islamist MP who said the love poems were un-Islamic. (*Cairo Times*)

Mohammed Abdel Sattar, himself detained on 12 September, three days after his brother was arrested for distributing leaflets against the US and Israel, died in jail from torture, reported the Egyptian Organisation for Human Rights. His body was returned to his family two days afterwards without explanation. (AFP)

EQUATORIAL GUINEA

Agence France Presse correspondent **Rodrigo Angue Nguema** was detained for eight days in connection with investigations into a rumoured *coup d'état*. Angue Nguema, one of the few independent reporters in the country, said he was threatened shortly after reporting the rumours. (CPJ, RSF, IRIN)

ETHIOPIA

On 1 October, **Araya Tesfa Mariam**, journalist for the Amharic-language weekly newspaper *Itiop*, was beaten up by three men in military uniform who jumped out of a police car. He suffered injuries to his head, arms, legs and teeth. He was dumped under a bridge where other police found him and took him to hospital. (EFPJA)

The Ministry of Justice department that registers NGOs warned on 4 November that it was going to take measures against the Ethiopian Free Journalists Association (EFJA) and on 10 November wrote to it, banning it from continuing its activities. EFJA was founded seven years ago. (EFJA)

FRANCE

An empty vehicle belonging to journalist **Christine Clerc** of *Le Figaro* was riddled with bullets in southern Corsica on the night of 4 September. (RSF)

Georges Lopez, the teacher featured in the hit cinema documentary *Etre et Avoir*, is suing director **Nicolas Philibert** for US$294,000 for the use of his image. If his suit is successful it could render documentary making in France impossible. (www.addoc.net, *Libération*)

GABON

Authorities suspended the satirical bimonthly *Sub-Version* and the newspaper *La Sagaie* on 17–19 September and renewed the ban on a third, *Misamu*. The bans follow earlier orders to the Interior Ministry to monitor the content of the papers. Local journalists linked *La Sagaie*'s ban to an article on the political influence of people from the south-eastern Haut-Ogoué region. *Misamu* was closed either by a dispute over ownership or for criticising the government, depending on perspectives. (CPJ)

GAMBIA

Abdoulie Sey, editor-in-chief of the *Independent* newspaper, was detained without charge for three days by NIA security police and interrogated about an article criticising President Yahya Jammeh. He alleged that his NIA jailers threat-ened to kill him if he continued and was told that his actions would be 'monitored'. (MISA, CPJ)

On 17 October, the *Independent*'s offices came under arson attack by men who assaulted a security guard at the building. The fire was quickly put out but staff had to publish the next issue from different premises. (MISA, CPJ, *Afrol News*)

Independent reporter **Pa Malick Secka** was attacked at a public city council meeting after he tried to report a brawl between councillors. They turned on him, seized his tape recorder and smashed a cassette. (allafrica.com)

GEORGIA

On 13 November, the National Election Commission cancelled the accreditation of independent TV station, **Rustavi 2**. The decision was provoked by broadcasts of a message from the Kmara student movement, calling on the commission to stop falsifying election results. Disquiet at the election abuses ultimately triggered the peaceful overthrow of President Eduard Shevardnadze on 23 November. (IFEX/RSF)

GERMANY

The German state of Baden-Württemberg has begun moves to ban Muslims from wearing headscarves in schools. The bill was proposed by the state following a supreme court ruling in September that allowed a Muslim teacher to wear a headscarf. Rights groups say a ban would hamper religious freedom but six other German states are planning similar laws. 'The aim of the law is to forbid state teachers from wearing symbols which could be regarded as political,' said Erwin Teufel, state premier of Baden-Württemberg. (BBC)

GHANA

Kweku Baako, editor-in-chief of *Crusading Guide*, received death threats suspected to have come from different factions of supporters of former president Jerry Rawlings. He had recently published an investigation into the finances of Rawlings's wife. (IFJ)

GREECE

Two people on a motor-cycle threw a petrol bomb at the Athens home of TV newsreader **Anna Panayotarea** on 29 September, an attack she links to recent threats and her investigations into the 17 November terrorist group. Greek TV has been accused of pro-government bias in reporting the group's prosecution. (RSF)

GUATEMALA

The Committee to Protect Journalists condemned the recent intimidation of the Guatemalan press. A five-day visit to the country was prompted by recent press freedom abuses in the months leading up to Guatemala's presidential elections. (CPJ)

GUINEA

Guinean media regulators, the National Communication Council, suspended bi-monthly newspaper *Le Populaire* for publishing an article featuring a picture of a man showing his severed genitals. **Ibrahima Diallo**, managing editor, and journalist **Abdallah Balde** have also been suspended. (MISA, MFWA)

HAITI

On 28 October, the independent station **Radio Caraibes** was attacked by gunmen, who allegedly drove off in a car with state official number plates. After the attack, the station decided to suspend its broadcasts for a brief period. (CPJ)

Privately owned **Radio Maxima**, in the northern city of Cap-Haitien, suspended news programmes on 27 October after threats from pro-government forces. Station director **Jean Robert Lalanne** is a local leader of the opposition to President Aristide. (RSF)

HONDURAS

TV journalist **Antonio Rivas**, 36, was gunned down on 26 November as he entered the offices of TV Canal 38, in Santa Rosa de Copan, 155 miles west of Tegucigalpa. Rivas, who had exposed environmental

damage caused by mining companies operating in the region, escaped uninjured from a similar incident in February when two shots were fired at him in front of his home. At the time he said: 'I wouldn't risk saying that it was because they want to silence me because of events I denounced on my programme, but I don't discount it.'

On 23 October, Attorney-General Roy Edmundo Medina called on the Supreme Court to rule the country's 'insult' laws unconstitutional. He said article 345 of the Criminal Code should be repealed so individuals and journalists could reasonably criticise the errors of state officials without fear of criminal charges. (PFC)

HUNGARY

Police were called to remove the decayed corpse of a man that builders and students at Budapest's University of Arts initially mistook for a modern art sculpture. The year-old corpse hung for a whole day in a garden building, packed with contemporary sculptures, which had just been reopened after repairs on 14 November before onlookers realised what it was and called the police. (Reuters)

INDIA

Punjab Kesari reporter **Parmanand Goyal** was shot dead by three unidentified men on 18 September,

shortly after he was warned to stop writing articles critical of the local police Harayana state Chief Minister Shri Om Parkash Chautala. (IFJ)

On 17 October, the BBC reported that up to 60,000 Hindu hardliners had been arrested in Uttar Pradesh in an attempt by the state government to uphold a court order banning religious activity in or near the site of the destroyed Babri mosque in Ayodhya. Thousands of Vishwa Hindu Parishad cadres still made it to the town, but were prevented from staging a rally there by police firing tear gas and rubber bullets. The 6 December 1992 destruction of the mosque led to over 2,000 people being killed in anti-Muslim violence in the country. (BBC)

On 29 October, Muslim professor **Syed Abdul Geelani** had his conviction for conspiracy overturned by the Delhi High Court. Geelani had been sentenced to death under the controversial Prevention of Terrorism Act for his alleged part in a December 2001 attack on the Indian parliament. The court ruled that there was not sufficient evidence to convict him. (*Christian Science Monitor*)

Distributors and cinema owners in north-east India defied separatist groups who wanted Hindi-language movies banned because they believed they undermined local culture. The Eastern India Motion Pictures Asso-

WHISTLE-BLOWER'S FATE: SATYENDRA KUMAR DUBEY

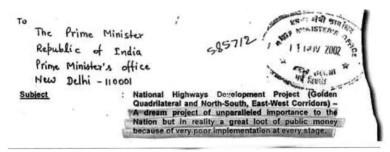

To

The Prime Minister
Republic of India
Prime Minister's office
New Delhi - 110001

585712   1 1 1 1 IV 2002

Subject   : National Highways Development Project (Golden
                Quadrilateral and North-South, East-West Corridors) –
                A dream project of unparalleled importance to the
                Nation but in reality a great loot of public money
                because of very poor implementation at every stage.

Hon'ble Sir,

Through this letter, I wish to draw your kind attention towards great lapse in the implementation of above project. Since such letters from a common man are not usually treated with due seriousness, I wish to clarify at the outset that this letter is being written after carefull thought by a very concerned citizen of the country who is also very closely linked with the project. I request you to kindly go through my brief particulars (attached on a separate sheet to ensure secrecy) before proceeding further.

This was the opening of a November 2002 letter by 31-year-old civil engineer Satyendra Kumar Dubey, then Deputy General Manager on the laying of a 60km section of the massive Golden Quadrilateral road construction project. In his note he detailed corruption in the handing out of subcontracts, but asked for his name to be kept secret. It wasn't. Instead, the letter, name attached, was bounced from one indifferent official to another for more than a year, until, as the police now suspect, the letter finally reached the hands of someone who was interested and was ready to act. On 27 November, Dubey was shot dead, presumably by a 'friend' of one of the corrupt contractors he had exposed.

As noted by Amitav Ranjan, the *Indian Sunday Express* journalist who broke the story, Dubey's request for secrecy would have had legal protection had India passed the Whistle-Blower Act recommended by the Constitution Review Commission in 2002. This would have ensured that Dubey was 'protected against retribution and any discrimination for reporting what he perceived as wrongdoing'. A designated authority would have probed without betraying his identity. It would also have been bound to protect him. ❑

ciation (EIMPA) said in September that more than 12 associations of distributors and cinema owners would defy the ban. (BBC)

The state assembly of Tamil Nadu sentenced five journalists from *The Hindu* and **S Selvam**, editor of the Tamil-language *Murasoli*, to 15 days in jail on 7 November for libelling Chief Minister Jayalalitha Jayaram in their reports last April. On 8 November, *The Hindu* journalists concerned, including editor **N Ravi**, executive editor **Malini Parthasarathy**, publisher **S Rangarajan**, chief of bureau **V Jayant** and special correspondent **Radha Venkatesan**, appealed against their conviction to the Supreme Court. That evening, a carload of policemen, identified by the Bangalore police as officers from Tamil Nadu, intercepted the car in which **N Ram**, editor-in-chief of *The Hindu,* and **N Murali**, joint managing director, were travelling before letting them go. The Supreme Court suspended the execution of the arrest warrants on 10 November. On 12 November, following a request from N Ram, the central government agreed to deploy federal security forces outside the paper's offices for security reasons. The request was withdrawn several hours later after the state government objected. (Reuters, BBC, IANS, *The Hindu, Times of India,* IPI)

On 16 November, unidentified persons attacked the Raipur home of a correspondent from the *Indian Express*, which had published video clips purportedly showing the Union Minister of State for Environment and Forest, Dilip Singh Judeo, accepting a bribe from an Australian mining company. (PTI)

Recent publications: *India: Report of the Malimath Committee on Reforms of the Criminal Justice System: Some observations*, by Amnesty International, 19 September 2003, pp 32; *India: Abuse of the law in Gujarat: Muslims detained illegally in Ahmedabad*, by Amnesty International, 6 November 2003, pp 20

INDONESIA

On 27 October, the executive editor of the daily tabloid *Rakyat Merdeka* was given a six-month suspended sentence for insulting the president. *Rakyat Merdeka* published four headlines that were deemed offensive to President Megawati Sukarnoputri. (CPJ, IFEX)

Indonesia's army commander General Ryamizard Ryacudu told political parties to stop their security men from wearing camouflage, saying ordinary people were confusing party workers with soldiers. Citing some party security men's reputation as swaggering bullies, he made clear he did not want his men associated with such behaviour. 'Wear anything . . . wear brown . . . as long as it's not a soldier's outfit,' Ryacudu said on 14 November. (BBC)

IRAN

Judges closed down the Kurdish weekly magazine ***Avay-e-Kurdistan*** ('Voice of Kurdistan'), published by former MP Ali Nemat Zadeh, after just four issues, it was reported on 21 October. The closure is said to be the first time a Kurdish-language paper has been banned in Iran. (KurdishMedia.com)

Five years on from the murders of prominent journalists and intellectuals in November and December 1998, Hossein Ansari-Rad, head of the Article 90 Parliamentary Commission tasked to investigate such cases, admitted that 'we have reached the conclusion that highly ranked individuals are implicated in this case, figures whom we cannot challenge'. Among the unsolved cases are the killings of **Daryush** and **Parvaneh Forouhar**, prominent liberal opposition figures; **Majid Charif**, an editorial writer for the monthly *Iran-é-Farda*, and writers and journalists **Mohamad Mokhtari** and **Mohamad Jafar Pouyandeh**. (RSF)

PEN Canada has launched a fund-raising campaign to send a Canadian observer to Tehran to observe the trial of Iranian security agent Mohammad Reza Aghdam Ahmadi, accused of murdering photographer **Zahra**

Kazemi. Kazemi was murdered in July while in Iranian custody after being arrested for taking photographs outside Evin Prison in Tehran. She died of a brain haemorrhage after suffering severe blows to the head. (PEN)

IRAQ

Iraq's US-appointed Governing Council banned satellite TV station **al-Arabiya** from working in Iraq on 24 November, accusing it of inciting violence against the coalition. Its Baghdad bureau was forcibly shut. 'Al-Arabiya incites murder because it is calling for killings through the voice of Saddam Hussein,' said a Council spokesman. On 16 November, the channel broadcast a recorded message said to be from Saddam Hussein that called for new 'resistance' against the US and British occupation forces. (BBC)

Criminal proceedings have been launched in Spain against three US soldiers responsible for shelling the Palestine Hotel in Baghdad on 8 April. The attack killed Spanish Telecinco cameraman **José Couso** and **Taras Protsyuk**, a Ukrainian cameraman working for Reuters. (RSF)

Ahmed Shawkat, editor of the weekly *Bilah Ittijah*, was shot dead on the roof of his office in Mosul on 20 October as he made a phone call. His daughter Roaa said Shawkat 'used to write against the resistance, against the Americans, against the local government and the former government'. Shawkat had received threatening letters telling him to close down his newspaper. (RSF)

Recent publications: Human Rights Watch, *Hearts and Minds: Post-War Civilian Deaths in Baghdad Caused by US Forces*, published 21 October 2003; *After the War: The report of the KHRP Fact-finding Mission to Iraqi Kurdistan*, published October 2003

IRELAND

The Irish government is considering jailing or fining police who pass information to the media, even if they believe the leak is in the public interest. Justice Minister Michael McDowell argues that the bill is needed to root out police graft, but Andrew Puddephatt of free-expression group Article 19 says police 'should have the right to be whistle-blowers like any other civil public servants'. (*Observer*)

Michael McDowell says the Irish press should be regulated by a state-appointed press council, applying a state-drafted code of ethics. He also proposes that telephone companies and internet service providers be required to pass on details about their users to the authorities. (*Observer*)

ISRAEL

A controversial documentary about the Israeli army's invasion of the Jenin refugee camp in the West Bank can be shown in Israel, a court ruled on 11 November. Israel's film board had banned *Jenin, Jenin* on the grounds that it presented a distorted version of events, but the Supreme Court rejected this argument. 'The fact that the film includes lies is not enough to justify a ban,' said Justice Dalia Dorner in her verdict. (BBC)

Israeli customs seized a shipment of 450 singing and dancing Osama bin Laden and Saddam Hussein dolls under a law banning incitement, it was announced on 26 November. The battery-powered Chinese-made figurines were confiscated at the northern port of Haifa, Customs Authority spokeswoman Idit Lev-Zerahiya said. An Israeli Arab businessman from the northern village of Qafr Qara admitted under questioning to importing the 400 copies of the al-Qaida leader and 50 of the deposed Iraqi ruler, as a 'gimmick' for sale to Jews and Arabs. (Reuters)

ITALY

Police seized 7,000 pages of print and digital files belonging to journalist **Gianmarco Chiocci** from the Italian daily *Il Giornale* in October. He had been investigating allegations that former Italian premier Romano Prodi and Foreign Minister Lamberto Dini took kickbacks during Telecom Italia's purchase of shares in Telekom Serbia in

BRIEF MOMENT OF FREEDOM

On the evening of 12 December 1944, a meeting attended by newspapers owners including Messrs Razooq Ghannam, Mohammed Mahdi al-Jawahiri, Yahia Qasem, Noor el-Din Dawed, Sadr al-Deen Sharaf el-Din, Rafael Batti and Kamel al-Jadergi was held in the headquarters of *Sawt al-Ahali*. It was agreed:

1   To found a Journalists' Association in Baghdad and demand that the Government issue a regulation vis-à-vis the founding of the Association. Messrs Mohammed Mahdi al-Jawahiri and Noor el-Din Dawed were given the task of petitioning the Government and inviting colleagues to approve this petition.

2   To complain against the Government's *ultra vires* acts of censorship and authority over newspapers. Accordingly, the presentation of a detailed memorandum, along with a list of such acts, was agreed. Both are to be signed by newspaper owners. Messrs Kamel al-Jadergi and Mohammed Mahdi al-Jawahiri were given the task of preparing the draft complaint and memorandum.

Signed: Noor el-Din Dawed, owner of *al-Nida'*, Yahia Qasem, owner of *al-Sha'b*, Sadr al-Deen Sharaf el-Din, owner of *al-Sa'a*, Razooq Ghannam, owner of *al-Iraq*, Rafael Batti, owner of *al-Bilad*

Signed subject to qualifications: I reserve my opinion as to paragraph 1: Kamel al-Jadergi, owner of *Sawt al-Ahali*, Mohammed Mahdi al-Jawahiri, owner of *al-Rai' el-Am*

Translated by Manal Mitri from the Baghdad press, December 1944

Three years before the publication of this statement, the British Army had moved into Baghdad to protect its interests and restore the regent Prince Abd al-Ilah and his ward, the five-year-old King Faisal II. Martial law and government censorship remained in place, but by late 1944, fuelled in part by the Regent's own support for liberalisation, there was renewed clamour for democratisation. This statement was part of that call. The demands were not met until the appointment of a new prime minister, Tawfiq al-Suwaidi, in February 1946. He ended martial law and censorship, closed the notorious al-Faw detention camp and allowed political parties to convene. This liberal spring did not last: by May, al-Suwaidi's government had fallen and repression returned. ❏

1997. Chiocci and editor **Maurizio Blepietro** are accused of violating the confidentiality of a judicial investigation. (RFS)

Deputy PM Gianfranco Fini of the neo-fascist Alleanza Nazionale party proposed to grant immigrants who had been in Italy for six years or more the right to vote in municipal elections, if they were paying tax and had no criminal record. Umberto Bossi, leader of the Lega Nord party, briefly threatened to resign and bring down the government in protest at the proposal. (*La Repubblica*)

Giulio Andreotti, the former prime minister sentenced last November (*Index* 1/03) to 24 years' imprisonment for ordering the murder of journalist **Mino Pecorelli**, was wholly absolved by Italy's Supreme Court on 30 October. (*La Repubblica*)

On 19 November, state-owned Rai 3 TV suspended satirist **Sabina Lutazzi**'s hit programme *RaiOt* after Silvio Berlusconi's television company Mediaset threatened to sue for defamation. (www.rai.it, *La Repubblica*)

JAPAN

The body of writer **Satoru Someya** was found on 12 September in Tokyo Bay. Someya reported on organised crime elements in Tokyo's red-light district, Kabukicho. (RSF, CPJ)

Mainichi Shimbun reporter **Tomoko Oji** received a second major award from the Japan Newspaper Publishers and Editors Association (NSK) on 15 October, for a story revealing the use of local government registers to recruit teenagers for the self-defence forces. The piece led to changes in the recently passed Personal Information Protection Law, which has been criticised for infringing freedom of the press. (*Kyodo News*)

KAZAKHSTAN

On 4 October, **Andrei Doronin**, correspondent for the independent daily *Ekspress-K*, was beaten up near his Almaty apartment by assailants who questioned him about his work and warned him to give up journalism. Doronin had written about losses to the national budget caused by vodka production in the untaxed shadow economy. (RFE/RL)

The Kazakh Justice Ministry announced the launching of a national campaign on 6 October to promote understanding of intellectual property rights. For two years, Kazakhstan has been on a US watch list of nations suspected of organised copyright piracy, leading to fears that the country might lose its most-favoured-nation trade status with Washington. (Interfax)

On 5 November, the Supreme Court turned down an appeal for a review of the case of journalist

Sergei Duvanov, sentenced to three years and six months in prison in January 2003 on charges of raping a minor. His supporters say the case was fabricated by the authorities to discredit Duvanov's critical articles. (RFE/RL)

KENYA

On 29 September, managing director **Tom Mshindi**, associate editor **Kwamchetsi Makokha** and Sunday editor **David Makali** of the daily *East African Standard* were arrested following the publication of a leaked police report detailing the confessions of the killers of Constitutional Review Commission expert **Crispin Odhiambo Mbai**, assassinated on 14 September. On 1 October, Makali and a policeman were charged with stealing a police tape of the confessions. Makali pleaded not guilty. (CPJ)

Women members of parliament in Kenya walked out on 20 November in protest at a ban on handbags in the chamber. The ban was imposed ten months earlier in response to fears that bags could conceal weapons. But when parliamentary speaker Francis Ole Kaparo refused to waive the ban on 20 November, 12 women MPs walked out to applause from other female MPs. (BBC)

KYRGYZSTAN

On 4 September, National Security Service officers in southern Kyrgyzstan banned the sale of journalist **Nuradil Bakashev**'s book on the killing of five anti-government demonstrators in the Aksy Raion of Djalal-Abad Oblast in March 2002. (RFE/RL)

The Kyrgyz media refused in August to publish a report on political and socio-economic conditions in the country, for fear of triggering state retribution, said parliamentarian Azimbek Beknazarov. The Kyrgyz opposition has no funds to print the report privately and relies on the media to put its case to the country. (RFE/RL)

Police in Kara-Suu in southern Kyrgyzstan are investigating the death of journalist **Ernis Nazalov**, correspondent for the Kyrgyz Ruhu and Kyrgyz Ordo national press. He was about to publish a report on high-level corruption in Kyrgyzstan when he was found dead on 15 September. His records have apparently disappeared. The US-based human rights group Freedom House has called for an independent investigation. (*Moya Solitsa*)

On 17 October, the Pervomai Raion Court in Bishkek fined the newspaper *Argumenty i fakty v Kyrgyzstane* five soms (12 US cents) for insulting the opposition Ar-Namys party. The paper had claimed National Guard commander Abdygul Chotbaev had said the party was financed by foreigners. The paper was also ordered to publish an apology to Ar-Namys. (RFE/RL)

Aktan Abdykalykov, head of the government's Media Council, said on 20 October that 95 per cent of Kyrgyz journalists wanted libel decriminalised. Officials bring criminal libel suits against the press and demand huge reparations for alleged damage to their honour – largely, it is alleged, in order to stifle the independent media. (RFE/RL)

LIBERIA

Independent FM station **Star Radio FM** in Monrovia is back on air thanks to an order from transitional government chairperson Gyude Bryant, three years after former president Charles Taylor banned it for allegedly broadcasting 'hate messages against the Liberian government'. Bryant said Star Radio could enhance the 'integrity' of Liberia's post-civil war media. (MISA, MFWA, IRIN)

LIBYA

The official daily newspaper *al-Zahf al-Akhdar* was banned between 13 and 27 October for 'damaging national interests'. It had published articles critical of other Arab states, including Bahrain and Kuwait, during a row over Libya's threat to withdraw from the Arab League. (RSF)

LITHUANIA

On 14 September, a Russian NTV film crew travelling by train to Kaliningrad filmed protests over new visa regulations between members of the National Bolshevik party and border patrol guards at Kena. They were detained, fined and sent back to Moscow. (CPJ, IFEX)

The Second District Court of Vilnius ruled on 30 September against the State Security Department's closing down of pro-Chechen independence website **www.KavKaz-Center.com**, requiring only that it be free of national and religious 'hate speech'. (CPJ, IFEX)

MALAWI

On 9 September, the Malawi High Court awarded US$457 in damages to journalist **McDonald Chapalapata** of *The Nation*. He was assaulted by National Food Reserve Agency financial controller Paul Chimenya when he quizzed him about improper sub-contracting during an interview in November 2002. (MISA)

On 28 October, director of public prosecutions Fahad Assani instructed police to drop charges against journalist **Frank Namangale** of the *Daily Times*, arrested on 16 September for 'publishing false information likely to cause fear and alarm to the public'. He had reported that President Bakili Muluzi's son had been arrested in connection with an armed robbery. It turned out to be his nephew. Said Assani: 'The story was not a fabrication and it did not warrant the arrest of a journalist . . . If there were no journalists, most things would be swept under the carpet.' (MISA)

MALAYSIA

On 6 October, the government said it had forwarded its nine-month-long investigation of news website **Malaysiakini** to the attorney general for a decision on whether to prosecute. The government began investigating the popular online news outlet for posting a letter to the editor on 9 January that criticised government policies favouring ethnic Malays. (HRW/IFEX)

On 16 October, Kuala Lumpur magistrates convicted rights activist **Irene Fernandez** of 'maliciously publishing false news' for issuing a ground-breaking 1995 report that documented beatings, sexual abuse and inadequate food in detention camps for migrant workers. Over the course of the seven-year trial, the longest in Malaysian history, Fernandez applied for a passport 42 times. The prosecutor urged the court to deny Fernandez's most recent request for a passport on the grounds that she would likely 'tarnish the image of the country' if allowed to speak about Malaysia's human rights situation at international conferences. (HRW/IFEX)

MALDIVES

Sparked by the 19 September death from torture of **Hassan Eemaan Naseem**, a prisoner at Maafushi Prison, protest riots erupted at the prison and on the streets of the capital, Male. One man was killed and least 100 wounded. Protests in the capital targeted government buildings, including the parliament, high court and at least two police stations. (AI, maldives culture.com)

Following the protests, security forces arrested **Ilyas Hussain**, one of 42 signatories to a petition demanding the right to register a political party in the Maldives. The following day actor-activist **Jennifer Latheef** was arrested after a non-violent protest against police brutality. Hussain was later released, but Latheef was still being held without charge at time of writing. (maldivesculture.com)

Mohamed Latheef (*Index* 2/96), former MP and father of detained activist Jennifer Latheef, officially launched the Maldivian Democratic Party on 10 November from exile in Colombo, Sri Lanka. Latheef said that the 17 October referendum to ratify the presidency of Maumoon Abdul Gayyoom was 'blatantly rigged' and called on him to 'step down immediately' to 'make way for free and fair elections'. (maldivesculture.com)

MALI

Radio director **Mamoutou Traore** and programme hosts **Cheriff Haidara** and **Gata Ba** from privately owned Radio Sido were detained after airing a report criticising a recent court ruling. They have been accused of criminal defamation by one of the parties to the court case. Their case has been taken up by the Higher Council of Communication in Mali. (CPJ, IRIN, *Afrol News*)

MAURITANIA

The newspaper *Essahifa* was banned on 23 September without official explanation, leaving editor-in-chief **Yahya Ould Hamoud** to speculate on the stories that might have triggered the ban: one about an exiled politician, one about the June 2002 attempted coup, and the third about an Islamist activist. (MFWA)

Essahifa was banned again in October, along with three other papers, *Le Calame*, *Le Journal du Jeudi* and *Le Sahara*, a week ahead of the start of official campaigning for the 7 November presidential elections. Incumbent president, Ould Taya, won the election after arresting his closest rival, Mohammed Ould Haidallah. (BBC)

MEXICO

On 10 September, Communications Ministry (SCT) officials attempting forcibly to close down **La**

Voladora community radio station were deterred by a human barricade of station staff. The incident broke a government promise to negotiate peacefully an end to a long-running licensing row with Mexico's community radio stations. (AMARC)

MOROCCO

On 22 October, **Ali Lmrabet** (*Index* 3/03, 4/03), editor of the banned news weeklies *Demain* and *Doumane*, was re-sentenced for publishing 'false information disturbing or likely to disturb the peace' after the public prosecutor appealed against his four-month jail sentence and fine of US$2,600 in 2001 as 'too lenient'. The month before, Lmrabet had sued state official spokesperson Nabil Benabdallah for defamation during a speech made in Paris on 18 June when he called Lmrabet a liar and suggested that he was mentally ill. (*El País*, RSF)

On 3 November, **Mustapha Kechnini** (*Index* 4/03), editor of the weekly *al-Hayat al-Maghribia*, was jailed for two years and journalists **Abdelaziz Jallouli** and **Miloud Boutriki** sentenced to 18 months' imprisonment for 'undermining the monarchy' and 'inciting people to subversion'. The charges related to the weekly's 20 May interview with Mohammed al-Abadi of the Islamist group al-Adl Wal Ihssan, who was jailed for two years at the same trial. (RSF)

On 7 November, King Mohammed VI was reported to have agreed to the formation of a 'justice and reconciliation commission' to pursue 'out-of-court settlements of past human rights abuse cases related to forced disappearances and arbitrary detention'. Five days later Amnesty International denounced increases in the use of torture by Moroccan security forces, alleging that at least ten detainees had died under torture over the last two years. (AI)

MOZAMBIQUE

On 3 November, unknown men assaulted German freelance journalist **Fritz Stark** as he photographed a march of migrant workers. His attackers tried to confiscate his equipment but failed. That night, while Stark was sleeping in the Catholic Church in Quelimane, they returned with weapons and took his camera and money. (MISA)

During the weekend of 8–9 November, supporters of the former RENAMO rebel movement held Radio Mozambique journalist **Salvador Januario** captive for three hours after he reported that RENAMO supporters had been illegally tearing down other political parties' election posters. (MISA)

NAMIBIA

On 8 November, Namibian Special Field Force (SSF) members arrested journalist **Paulus Sackarius** and driver **Simon Haimbodi** of the Afrikaans-language daily *Republikein* and a 12-year-old guide as they travelled to cover a memorial service for a police officer. The SSF members first accused them of entering a restricted area, then changed the charge to a vehicle registration offence. Sackarius and Haimbodi were also charged with falsely representing themselves as reporters for the state-owned *New Era* newspaper despite Sackarius's *Republikein* press card. While in custody, the boy was assaulted. All three were released four hours later. (MISA)

NEPAL

Popular poet and journalist **Balaram Sharma**, also known as Poorna Biram, was arrested by soldiers on 29 August. On 16 September, Sharma's wife filed a writ of habeas corpus demanding that his whereabouts be revealed. The army released Sharma on 13 November. (CEHURDES, AI, RSF)

Following the breakdown of talks between Maoist rebels and the government on 27 August, the authorities on 2 September issued a 'prohibition order' in parts of the Kathmandu valley banning all rallies, gatherings and sit-ins of more than five people in public places, and the publication of pamphlets for three weeks. The ban was extended for three more days on 23 September. (CEHURDES)

Shanta Shrestha, an elderly feminist leader and activist, was detained at Chhauni army barracks in Kathmandu between 31 August and 18 September on suspicion of support for Maoist rebels. **Shubhashankar Kandel**, managing editor of *Janadharana*, was arrested at his home on 9 September by plainclothes security forces. He was also held at Chhauni and interrogated in connection with his alleged membership of the banned Maoist party. He was released on 1 October. (AI, *Nepal News*)

Binod Sajana Chaudhary, correspondent for the weekly *Nepalgunj Express* in the western district of Kailali and the weekly Maoist-linked paper *Janadesh*, was shot dead on 27 September by security forces on his way to the town of Kegaun for an assignment. Chaudhary was allegedly killed after he identified himself as a journalist. (*Nepal News*, One World South Asia)

Among several journalists detained by security forces whose whereabouts were still unknown at time of writing: **Prem Nath Joshi**, of the weekly *Jana Dristi* and *Shangrila Voice*, arrested on 13 September; **Subindra Budhamagar** of *Nischhall Masic Patrika*, arrested in Balaju on 11 October; **Hari Regmi**, a freelance photojournalist, arrested on 16 October in his Kathmandu studio; **Raju Chhetri**, managing editor of the

weekly *Rastriya Swaviman*, arrested on 18 October near the town of Pokhara; **Yogesh Rawal**, of the daily *Rajdhani* and a member of Amnesty International's Nepal country section, arrested by 20 members of the paramilitary armed police force in the western Kailali district, on 24 October; **Himal Sharma Chapagain**, general secretary of the All Nepal National Independent Student Union (Revolutionary), linked to Maoist rebels, arrested by security forces in Asan, Katmandu, on 21 October, and **Sharita Devi Sharma**, his sister, arrested two days later. (AI, RSF)

On 9 October, it was reported that Maoist rebels had warned journalists in the western Mygadi and central Dhading districts not to report critically on their activities. **Keshav Adhikary**, a local reporter in Dhading district, and journalist **Resham Birahi** in the western Banke district, were both threatened with death by the Maoists. On 8 November, Maoist rebels expelled reporters **Ishori Neupane** of the *Kathmandu Post* and **Kishor Jung Thapa** of *Gorkhapatra* from their Khanibas stronghold in the northern Ghorka district because they did not have permission to be there from the 'People's Government'. (CEHURDES, OneWorld South Asia)

Recent publications: *Trapped by Inequality: Bhutanese Refugee Women in Nepal* by Human Rights

Watch, 24 September 2003, pp 79; *Nepal: Widespread 'disappearances' in the context of armed conflict* by Amnesty International, 16 October 2003, pp 26; *Nepal: Back to the Gun* by the International Crisis Group, 22 October 2003, pp 15

NICARAGUA

A briefing paper on Nicaragua given to reporters touring with US Secretary of State Colin Powell on 5 November divided the country into an Americanised elite and the hungry rest. 'Most Nicaraguans are subsumed by the struggle to find the next plate of rice and beans and, therefore, have little time to think about the United States or world affairs in general,' it said. By contrast, members of the educated, pro-US elite 'prefer to dress in Ralph Lauren shirts, drive large Ford SUVs, watch American movies, and when going out for a meal brag that they go to TGI Friday's.' (Reuters)

NIGERIA

On 26 November, **Kayode Fasua** and **Tunde Ajayi**, editors of the *Contact* and *Class* newspapers respectively, were arrested along with Justice Ministry officials **Michael Dada** and **Bola Fatile**, allegedly for being in possession of copies of the banned *Ekiti Razor* newspaper, which was said to contain material intended to 'disparage the reputation' of the state governor, Ayo

Fayose. Police intercepted the four at a roadblock and found several copies of the newspaper in their vehicle. (MRA)

On 24 November, Lagos police detained *Insider Weekly* editor-in-chief **Osa Director** and executive editors **Chuks Onwudinjo** and **Janet Mba-Afolabi** over the magazine's allegation that top officials were illegally storing crude oil. On 26 November, after pressure from the Media Rights Agenda and other pro-democracy advocates, they were released on bail of N200,000 (about US$1,515). They are scheduled to reappear in court on 12 January 2004. (MRA)

NORWAY

The Norwegian Board of Film Classification has replaced its 80-year-old system of direct censorship with a classification system, allowing the release of more than 300 banned films including Arnold Schwartzenegger's movie *Commando*, judged at the time to have failed to meet 'moral criteria'. (www.indexonline.org)

PAKISTAN

On 10 September, the entire staff of the assembly of the North-West Frontier province attacked journalists covering legislative proceedings. According to the Pakistan Press Foundation, staff members allegedly launched the attack on the orders of the speaker of the assembly. (PPF)

President **Nasrullah Afridi** and Vice-President **Aurangzeb Afridi** of the Tribal Union of Journalists in the Kyber Agency, and local correspondents for the Peshawar-based Urdu-language dailies *Mashriq* and *Subah*, were briefly detained by the outlawed Tanzeem Ittehad-e-Ulema on 18 September. They continue to receive threats from the group. (RSF)

RSF expressed serious concern on 26 September for the health of **Rehmat Shah Afridi** (*Index* 3/99, 6/99, 4/01), the former editor of the Punjab daily papers *Frontier Post* and *Maidan*. Afridi, who is in jail awaiting execution for suspect drug-trafficking convictions, has a serious heart condition. (RSF)

On 3 October, **Ameer Brux Barohi**, a local reporter for the Sindhi-language daily paper *Kawish* and Kavish Television News, was shot five times by three unidentified armed men. Barohi, who had apparently angered local strongmen with his critical reports about their activities, later died of his injuries in hospital. (CPJ, PPF)

Recent publication: *Pakistan: Denial of basic rights for child prisoners* by Amnesty International, 23 October 2003, pp 36

PANAMA

President Mireya Moscoso was blamed for forcing musician, movie star and former presidential contender **Rubén Blades** off the bill for Panama's official 3 November Independence Day celebrations. Blades, a critic of Moscoso, played instead at an alternative concert backed by Panama City Mayor Juan Carlos Navarro. (*Panama News*)

PARAGUAY

In September, *ABC* daily newspaper journalist **Vladimir Antonio Jara** alleged that Judge Héctor Capurro had tried to intimidate him into revealing the source of his story on the November 2001 kidnapping of María Edith Bordón de Debernardi, wife of a powerful Paraguayan businessman. Jara stood by his constitutional rights and refused. (SPP)

On 17 October, **Aldo Zuccolillo**, director of *ABC Color* newspaper, was ordered to pay combined compensation of US$27,612 to the state and former state reform minister Juan Ernesto Villamayor. The paper had accused Villamayor of fraud. Since 1998, Zuccolillo has faced some 20 lawsuits for defamation, most brought by state officials and politicians. (PFC)

On 22 October, **Rosendo Duarte** of *Última Hora* in the city of Salto del Guairá, complained to the public prosecutor, alleging that he had received death threats in connection with his reports of corruption at border posts near the city. (PFC)

PERU

On 6 September, journalists **Marco Antonio Vásquez** and **Diego Fernández Stoll** from the Frecuencia Latina TV show *La Ventana Indiscreta* ('The Indiscreet Window') were detained for nearly three hours on order of district attorney Nelly Calderón Navarro after they tried to film the attorney-general's birthday party in Lima. On 14 September, the programme alleged that Peru's National Intelligence Council (CNI) was spying on station staff and staff at other stations. (IPYS)

Cameraman **Renato Fernández** and reporter **Andy Ortiz** of Canal N TV were attacked by a National Police officer on 24 September in the city of La Oroya in central Peru as they covered protests by workers dismissed by the locally based Doe Run Perú mining company. (IPYS)

PHILIPPINES

On 6 September, radio commentator **Juan 'Jun' Pala** of DXGO in Davao City was shot and killed. He had criticised various government officials, including Mayor Rodrigo Duterte, whom he had cited as the likeliest culprit in an earlier attack on his life. He is the sixth journalist slain this year in the Philippines. (RSF)

On 17 October, Article 19 and the Manila-based Center for Media Freedom and Responsibility made a submission to the UN Human Rights Committee on freedom of expression in the Philippines. It cited issues such as laws threatening freedom of expression, the high rate of murdered journalists and the lack of a freedom of information law. (A19, CMFR, IFEX)

POLAND

The International Press Institute (IPI) has condemned Polish authorities' persecution of the daily *Rzeczpospolita* in Warsaw. Continued legal wrangling threatens the independent newspaper with renationalisation. (IPI, IFEX)

Poland's Press Freedom Monitoring Centre is to raise international concern at a wave of indictments that they say are intended to harass Polish investigative journalists. Civil rights ombudsman Andrzej Zoll said he would take up the cases of authors of articles in the dailies *Zycie Warszawy*, *Super Express* and *Rzeczpospolita*. (BBC)

RUSSIA

On 10 November, Russia's Supreme Court upheld the decision of Perm district court in the Urals to acquit journalists **Konstantin Bakharev** and **Konstantin Sterledev** of revealing state secrets. The court instead sentenced a police officer, who was the original source of the information on a corrupt informant of the Federal Security Bureau, to two years' imprisonment. (CPJ, IFEX)

On 23 September, investigators searched the computers of Moscow-based independent news website **www.grani.ru** on behalf of the Chechen Prosecutor General's Office. Staff produced a copy of an anonymous email showing video footage of two Russian prosecutors, abducted by unknown individuals in Chechnya on 27 December 2002. The video shows them appealing to Boris Berezovsky (*Index* (1/02, 2/02, 4/03), the exiled businessman and majority shareholder of the website. (IFEX, CPJ)

On 28 September, the offices of long-established magazine *Novoye Vremeye* were occupied by armed personnel representing a company called Primex Ltd. Claiming to be the new owners of the building, they unsuccessfully attempted to evict the magazine's staff. (RSF, CPJ)

On 13 November, a Chelyabinsk court reduced the sentence of **German Galkin** (*Index* 4/03) from one year's hard labour to probation, for libelling the governor of the Urals region. Ann Cooper, executive director of the Committee to Protect Journalists (CPJ), said: 'Galkin's conviction should now be overturned, and parliament should move quickly to decriminalise Russia's antiquated libel laws.' (RSF)

Aleksei Sidorov, editor-in-chief of independent daily the *Togliatti Review*, was stabbed to death outside his home in the city of Togliatti, Samara region, on 9 October. The killing comes 18 months after the murder of Sidorov's predecessor **Valery Ivanov**. Despite official explanations that the murder was the result of 'hooliganism', editorial staff claim it was linked to investigations of local criminal elements and government corruption. (RSF, CPJ)

Russia's constitutional court ruled on 30 October that amendments to election laws forbidding 'political agitation' in the media were unconstitutional and that the term 'campaigning' had been defined too broadly to allow a clampdown on journalists. The much-criticised clause had effectively barred coverage of candidates' backgrounds, speculation on the results and analysis of policies. **Konstantin Katanyan** of Vremya MN broke the law deliberately with an article about the election of the governor of Mordoviya but has not been reprimanded, fuelling speculation that the law was applied arbitrarily. (IFEX, CPJ, *Guardian*)

Russia's Education Ministry considered banning a school textbook on modern Russian history in November because it included criticism of President Vladimir Putin. The book, **20th Century History of the Fatherland**, invites students to comment on statements that accuse Putin of being an authoritarian leader. It has been in

circulation as a ministry-approved textbook for two years. (BBC)

Moscovites caught kissing in public could be fined if city authorities pass a new law under consideration, claimed a Russian newspaper in November. The kissing ban could even extend to lawfully wedded spouses, the *Stolichnaya Vechernyaya Gazeta* claimed. Quoting unnamed sources, it said the plan was aimed at raising levels of public morality in the Russian capital. (BBC)

Mikhail Komarov, deputy editor of the Ryazan edition of the newspaper *Novaya Gazeta*, was severely beaten outside his home by two men. Earlier that day, local businessman Sergei Kuznetsov had filed a lawsuit against Komarov, accusing him of libel in a story about botched plastic-surgery operations performed at a private clinic owned by him. (RFE/RL)

SENEGAL

Radio France International correspondent **Sophie Malibeaux** was arrested as she attempted to cover a meeting of the armed independence group Movement of Democratic Forces of Casamance (MFDC). She was ordered to leave the country. (WAJA, CPJ, *Afrol News*)

SIERRA LEONE

Paul Kamara, founder of the newspaper *For Di*

People, was jailed for six months on 12 November for defaming Judge Tolla Thompson in an article criticising his management of Sierra Leone's soccer association. Kamara, who also owns a football club, was convicted on 18 counts of criminal libel. The court recommended that the government ban his paper for six months. (CPJ, MISA, MFWA)

SINGAPORE

On 6 October, a web saboteur targeted the **Singapore Review**, an online discussion forum known for lively criticism of the government. Two days after the forum was profiled in the Singapore daily *Straits Times*, the hacker broke into the forum moderator's account and bombarded members with hundreds of fake messages, forcing some 200 to unsubscribe from the group. (RSF)

The Rocky Horror Picture Show, banned in Singapore for nearly 30 years, finally made its debut in the country. The 1975 film of the musical, starring Susan Sarandon, was banned by Singaporean authorities because of its 'sexual and masochistic content'. The movie was shown for the first time at an outdoor Halloween party on 1 November, the *Straits Times* reported. Only people who could prove they were over 21 were allowed to watch it. (BBC)

SLOVENIA

A court sentenced a man for 'terrorist' crimes for sending hate email to President George W Bush. **Tomi Sluga**, 29, told a court in the north-eastern town of Murska Sobota that he was drunk and only joking when he sent the email to the White House website before a June 2001 Bush visit to Slovenia. 'President, save the Earth, you ass, you will be killed in Ljubljana. Welcome!' the email read. But the court found Sluga guilty of 'endangering a protected person' and gave him a two-year suspended sentence on 16 November, the first conviction under Slovenia's new anti-terrorism laws. (Reuters)

SOUTH AFRICA

South African MPs have appealed to the legislature's joint rules committee to ban TV cameras from focusing on MPs who fall asleep in the debating chamber. Speaker Frene Ginwala pointed out that if the committee tried to stop television stations from capturing the images they would also have to censor the print media. (*Southern Africa Report*)

South African Broadcasting Corporation public service radio chief Judy Nwokedi warned managers to avoid shows that 'may veer in the direction of political discourse'. One manager then tried to bar programmes of a 'political nature' outside scheduled news and current affairs spots. On 2 September, SABC chief executive Peter Matlare blamed 'mischief-makers' for misconstruing instructions. (*Southern Africa Report*)

On 11 November, the Bloemfontein high court upheld a lower court ruling requiring journalist **Ranjeni Munusamy** to testify before a special investigations commission despite threats to her life if she does. Munusamy had worked on the story at the heart of the commission investigation, that National Director of Prosecutions Bulelani Ngcuka had been an informer for the apartheid-era secret services. (MISA, FXI)

SRI LANKA

On 10 September, Fisheries Minister Mahinda Wijesekera led an attack against hunger-striking graduate students demanding employment. Wijesekera has also uttered death threats against **Lasantha Wikramathunga** (*Index* 2/95, 5/98, 2/00, 6/00, 4/03), editor of the *Sunday Leader*, and **Lucien Rajakarunanayake**, former chairman of the state-owned Lake House publications group. (Free Media Movement, Asian Human Rights Commission)

On 26 September, the Free Media Movement condemned an attack by students from the University of Sri Jayawardenapura against a camera crew from Independent Televison News. (*Lanka Academic*)

Trade union activist **Michael Anthony Fernando** (*Index* 2/03) was released early from prison to a hero's welcome on 17 October. Jailed for a year for contempt of court in February by Chief Justice Sarath Silva, a party to Fernando's complaint, he was awarded the Asian Human Rights Commission's inaugural Human Rights Defenders Award the day before his release. (AFP, *Sunday Observer*, Asian Human Rights Commission)

On 30 October, a group of Sinhalese extremists attacked participants at a Sinhala–Tamil cultural conference advocating greater links between the country's two main ethnic communities. **Atula Vithanage**, a reporter for Hiru FM radio station, and **Yamuni Rashmika**, a reporter for *Lanka* newspaper, were injured in the attack. (Free Media Movement)

On 4 November, President Chandrika Bandaranike Kumaratunga suspended parliament, fired three top ministers and their senior aides, declared a state of emergency, and stationed troops around key installations in the capital. State television and press changed their editorial policies overnight by taking a pro-president line. After veiled international criticism of her actions on 7 November, Kumaratunga declared that the state of emergency had never been in effect since she had not signed the proclamation. (Free Media Movement, *Sunday Leader*, National Peace Council of Sri Lanka, BBC)

Recent publications: *Study of Media in the North-East of Sri Lanka* by the Centre for Policy Alternatives & International Media Support, Denmark, June 2003, pp 46; *Rewarding Tyranny: Undermining the Democratic Potential for Peace*, Special Report No 17, by University Teachers for Human rights (Jaffna), 7 October 2003; *Constitutional Coup in Sri Lanka: Back to the bad old days* by the Asian Centre for Human rights, 6 November 2003, pp 8

SUDAN

On 30 September, Public Prosecutor Mohammad Farid Hassan, citing article 130 of the 1991 legal procedure code, suspended the daily newspaper *al-Azminah* pending investigations. The courts are studying the publication of reports about pro-government militias that apparently upset senior army commanders. (RSF)

On 1 October, the National Press Council suspended the daily newspaper *al-Sahafa* for three days for publishing an advertisement by Ethiopian Airlines praising the quality of wines on its Khartoum–Paris flights. Alcohol was banned in Sudan in 1993. (RSF)

Sudanese officials freed Islamist leader **Hassan al-Turabi** on 13 October after more than two years in detention and lifted a ban on his party's activities. Turabi was arrested in February 2001 after a power struggle with his former close ally, President Omar al-Bashir. Turabi, leader of the Popular National Congress (PNC), was accused of crimes against the state. (BBC)

TAJIKISTAN

On 5 September, Tajik state TV licensing commissioners deferred for six more months their promised ruling on independent media group Asia Plus's bid to launch a television station. State officials claim the group lack the technical and staff capacity to run a TV network. (Deutsche Welle, RFE/RL)

THAILAND

Prime Minister Thaksin Shinawatra curtailed his citizens' civil rights and liberties during the 14–24 October Asia-Pacific Economic Cooperation summit in Bangkok. He warned rural protesters they would be denied access to funds from the government's poverty-eradication programmes and threatened to 'blacklist any non-governmental organisation taking part in a street rally during the meeting'. (Article 19)

TUNISIA

Lawyer and human rights activist **Radhia Nasraoui** (*Index* 4/02) began a hunger strike on 15 October to protest against 'systematic government harassment, beatings and police surveillance'. Nasraoui still suffers the effects of a 38-day fast she maintained last year, and was admitted to hospital on 12 November after 29 days without food. (*Vanguard*)

Internet dissident **Zouhair Yahyaoui** (*Index* 4/02) was released on 18 November after serving 18 months of the 28-month prison sentence he received for spreading 'false information' on his website TUNe ZINE. Yahyaoui set up the website in July 2001 in order to circulate news about the fight for democracy and freedom in Tunisia. (RSF)

Journalist and rights activist **Néziha Rejiba**, better known as Om Zied, was found guilty of currency offences on 19 November, given a suspended sentence of eight months and fined US$970. Rejiba writes for the foreign-based online magazine Kalima, access to which is banned in Tunisia. A printed version has been secretly distributed in Tunisia. (RSF)

TURKEY

Most of the Turkey's governing party boycotted a presidential reception marking the secular republic's 80th anniversary in a row over Islamic headscarves. Members of the Justice and Development Party, whose origins are in a banned Islamist movement, protested against President

Ahmet Necdet Sezer's refusal to invite headscarf-wearing wives of senior officials, including Prime Minister **Recep Tayyip Erdogan**, to the 29 October event. Headscarves are banned in official ceremonies and in public buildings such as schools and courts. (BBC)

Sisters **Nurcihan** and **Nurulhak Saatçioglu** were jailed again four years after serving seven months for their crime — protesting against the prohibition on headscarves in 1999 — for which they were charged with 'attempting to change the constitutional order by force'. Malatya State Security Court decided a stricter sentence of four years and two months was needed under the Meetings and Demonstration Law and the pair were arrested and re-jailed on 3 October. Their mother **Huda Kaya**, who was arrested at the same protest, is still serving a three-year jail sentence. A third sister, **Intisar Saatçioglu**, was jailed on 28 October. (*Kurdistan Observer*)

Dicle Press Agency journalists **Sabiha Temizkan**, **Sertaç Lalelioglu** and **Umut Sener**, of the journal *Emek ve Adalet*, were detained during October's Republic Day celebrations in Ankara on suspicion that they planned to hold up a placard. Police released them after five hours, saying they detained them 'by mistake'. (BIA-TIHV)

A concert by **Koma Rewsen** in the town of Van was banned on 22 October because, claimed centre director Turan Özgüner, the band used the letter W which exists in Kurdish, but not Turkish. On 27 October, leaders of pro-Kurdish parties filed to the courts to secure the right to have Kurdish first names that include X and the other letters, W and Q, that are not in the Turkish alphabet. (*Özgür Gündem*)

In October, an Ankara court ordered a ban on access to the websites **www.ozgurpolitika.org** and **www.ekmekveadalet.com**, run by the newspaper *Özgür Politika* and the journal *Ekmek ve Adalet*, on the grounds that their sites 'insulted the army'. There are no provisions within the Turkish Penal Code to cover prevention of access to an internet site. (*Radikal*-TIHV)

Professor **Fikret Baskaya** (*Index* 5/00, 3/03) and Maki Publications editor **Ismet Erdogan** were acquitted on 11 October of charges relating to the publication of Baskaya's political study *Collapse of the Paradigm: An Introduction to THA Criticism of Official Ideology*. The ruling followed the adoption of new rules allowing retrial of cases heard by the European Court of Human Rights. (*Milliyet*-TIHV)

Kurdish music albums by **Koma Azadi**, four albums by **Sivan Perver** (*Index* 1/00, 1/02), **Koma Amed**, **Koma Agirê Jiyan** and **Xelil Xemgin** were banned in September in the eastern provinces of Hakkari and Van on the grounds of 'making propaganda for an illegal organisation'. (*Özgür Gündem*-TIHV)

TURKMENISTAN

President Saparmurat Niyazov ordered the closure of the country's cable TV networks for a second time in two years on 15 September, now as then in response to programmes that criticised his rule. Observers suspect that satellite TV dishes will soon be banned. (RFE/RL)

Researcher **Caroline Giraud** claimed on 20 October that Reporters Sans Frontières did not get many reports of censorship or journalists being harassed in Turkemenistan, but added that 'such instances only happen in a country struggling to establish an independent press — something that clearly isn't happening in Turkmenistan'. (RSF, IRIN)

On 10 November, a new, more restrictive, law on religious activities came into force, effectively criminalising all religious activities bar those carried out by the state-sanctioned Sunni Islam and Russian Orthodox Christian faiths. Violators may be sentenced to a year's corrective labour. The private teaching of unsanctioned religion is also criminalised. (RFE/RL)

UKRAINE

On 18 November, Ukraine's parliament approved new media controls designed, according to the opposition online news site Ukrainskaya Pravda, to control information on the web ahead of presidential elections due in October 2004. The Ukrainian Centre for Information Technology, created by the state communications committee and the SBU secret police, assumed control on 22 July of the country's '.ua' domain name and through it Ukraine's internet access. Telecom operators and internet service providers have been ordered to install equipment to monitor internet traffic. (AFP, RSF)

On 17 November, the International Federation of Journalists (IFJ) launched an independent inquiry into the unresolved case of murdered journalist **Gyorgy Gongadze** (*Index* 1/01, 2/01, 1/02, 2/02, 1/03, 3/03, 4/03). It will 'examine the apparent failure of legal and judicial processes . . . and the reactions of institutions and civil society to the case'. (IFL, IFEX, RSF)

On 3 October, half a dozen men broke into the offices of *Moloda Galychyna*, a newspaper close to the Ukrainian Social Democratic Party in the western city of Lviv. They destroyed computers and attempted to set fire to the premises. Lviv police have launched an investigation. (IFEX, RSF, AFP)

UNITED KINGDOM

The number of officers serving with the UK's anti-subversion and terrorism Special Branch police unit has more than doubled in 25 years despite the end of the Cold War and the cooling of the Northern Irish conflict, says *Statewatch* bulletin editor Tony Bunyan. He said the growth has come about in response to the rise in protests across Europe on issues such as war, the environment and global capitalism. (*Guardian*)

The London Metropolitan Police were criticised for using anti-terrorist legislation to stop and search demonstrators at an arms fair protest on 10 September. Twenty-three people were arrested. Section 44 of the Terrorism Act 2000 allows police to stop and search where they 'consider it expedient for the prevention of acts of terrorism'. According to figures given to Parliament there were 10,186 such stop and searches of cars, drivers and pedestrians in England and Wales during 2001–2, resulting in 189 arrests for various offences. (*Statewatch*, *Hansard*)

Serial killer **Denis Nilsen** is seeking to mount a legal defence of his right to free expression after a partial copy of his autobiography was confiscated by prison authorities. Nilsen's lawyer Alison Foster said that restrictions of free speech should only be allowed if there was 'considerable justification'. (*Guardian*)

Edinburgh City Council has withdrawn a ban on the video recording of school events such as nativity plays unless all the parents of the children involved had given their consent, a rule passed amid fears that paedophiles might gain copies of the tapes. (*Herald*)

Guardian journalist Rob Evans called for a judicial review after government ministers imposed a gagging order on ombudsman **Ann Abraham** to prevent her from disclosing information about ministerial conflicts of interests. Evans had sought Abraham's help in his own investigation but her inquiries were also blocked. (*Guardian*)

The *Mail on Sunday* newspaper was prevented by a court order from publishing a story about the royal family at the request of former royal servant Michael Fawcett. That ban remained in place even after an injunction barring the *Guardian* from naming Fawcett was lifted after three days. A *Mail on Sunday* spokesman said the use of the courts to 'suppress information and prevent proper public debate' was 'deeply disturbing'. (*Guardian*)

The National Union of Students embroiled itself in a row over a motion proposing that academic boycotts of 'Zionists' or Israelis were anti-Semitic and condemned attempts to 'demonise and ostracise' them. Students at London's School of Oriental and

SAUCE FOR THE GOOSE

CLIVE SOLEY

The following is a transcript of a Point of Order by Clive Soley MP, raised in the UK House of Commons on 11 November 2003

'Mr Speaker, I raise this point of order because I am concerned about a letter I received from an editor of a major newspaper following queries I had raised about sexual harassment and bullying at News International [the UK press wing of the media empire run by Rupert Murdoch. Ed]. This letter was a thinly disguised attempt to warn me off.

'Recently I received an unsolicited copy of a letter to News International's lawyers from a firm representing a victim of serious sexual harassment. The allegations had been made against Stuart Higgins, one-time editor of the *Sun* newspaper. I understand the eventual settlement involved a payment of about £500,000, with a condition of silence imposed on the victim.

'As far as I am aware no proper disciplinary hearings took place and other senior staff appear to have colluded with what was by any standard extremely offensive and destructive behaviour. The police were not called when hate mail was being sent on News International stationery to the victim.

'I do not know if either the offence or the settlement were reported to Rupert Murdoch although I think that would have been likely. There was no attempt to deal with the underlying problem of sexual harassment and bullying, and my contacts tell me it was not an isolated case. The solicitor's letter confirms that.

'Mr Speaker, I have to raise this with you because after I had written to Les Hinton, the chief executive of News International, I then received a letter from Rebekah Wade, editor of the *Sun*. The letter asked me how many complaints of sexual harassment had been made to me while chairman of the PLP [Parliamentary Labour Party] by PLP staff and by MPs' staff. In fact I had received none.

'It is impossible to see this letter as anything other than a threat, as I had not approached any editors. I had only approached the chief executive's office. It must be a matter of serious public concern when a major multinational media group uses its editors to threaten a Member of Parliament who is carrying out a legitimate inquiry into that group's employment practices.

'As I am asking other employees who also suffered abuse to contact me or their lawyers it is important that editors and management understand that this House will not tolerate explicit or implicit threats against its members when carrying out their proper duties.

'I am asking you to make it clear that MPs do have these duties and that they should be allowed to pursue them without threats or warnings of any type.

'I am a very strong defender of legitimate investigative journalism. The press cannot and should not expose others while covering up their own problems.'

The Speaker of the House of Commons has offered to investigate the allegations. ❑

African Studies countered by stating that 'criticising any state's policies doesn't amount to racism or anti-religious discrimination'. (NUS, SOAS)

Burger chain **McDonald's Corp** was banned on 26 November from repeating an advertisement about its french fries which said that after selecting certain potatoes 'we peel them, slice them, fry them and that's it'. The UK Advertising Standards Authority agreed that less savoury parts of the process had been omitted, such as par-frying, freezing and adding salt and a dextrose sugar solution. (BBC)

UNITED STATES

On 7 October, journalists travelling to Guantánamo Bay were made to sign a statement promising not to ask questions about investigations under way at the base on pain of being removed and stripped of their Defense Department press accreditation. (RSF)

The influential Albert Shanker Institute educational think tank produced a report, *Education for Democracy*, demanding that students be taught to show more 'gratitude' and 'loyalty' to US political institutions and calling for an end to 'moral relativism in which every idea is deemed equally worthy'. Former president Bill Clinton, NAACP President Kweisi Mfume and Sandra Feldman, president of the American Federation of

Teachers, are among the signatories, alongside a host of neo-conservatives. (*Statewatch*)

Dictionary publisher Merriam-Webster came under fire from McDonald's Corp over the inclusion of the word 'McJob' in its latest collegiate dictionary, which it defined as 'a low-paying job that requires little skill and provides little opportunity for advancement'. Chief executive Jim Cantalupo complained on 11 November that the definition was 'a slap in the face to the 12 million men and women who work hard every day in America's 900,000 restaurants'. (AP)

Diebold Election Systems, which operates touch-screen voting machines in 37 states, is threatening websites that link to documents citing Diebold staff concerns about the machines' reliability and experts' views that they could be hacked by election fraudsters. (*New York Times*, www.eff.org)

A 16-hour Elvis Presley documentary was banned on 7 November by a US appeals court which ruled it had violated copyright. *The Definitive Elvis* video sold for US$99 and included various TV appearances by Presley. Elvis Presley Enterprises and Jerry Leiber and Mike Stoller, who wrote hits such as 'Jailhouse Rock' and 'Hound Dog', objected to their use. 'The king is dead,' 9th Circuit Court of Appeals Judge Richard Tall-

man wrote in the decision. 'His legacy, and those who wish to profit from it, remain very much alive.' (BBC)

URUGUAY

On 29 September, journalist **Julio Toyos** announced, during the TV Libre television programme, that he had received death threats because of an investigation he was conducting into alleged police links to a mafia ring in the city of Paysandú. (PFC)

UZBEKISTAN

On 11 September, the Committee to Protect Journalists reported that **Ruslan Sharipov**, jailed Uzbek journalist and rights activist, had confirmed that he pleaded guilty at his trial in August after torture. Homosexuality is a criminal offence in Uzbekistan but Sharipov's main offence has been his critical articles for the Russian media describing police abuses and press freedom violations. (CPJ, CJES)

On 18 September, the State Departments of Social Relations and Information Analysis organised special seminars for journalists to 'teach' them how to report correctly the country's reform programmes. According to the organisers, the seminars are supposed to ensure that journalists 'do not remove individual events from their context'. (RFE/RL)

COMING UNPLUGGED

Subject: *IDENTIFICATION OF EQUIPMENT SOLD TO LA COUNTY*
Date: *Tue, 18 Nov 2003 14:21:16 -0800*
From: *'Los Angeles County'*

The County of Los Angeles actively promotes and is committed to ensure a work environment that is free from any discriminatory influence be it actual or perceived. As such, it is the County's expectation that our manufacturers, suppliers and contractors make a concentrated effort to ensure that any equipment, supplies or services that are provided to County departments do not possess or portray an image that may be construed as offensive or defamatory in nature.

One such recent example included the manufacturer's labeling of equipment where the words 'Master/Slave' appeared to identify the primary and secondary sources. Based on the cultural diversity and sensitivity of Los Angeles County, this is not an acceptable identification label.

We would request that each manufacturer, supplier and contractor review, identify and remove/change any identification or labeling of equipment or components thereof that could be interpreted as discriminatory or offensive in nature before such equipment is sold or otherwise provided to any County department.

Thank you in advance for your cooperation and assistance.

Joe Sandoval, Division Manager
Purchasing and Contract Services
Internal Services Department
County of Los Angeles

The term 'master/slave' is used by engineers working with electronic and mechanical devices to describe the unidirectional control of one device or process by another. But in May 2003, an African-American probation department employee filed a discrimination complaint with the county's Office of Affirmative Action Compliance after spotting 'master' and 'slave' labels on a videotape machine. Joe Sandoval, the division manager who issued the memo above, first published by the www.snopes.com website, told Reuters: 'I do understand that this term has been an industry standard for years and years . . . It appears that some folks have taken this a little too literally.' ❏

On 6 October, the only independent television station for young people in the Ferghana Valley city of Andijan stopped producing its own programmes because of a lack of money. The station, Andijan, dismissed its remaining journalists on 1 October. The station continues to exist, rebroadcasting programmes from Russia's ORT TV. (RFE/RL)

VENEZUELA

On 3 October, National Telecommunications Commission (CONATEL) officials confiscated equipment belonging to **Globovisión TV**, alleging that Globovisión was using unauthorised frequencies. Globovisión is one of four stations now under investigation that are seen as critics of the government of President Hugo Chávez Frías. A few hours after its equipment was confiscated, a man threw a grenade at the CONATEL HQ. No one was hurt. (IPYS, RSF, CPJ)

During the night of 27 September, unidentified men attacked **Horizonte 1260 AM** radio station in west-central Yaracuy state. Station manager Félix Morillo could not identify the assailants but recalled that pro-government supporters forcibly occupied the station on 13 April when President Chávez was temporarily removed by a coup. (IPYS)

On 11 October, five men destroyed equipment belonging to the **Parroquiana 90.1 FM** community radio station in the town of San José de Perijá in south-western Zulia state. Station director Hercilia León linked the attack to the broadcasting of community leader Omaira Petit's allegations of corruption by a member of the town council. (IPYS)

VIETNAM

A year after his arrest on 25 September 2002, journalist and cyber-dissident **Nguyen Vu Binh** has still not been put on trial, said Reporters Sans Frontières in an appeal to the Hanoi authorities. Nguyen was arrested after criticising a 1999 border pact with China. Since May a special state agency has tightened control of internet access inside the country and monitored web usage. (RSF)

On 12 November, the Hanoi People's Court sentenced writer **Tran Dung Tien** to ten months in prison. Tien, 74, who was arrested on 22 January, was convicted on charges including 'abusing democratic freedoms' and faced a possible sentence of up to seven years. (CPJ, IFEX)

ZAMBIA

On 1 November, police raided privately owned Lusaka-based **Omega TV** on the orders of Solicitor-General Sunday Nkonde and ordered staff to cease test broadcasts, saying the station was operating illegally. Three days later, Lusaka Police Commanding Officer Chendela Musonda rescinded the order and the station reopened. On 11 November, the high court reversed this decision and the TV station was closed again. (IFEX)

ZIMBABWE

On 15 September, photographers **Tsvangirai Mukwazhi** of AP and **Paul Cadenhead** of Reuters were arrested at the *Daily News* offices as they pictured police seizing the paper's equipment. The photographers were held for seven hours and then ordered to pay an 'admission of guilt' fine of US$6 each. (MISA)

On 3 October, members of the Chipangano vigilante group attacked *Financial Gazette* journalist **Cyril Zenda** after they took offence at his T-shirt, which bore the slogan 'Free My Voice: Free the Airwaves'. They tore the T-shirt from his body, burnt it, and then stole his mobile phone and money. (MISA)

On 12 October, lawyer **Beatrice Mtetwa**, who acted on behalf of *Guardian* journalist **Andrew Meldrum** and the embattled *Daily News*, called the police after her car was attacked by thieves but was instead accused of drink-driving. She was arrested and beaten, suffering bruises and cuts. Mtetwa later tried to press charges, without result. (MISA)

On 12 October, journalist **Blessing Zulu** of the *Zimbabwe Independent* newspaper and freelancer **Newton Spicer** were arrested while covering a demonstration organised by the National Constitutional Assembly (NCA). Heavily armed police put an end to the protest and arrested more than 300 NCA members. (MISA)

On 12 November, Associated Newspapers of Zimbabwe (ANZ) filed a high court application to resume publishing the *Daily News*, closed by police on 12 September. On 25 October, ANZ chief executive **Washington Sansole** and directors **Rachel Kupara**, **Stuart Mattinson**, **Sipepa Nkomo** and **Brian Mutsau** were arrested then released after posting US$63 bail each. The same day police arrested 18 of the newspaper's journalists and released them a few hours later. The day before, Zimbabwe's administrative court had ordered that the *Daily News* be granted an operating licence, reversing the closure order. (MISA, Reuters, RSF, *Daily News*)

Compiled by: James Badcock (North Africa); Ben Carrdus (East Asia); Gulliver Cragg (Western Europe, North America); Ioli Delivani (Eastern Africa); Veronique Dupont (South America); Sam Holden (Russia, Poland, Ukraine, Baltic States); Patrick Holland (Britain and Ireland); Billie Felix Jeyes (Southern Africa); Monica Gonzalez Correa (Central Asia and Caucusus); Javier Gonzalez-Rubio (South East Asia); Andrew Kendle (India and subcontinent); Gill Newsham (Turkey and Kurdish areas); Jason Pollard (Gulf States and Middle East); Melanie Rawlingson (Western Africa); Jugo Stojanov (Eastern Europe); Mike Yeoman (Central America and Caribbean)

Edited by Rohan Jayasekera and coordinated by Natasha Schmidt

THE FIRE NEXT TIME: AIDS IN RUSSIA

**RUSSIA HAS ONE OF THE FASTEST
GROWING HIV INFECTION RATES IN
THE WORLD. YET THERE IS NO SEX
EDUCATION IN SCHOOLS, NO HIV/AIDS
AWARENESS PROGRAMME AND A
PROFOUND RELUCTANCE TO ADMIT
TO THE PROBLEM AT OFFICIAL LEVELS**

Kaliningrad, Russia: Aids poster promoting safe sex.
Credit: Lehtikuva Oy / Rex Features

IGNORANCE, EXCLUSION AND DENIAL
IRENA MARYNIAK

There was relief tempered with incredulity in Russia when deputy health minister Gennadii Onishchenko announced a 50 per cent decrease in the number of new HIV cases for 2002: just 41,000 as opposed to the 77,200 registered the previous year.

This remarkable drop was put down to tougher law enforcement and the collapse of the Taliban leadership in Afghanistan. The regime had been a major supplier of drugs to Western Europe via Kazakhstan, and Russia was becoming a dumping ground for cheap heroin. Records showed that the spread of HIV/Aids doubled in 1999, a year when heroin consumption here also rocketed. But now all that was under control. The total number of deaths was still just a little over 2,000, and about 5,000 Aids patients were being treated by the state. The first Aids hospice was opening in St Petersburg; HIV-positive foreigners were being deported; and the Baltic enclave of Kaliningrad was holding a Live Aid-style concert to raise money and awareness. Five thousand people came, including Russia's First Lady, Liudmila Putin. The president himself hadn't once mentioned the issue in public, it is true, but this is a big and complicated country of 144 million people with an ingrained tradition of public discretion. He probably had other priorities and who could complain that nothing was being done?

Vadim Pokrovskii, director of Moscow's Centre for Aids Prevention and Treatment, for one. The 50 per cent fall in the HIV infection rate was a very misleading statistic, he told journalists. The health ministry had stopped paying for HIV tests, forcing regional authorities to pick up the cost. Fewer people than ever were being tested. Pokrovskii estimates that up to 1.2 million Russians are infected with HIV (official figures currently stand at 250,000). Unless urgent measures are taken there could be 5 million HIV-positive people living in Russia by 2007. Two million are expected to die within 15 years, but there are fears the figure could rise as high as 7 million. Along with Ukraine, India and China, the Russian Federation has the fastest

c700,000 people live with HIV/Aids in Russia; official figure 200,000 | This could rise to 8m by 2010 | Adult prevalence rate (15–49 age group) is 0.9%; 26% (180,000) are women | 60% of infected men are between the ages of 17

growing HIV infection rate in the world. A 6 per cent fall in population is expected if 3 per cent are infected: a demographic crisis could be imminent.

Russia's birth rate is low, its mortality rate high and, as Valerii Abramkin warns (p178), a TB epidemic is growing. But for the moment, on street corners, in hotel lobbies, nightclubs, subways, markets, libraries and schools, Aids is but a latent presence. The untreated will not begin to die in their thousands for a decade: that is when the labour force, higher education and the military will be hit. In December 2002, United Press International reported that one-third of conscripts were already deemed unfit for service because of HIV or hepatitis. In some areas around Moscow, 5 per cent of young people have Aids. Up to 15 per cent of Moscow's prostitutes may be infected. Figures are unreliable because the vulnerable do not come forward for testing or treatment. They fear ostracism; they fear the facts; and, most immediately, they fear arrest.

An estimated 90 per cent of HIV-positive Russians are intravenous drug users and, according to a law passed in 1998, addiction is a crime. The possession of 0.005 grams of heroin can give a user three years in prison. Sentences for hoarding drugs can extend up to 15 years. Sterile injecting equipment is available without prescription, but with such draconian laws still in place who would want to advertise the habit by running to a pharmacist? Sharing needles is part of the lifestyle and to refuse to do it can cause deep offence.

In areas where joblessness and poverty are the norm, the drugs trade offers enormous economic incentives. Intravenous users are estimated to infect two or more people with HIV every year. A significant proportion of those affected are occasional, 'social' injectors – and the virus spreads to partners, children, hospitals. Many victims are women from the provinces working as prostitutes in big cities. Most are under 25. Those who are arrested may shuttle between prison and the streets for years. An overcrowded and corrupt penal system fuels drug abuse, prison regulations notwithstanding. Home-made drugs and syringes are passed from hand to hand; condoms are restricted because of a notional prohibition on sex. Methadone treatment for heroin addiction is illegal. The number of HIV-positive prison inmates has risen ten times over the past 30 months.

and 25 | In 2001 there were 9,000 HIV/Aids-related deaths | HIV epidemics have been discovered in 87 of the country's 89 regions | 80–90% of all infections in Russia stem from intravenous drug use (IDU) | In 2002 IDUs

According to the Moscow Centre for Prison Reform, 50 per cent of Russians infected with HIV are former prisoners.

A survey taken last year showed that one-third of Russians think that anyone known to be HIV-positive should be isolated from the community. There have been reports of fearful doctors refusing to provide care and schools refusing to admit infected pupils. A law passed in 1995 guarantees people with HIV anonymity, medical care and counselling, and the public information, epidemiological surveillance and education. Yet the HIV-positive sector of the community is shunned, sacked, mistreated and branded as degenerate. When Médecins Sans Frontières launched a pioneering needle-exchange programme in Russia in 2002, its vehicles were torched. Aids is widely viewed as a 'foreign' problem that has infiltrated communities of drug users, gays and prison inmates, and will stay with the undesirables if decent people are careful. The Russian Orthodox Church has objected to cinema ads promoting safer sex, and billboards promoting the use of condoms raised complaints from the authorities that they were harming public morals. But official prudery apart, Russians take pride in sleeping around, and the possibility of heterosexual transmission raises few real qualms. Sex is freedom, risk is joy, and hygiene or sanitation are not always the highest priorities. In 2000, 3 per cent of HIV transmissions were from heterosexual sex. By August 2002 this had leaped to 11 per cent.

The upshot has been a rude awakening in the Duma to the fact that 80 per cent of those infected with HIV are under 30. In June, the Moscow Healthcare Department called for compulsory measures to register and treat all HIV/Aids patients. Of the 22,000 already registered in the capital, only about 1,000 are coming forward for treatment. There is widespread mistrust of the medical establishment, its attitudes and the insanitary conditions in which health workers operate.

According to Pokrovskii, the long-term danger lies above all in public ignorance about living with Aids and the state's reluctance to put funds into a national information campaign that would raise awareness. Even though about 30 NGOs have been working on HIV/Aids in Russia since the mid-1990s, networking has been poor and information fails to reach those who need it most. Future costs of treating people could be prohibitive for

accounted for 53.9% of new infections | In a recent survey of IDUs in Togliatti over 50% of the respondents were HIV-positive | 20–25% of IDUs in prison are HIV-positive | Frequent prison amnesties spread the infection into the general

government. At present, Russia spends about US$5million a year on HIV/Aids – an amount that covers the treatment of just 500 patients. An adequate public information campaign would cost US$75 million.

In 2003, Russia committed less than US$6 million to its domestic Aids programme, but gave a grand US$20 million to the Global Fund To Fight Aids, Tuberculosis and Malaria. Two years ago, it blocked a US$150 million loan offered by the World Bank to fight Aids and TB on the grounds that it did not wish to incur any further foreign debt. Apparently, the government does not want to be seen to be begging for funds from the international community – especially for this.

Under the Soviet regime, the euphemism for sex most favoured by official writers was 'this . . . business' (*eto delo*). There is still profound reluctance to discuss sex-related issues publicly in Russia. It is inappropriate; the context is wrong; you just don't do it. There is no effective sex education in schools. So it comes as no surprise that not a single public figure has acknowledged being infected with HIV – though Pokrovskii is reported to have treated 'a handful'.

Thankfully, behind the scenes, there are signs of a tentative awakening. Earlier this year, the Duma passed the first draft of a law which may at last differentiate between drug users and drug pushers, treat addicts more leniently, and significantly cut the numbers of people with HIV in penal institutions by 2005. The question then will be whether the government can provide the necessary medical and welfare support for all those released from prisons and penal colonies into towns, cities and villages where people are suspicious, anxious, impoverished, ill-informed and, sometimes, angry. ❏

Irena Maryniak

population | 33% of prospective army conscripts are deemed unfit for service because of chronic hepatitis or HIV | 15% of Moscow's commercial sex workers are HIV-positive | Treatment for 3m infected adults would cost US$30bn pa

VISIT TO KOZLOVKA

LIUDMILA ALPERN

A RUSSIAN PRISON MONITOR VISITS
A WOMEN'S PENAL COLONY IN THE
HEART OF THE RUSSIAN FEDERATION

We got in quite late: the train from Moscow took us only as far as the Chuvash capital, Cheboksary. It was nearly another 100km to Kozlovka [in Chuvashia, about 50km from Kazan in Tatarstan. Ed]. We drove for more than an hour after I'd bought some pharmaceuticals by way of a gift for the administration and 'soapy things' for the inmates. I had chosen medicines against women's sexual infections – trichomoniasis and syphilis – and disposable needles.

There are about 36 women's penal colonies in Russia and I had decided on Kozlovka because of Nastia, a minor from the Novyi Oskol Educational Colony [on the Ukrainian border. Ed] who had been transferred there from Kazan, not long before our first visit in March. She arrived and discovered she was HIV-positive. It was the day we met. I shall never forget her face. Her eyes were round and black like a child's, deeply sad. She didn't smile like the other girls with HIV. There were seven of them in the colony. We had managed to persuade the educational colony administration, which was perfectly humane and reasonable, to give the girls more freedom. When we visited for the second time we found them in different quarters and they were no longer locked up. The next step would be to put them in dormitories with non-HIV girls. This was causing the infected girls anxiety.

By then Nastia had got used to her condition, but the sadness in her eyes remained.

'I'd like to go into the adult sector when I'm 18,' she said. 'It's closer to home. Mama will come and visit.'

'Do you know where you'll be sent?'

'They've told me it'll be Kozlovka in Chuvashia, near Kazan. Can you find out what it's like?' So I promised.

I tried to see things at Kozlovka through Nastia's eyes, which wasn't easy. There were a lot of young women, well dressed in short skirts and quite good shoes. There are no uniforms, but everyone wears a label. The girls are nice-looking, they wear make-up.

We started our visit with the needlework shop. There are workshops like this in every women's colony. The pay is low but the food seems good. The colony houses the republic's hospital so there are doctors and medicines on site. They receive 30,000 pharmaceuticals a month.

Someone called out to me in the courtyard and a pleasant young girl approached.

'I saw you in Novyi Oskol.'

'Is that where you've come from? So do you like it here?' She said regretfully that they'd persuaded her to move here. They told her women's colonies were freer, so she got out. It was clear she regretted it. She was on the verge of tears. Once you're here it's hard to leave before the end of your term. Every colony has its own laws, and life here is certainly no easier than in Novyi Oskol where the supervisors at least treat the inmates like children. A little later I found another girl like her in a punishment cell.

Despite a well-groomed exterior and a health-oriented timetable, punishment in the colony is harsh. 'There are 48 people in the Kozlovka strict regime sector,' they told me in the main office. I'd never known this in a women's penal institution. Prison is hard enough for a woman; extreme isolation can destroy her will to live. Yet many of the inmates said there was little in the way of illegal punishment here – secret beatings and so on.

The day we visited, 53 prisoners had already been relegated to 'strict conditions'. Twelve of them were sweating it out in airless stone barracks that were steaming in the heat. Even the loathsome loose black overall, reminiscent of the inquisition, that serves as punishment-cell dress seemed appropriate here. Most of the inmates had been punished for a quarrel, usually a verbal one, with a friend in the next cell. Several had refused to work or, more likely, not fulfilled their targets. There was another teenager from Novyi Oskol among them. She told us she'd made a mistake leaving the educational colony. She'd have been home by now. But here she'd got into mischief because she couldn't cope with the work.

The women in solitary were physically and psychologically worn out. They had all got 15 days, longer than in most other colonies.

We visited different sectors: the tuberculosis wing and the sick bay where the HIV prisoners had been brought. The women's hospital for the whole of Chuvashia is based inside the colony, so there were about 70 tuberculosis patients. They are held in a separate area where they get their treatment. There were just six HIV patients who had arrived a few days earlier. Before that, all women diagnosed with HIV had been sent to

Kozlovka women's penal colony, Russia: inside the prison laundry.
Credit: Liudmila Alpern

another women's colony in Chuvashia (there are three in all), but now the policy has changed and they are preparing to set up a local HIV sector for 80 people in Kozlovka itself. They need space, medical equipment, personnel and information.

For the colony's personnel this is a new departure, implying further problems. Few are willing to work with people who have HIV/Aids. There are prejudices and anxieties. Even medical personnel have misgivings. We were surprised by a question about mosquito bites put by a doctor.

The HIV patients are young and good-looking; their crime, generally, is taking drugs. Many are educated; some may not live to be released. In the Krasnodar colony there are already about 400 people with HIV. They live in the prison community and are permitted to work, which means they may receive an early, conditional release. This is evidently a better solution than complete isolation, though I'm aware that in the Shakhov Women's Colony some HIV-positive inmates are already grumbling and don't want to work.

But in the Riazan Educational Colony, for instance, HIV girls are held under full prison conditions. They told me that during the day they are not permitted to sit down on their beds; they may only sit on stools. The stools have thin cushions to make them softer. The girls walk for just two hours a day in a special courtyard (a two-by-two-metre cellar, with a concrete floor, high grey wall, a net – not a single bench or blade of grass). The authorities won't give them permission to work. Many attendants even reject their requests to be allowed to wash the floor in the corridor. The thought of physical contact with an infected inmate through so much as a floorcloth terrifies them.

The girls watch television three hours a day. That is all. Books, of sorts, are apparently provided and medicines. They are given some sort of concoction. Three of the girls are locked up all day. One is 16, the others 17. They are drug addicts, psychologically disturbed. Their minds are being dulled sitting in their cell. One has been in for more than a year. They recently had a fight, the operative told us, when we asked why the lavatory in the cell didn't have a cubicle. 'We asked, but they don't allow it,' the girls responded. They said they had their fight because of the isolation, because it was unbearable.

Three weeks after my visit to Kozlovka I went back to Novyi Oskol to see Nastia. I brought a stack of photos from Kozlovka. The HIV girls were all very keen to see pictures of the women's colony. They have to make some kind of choice – stay here or move closer to home – after their eighteenth birthday. What do they gain? Their parents won't necessarily come more often, especially as the number of visits allowed is limited, and it's much harder to leave a women's colony before the end of your term. The rules are harsher too. Now their position in their educational colony is stronger, they live in an ordinary room, on the same floor as other inmates. Perhaps they'll get work; it's what they want. Nastia has decided not to move to the adult colony. At any rate, she'll think it through carefully before making a decision. ❏

Liudmila Alpern *is deputy director of the Moscow Centre for Prison Reform and a member of Penal Reform International*

Translated by Irena Maryniak

TALES FROM NOVYI OSKOL

OLGA, AGED 16

I got into pushing when I was very young and started injecting myself when my father died. My mum got arrested first and they gave her seven years. I went on pushing because I needed to help my grandmother – I've got a lot of brothers and sisters. But it wasn't long before they put me inside too. I was appalled, I wasn't ready, though I should have expected it I suppose. After I'd been in eight months they found I had HIV. At the time I didn't understand this was Aids. I still can't believe it. They convicted me and they didn't know I had Aids. I got five years. If they'd known I was seriously ill maybe they'd have given me less. I'll be going somewhere nearer Mama on 18 March. We'll be really close. They put her in prison for nothing at all, as an addict. She's in a colony in Chelyabinsk at the moment.

GALIA, AGED 17

It all started when my parents got arrested. My dad got 11 years, and Mum got seven. I was left alone with my three sisters. My elder sister got keen on drugs and we were always having rows and then she left home and I was left with my two younger sisters. I tried to be like a mother to them and make sure they had food and clothes and did their homework. Then the police started coming round and saying that my sisters should have a guardian, but I was too young because I was 16. Everyone knew my elder sister was an addict so she couldn't do it. Then my grandmother became the guardian, and we started going round to see her and things got easier. But my elder sister came back saying that she'd quit the drugs and I let her come and live with us. It didn't last long. She started injecting herself again. I was always against drugs. But I was out with her once and tried heroin. I liked it and started injecting myself and then pushing so I'd always have a fix. But no matter how often I injected myself, I never left my sisters. I didn't do it very long – just six months. Then I was convicted under article 228 part 4 and sentenced to five years. My younger sisters have supported me since I've been in prison, and my grandmother too. My elder sister hasn't written once. She doesn't need me any more.

Novyi Oskol Educational Colony, Russia: 'I want to live like ordinary people . . .'
Credit: Liudmila Alpern

I'd been in prison four months when they found I was HIV-positive. They put me in a punishment cell and I was there on my own for three months because there were no other HIV-positive girls in the prison. Then they made a kind of room for me and moved me in there. I was in pre-trial detention for seven months and then they transferred me to a penal colony. And here I am. I've got HIV but I try not to think about it too much. I hope to survive at least 15 years.

MASHA, AGED 16

I've got this awful disease – HIV. I'm very frightened and can't forget about it for a moment. How can I go on living? I don't even want to think about my release, though I know they're fond of me at home and that they're waiting for me. Mama . . . I love her so much . . . I never thought about her when I was free. It's only here, in all this, that I've understood what I've done. And there's no going back. That's something I have to accept. It's very hard if you're living with other girls who are OK. You forget for a while and feel like an ordinary human being, and then someone reminds you you're an 'Aids victim' and you suddenly feel like crying. If I could turn the clock back I'd do things differently. But I'll never be able to do that now. I wanted to be a vet, and to be like Mama. But that's impossible now. Maybe it's for the best. Maybe God has punished me with this illness and will reward me with something else. I never did upset anyone much. I wasn't malicious. Why me? It's very hard morally speaking. I never knew you could wipe out a whole life with a single prick. It seems so silly to me now, to inject yourself and destroy your life for a moment's high.

LIUBA, AGED 16

My mother stopped trusting me altogether in the end and all I could do was become a prostitute or steal. I'm not the sort to go into prostitution but I did get into stealing and I was quite good at it. I liked getting money without effort, I had enough for my drugs and I didn't need anything else. That was when they first took me to court. I was found guilty and they gave me two years conditionally with two years' probation, and after a while I was amnestied. That was when I felt my freedom; I thought I could really do what I wanted. So I went back to stealing and they caught me and there was a criminal case and it all became a pattern and then the officer sent me for a blood test for HIV and syphilis. I went with my brother, and we went back after a week to get the results. He got his HIV result straight away and they said there was no problem; I was told to come back in a week. I got the syphilis result and they said I was OK. I was really glad. I thought the HIV test hadn't come back yet. I thought there couldn't be anything much wrong. I had all these terrible thoughts but I kept pushing them away and hoped for the best. A week went by. I was supposed to go and pick up the result, but I didn't. I got a summons at home telling my mother to come to the children's clinic immediately. My mother went and came back in tears and said: 'Sweetheart, you've got Aids.' We started crying together, I suppose it was the shock. Then Mama calmed down and said: 'Liuba, it's all right, people live with it, and so will you.' Mama wasn't afraid of my illness. I ate and drank with everyone at home; no one excluded me. A bit later on I started stealing again. I didn't care any more. I lost my head. I didn't understand what I was doing and didn't think that I might end up in prison. But I did.

IRINA, AGED 17

My friend Vera met this guy, his name was Sasha, and at first he didn't know that we injected ourselves, but then it all came out into the open. He found out that we were both addicts. At first he wouldn't let Lena inject herself, but later he suggested that we pushed what he had. So we started pushing heroin. I did most of it – Vera just helped. I was injecting myself once a day, then it was three or four times a day. I ended up needing a heavy fix. We pushed drugs so we could get them for ourselves. We didn't even have enough money for our basic needs. We spent everything we had on injections. We got thin. I suppose we didn't look too well. I didn't push for very long. They caught me, but it was OK – there wasn't enough evidence and they dropped the case. But that didn't stop me. I went on pushing.

I didn't know I was dying, and that others were dying too. I pushed for about a year. They caught me and put me inside. Before I went in I heard that my friend Lena had been diagnosed with HIV. I suspected I might be ill too, but tried not to think about it. A month went by. Exactly a month after I was imprisoned they told me I was HIV-positive. I wanted to die there and then. It would have been better to have served a long sentence than to know that I'd die so much sooner than my friends. I went to a technical school that specialised in commerce. At least I'm educated. I don't want to die. I want to live like ordinary people and I never shall. ❑

Excerpts from contributions to an essay competition written by HIV-positive girls from the Novyi Oskol Educational Colony

Translated by Irena Maryniak

DESPERATE MEASURES

The Russian Ministry of Health has reached an agreement with the Orthodox Church on joint work on HIV/Aids, announced Russia's NTV channel on World Aids day (1 December). This agreement is not new: back in September it was discussed by the newspaper *Izvestiya*, which reported that an Orthodox taskforce 'was preparing an anti-Aids "blueprint" to be ready by the end of the year'.

The taskforce's secretary bears the splendidly Bunyanesque name of Margarita Nelyubova: her surname means 'No-Love' and St Margaret of

Antioch, a repentant harlot, is traditionally invoked against sex-related illness. According to Nelyubova, the Orthodox Church has been involved in anti-Aids work for almost two years – educational among the uninfected, mostly children, via Church-affiliated summer camps and youth clubs; and pastoral help for victims and their families. Special training courses are available for parish priests, prison chaplains and church-affiliated carers working with the terminally ill, she said – though, to judge from the TV programme, for some priests 'help' goes no further than reading the names of the sick during the litanies.

Russia's chief medical officer of health, Dr Gennadii Onishchenko, welcomes Church participation; indeed, he would like to involve Russia's other, non-Orthodox confessions too. How far the Churches will respond to his call for greater involvement with 'the most vulnerable, drug addicts and persons providing paid sexual services' is unclear. The taskforce is currently addressing the 'moral theology' of Aids: it should not be considered a direct punishment for sin.

Nevertheless, according to a leading Orthodox theologian, Vladimir Shmaliy, 'diseases, in a way, are generally symptomatic of a society's sinfulness. And the fact that disease does not provoke compassion in society is an important indicator of society's malaise.'

On the vexed issue of condoms, medics and Church have agreed to differ. The latter's stand is 'implacable', says Vsevolod Chaplin, spokesman for the Holy Synod, the governing body of the Orthodox Church. Ironically, it was not always so. Until recently, the Orthodox Church made no public statements on contraception, or on the form of 'birth control' most prevalent in the Soviet era – abortion. Only recently has it pronounced on such matters, many of the less fervent faithful grumble.

Had the state involved the Church in back in 1987, when HIV was first admitted to exist in the then Soviet Union, agreement now might be easier. ❑

Vera Rich

*Opposite: Russia 1988: priests celebrate 1,000 years of Orthodoxy –
now they have to deal with Aids. Credit: Sipa Press / Rex Features*

LETHAL WEAPON TWO

VALERII ABRAMKIN

THE LATEST IN BIOLOGICAL WEAPONS
IS ROLLING OFF THE ASSEMBLY LINE
AND OUT OF THE PRISONS AND PENAL
COLONIES OF THE RUSSIAN FEDERATION

Every year, 300,000 Russians are released from incarceration. Of these former prison inmates, 30,000 have tuberculosis; one in four carries an incurable form of the disease and that carrier is likely to infect another 50 people in the course of a year. A single air traveller carrying the multi-drug-resistant tuberculosis (MDR TB) bacillus could infect every passenger on the plane. It could land anywhere in the world, and the Koch bacillus – a mutant killer – is impossible to isolate. The potential for devastation and death dwarfs memories of radiation sickness, bombs, even Chernobyl.

Unless the tuberculosis and MDR TB epidemic is brought under control, 2 million Russians will be carriers of the infection by the end of the next decade. In addition, the number of HIV-positive prisoners has grown eight times in two years (from 4,100 in early 2000 to 33,000 in 2002). HIV weakens the immune system, increases the risk of TB and affects the development and spread of MDR TB. The number of HIV-positive inmates in Russian prisons could well lead to the appearance of TB 'super micro-organisms' (the TB 'superbug'), resistant even to 'second line' drugs. By then, we shall be facing a form of tuberculosis that no known pharmaceutical product can treat.

According to Médecins Sans Frontières, the likelihood of developing TB is 25–30 times higher than normal if you are HIV-positive; the chance of developing an active form of the illness is multiplied by a factor of ten. And while it is widely believed that prisoners infected with HIV are most at risk from discrimination and human rights abuses in their daily lives, absence of discrimination can be just as dangerous: when an HIV-positive prisoner is allocated a cell with prisoners who may be TB carriers, for instance. One in

HIV/Aids could cut annual economic growth in Russia by 0.5% by 2010 and 1% by
2020 | HIV/Aids is projected to increase health expenditures by 1–3% pa | By
2010 GDP in Russia could be reduced by 4.15%, and by 2020 by 10.5% because of

Russia 1998: segregated HIV prison hospital ward. Credit: John Ranard / Panos

ten prisoners in Russia has TB: 60–70 per cent are bacillus carriers; 25–35 per cent are MDR TB carriers. Putting HIV-positive prisoners with other inmates can be their death sentence. Isolation can increase their chances of survival. The right to life and health of the population at large is also threatened, as thousands of HIV-positive prisoners pass through the tuberculosis sectors of penal institutions and later into the wider community.

HIV-positive prisoners are stigmatised twice over. They leave prison branded as criminals and as lepers. Assistance and rehabilitation are made

HIV/Aids | Investment could be 5.5% lower in 2010 and 14.5% in 2020 | In 2001, Moscow refused a World Bank loan to fight TB and HIV/Aids because it did not wish to increase its debt; it has recently re-opened negotiations for the loan |

harder by their isolation. Prisoners suffering from both HIV and TB are, of course, the hardest hit and the most helpless. An article in the Russian penal code ensuring the separation of HIV-positive inmates from other prisoners was removed in March 2001; in practice, most penal institutions continue to keep them in isolated areas of the prison. HIV-positive prisoners are generally given no work, and are deprived of education and medical help. In addition, they are held with groups of people such as drug addicts, who are inclined to be deeply withdrawn; this desocialises them further. This last factor will be mitigated in part by a proposed set of amendments to the criminal code, currently still in draft, which includes proposals to break off compulsory treatment for addicts (who account for 90 per cent of HIV-positive prisoners) and extend opportunities for their early release. The number of addicts and HIV-positive inmates in penal institutions should fall.

However, officials argue that conditions for diagnosis and treatment are better in penal institutions than outside. In prison, they say, it is easier to maintain treatment and harder to procure alcohol and drugs. This is seriously misleading. Under normal conditions, just 5–10 per cent of those infected with TB become ill. Given the stress, poor diet, restrictions and boredom, the chances of developing the disease is greatly increased; add to this the presence of HIV and the likelihood of infection can reach 100 per cent. Furthermore, the rise in the number of HIV cases in penal institutions can be linked directly to state policy on crime: prisoners are seldom found guilty of drug production, they are simply drugs users. Addiction is classified as criminal. Yet between 1997 and 2000, more than three times as many crimes were committed by people who had been drinking than by people who had taken drugs. This includes alcohol-induced crimes such as murder (71–78 per cent), grievous bodily harm (74–80 per cent), rape (70–78 per cent) and hooliganism (72–75 per cent).

Russia's zero-tolerance policy against crime was launched at the end of 1994. It was a time when losses suffered by Russian investors from corrupt banks and joint stock companies were estimated at 20 trillion rubles, although crimes that were officially registered in 1994–5 led to losses totalling a mere 9.5 trillion rubles. I am reminded of something Nils Christie, professor of criminology at Oslo University, said to the effect that

Sources: AP, amFAR, National Intelligence Council (CIA), Russian Federal AIDS Center, World Bank, UNAIDS

'effective' politicians most frequently survive by inventing an enemy: 'Enemies are not always a threat; they can be extremely useful. Enemies unite, allow governments to change their priorities, focus public attention on a single issue so others are forgotten. Crime is something a weak state cannot live without. Governments can rule through crime.' As enemies, drug addicts are even more convenient than run-of-the-mill criminals. It can hardly be coincidental that the battle against drugs became most intense after the August 1998 financial crisis that saw poverty rates rise to cover 40 per cent of the population.

The Russian situation is unique. I am unaware of any country in the world with as many people with HIV and TB held in prisons. In US prisons 2 per cent of prisoners are HIV-positive, though this rises to 10 per cent in some states, Florida and Texas for example. But the numbers of inmates with TB are not as high, and the penitential system of Western countries ensures that bacillus carriers can be separated from other prisoners effectively and in time. In Russian conditions this is impossible. About one-third of prisoners with TB (not counting latent cases) are held with other prisoners. Even with international help in the region of US$450 million in 2001, Russia will not be in any position to bring its TB epidemic under control if it cannot significantly lower the number of HIV-positive inmates in its prisons. As the figures for HIV rise, the battle against TB needs ever more resources. If current levels of infection with HIV and TB are maintained, the Russian prison system will imperil the entire world. ❏

Valerii Abramkin is the director of the Moscow Centre for Prison Reform

COCK

ALEXANDER 'ROACH' ANASHEVICH

i can do him right here, he's easy:
cock stop cock stop cock stop cock.

girls dream: if only cocks could fly like birds
liubochka says: i don't like a big cock, it hurts
sveta says: i will never take a cock in my mouth, and if i do i'll be sick
lena says: i have never seen a cock, i mean a real one, only at the
movies and in magazines
ira says: cocks have a very odd smell
nastia says: i would like to have a cock so i could pee standing up
marina says: the first person who told me about cocks was my mum,
so i would know what it was and not be scared
tania says: my friend has an interesting cock, it's curved, i like that,
i can't imagine a straight cock, cocks should be curved
lida said: go suck cock, suck cock

suck cock
suck cock

(it was summer, the graduation ball, boys were pissing from the deck
into the water, the sun was almost coming up)
liubochka says: all men have a cock, even the president
galia says: i have an artificial cock, i bought it for a hundred rubles in
a shop
lida says: i sucked a cock one time, and another a second time, and
another a third time
ira says: i've sucked cock
lida says: no you haven't, because nobody would let you
(an old woman lived on vasily island, she had a louis xiv clock. she was
very proud of the clock but afraid someone might steal it, just come in, kill
her, and take it away. she wrote a letter to her nephew: come and get the
clock. when the nephew came she said: you can't have the clock just yet.
she did that several times, then she must have fallen ill, she wrote a last
time: vanya, my dear nephew, come back, but he sent her a note saying: go
suck cock. you know yourself what soldiers are like, no beating about the
bush, always so in your face)

Credit: Genia Chef

misha liked his cock

misha washed his cock

igor thinks: that's odd, what's wrong with my cock

igor says: some infection has got on my cock, first there was like a spot, small, red, then my whole cock swelled up

oleg says: his cock was always hard, it was an illness and the doctors couldn't do anything. one doctor told him: i can't give you a prescription, i can only envy you

andrei says: i was working on the ambulances then, we were called out to an old guy, he was ninety, his daughter opened the door and said: he wanks his cock for days at a time, please help. What were we supposed to do, we laughed and shrugged. he was ninety, and we were twenty-five . . .

dima says: so she's completely crazy, right, but they didn't keep her in hospital, she really didn't know what she was doing, went up to a policeman, grabbed his cock and looked him in the eyes, he couldn't move, even though everybody going by was watching

lera says: i had two tomatoes and an egg for breakfast, i got a hard-on! lucky my trunks were nylon or they would have burst

igor says: my brother's cock is smaller than mine, mine is longer and thicker lena relates: i was walking along and he turned round and pulled his cock out, i was scared, i screamed, he ran away, and afterwards i dreamed about his cock all night

ira says: you know, galia is so stupid, she would sell her own mother for a cock

right, there's this guy with an enormous cock and he can't get sex from anyone. he goes to the hospital and says: help me. right, they say, we'll cure you, and put him in a ward. in the evening he's going along the corridor and sees a nurse scrubbing the floor, whips his cock out and fucks her, and the nurse says to him: you think because I'm working class you can fuck me with your foot?

liza says: there was this soldier, right, govorov he was called, and he had a cock, i've never seen anything like it, very big, a woman comes to him in his unit and govorov fucks her in the garage, she screams and they call an ambulance, because he's torn everything inside her, anyway he didn't go with any more women after that, he was a decent guy, didn't want to hurt anyone, and then later liusia slept with him several times and it was all right, and to this day she's pining for him, but he was something else, after the army he went off to kalmykia, or maybe it was the komi republic, i don't remember

gosha says: one year i went on a field trip for a questionnaire survey but i didn't have the papers i needed, so i had to spent the night in a dosshouse, and there was a kirghiz in the next bed, and i couldn't get to sleep, and he was wanking under the sheet, and i remembered people used to say 'go suck the cock of a dead kirghiz', so it was a bit disgusting and anyway he was quite dirty, but i was interested so i said: show me your cock and he did, and it was perfectly ordinary, only small

serafima says: i read in the paper that some stupid girl bit her lover's cock off

lena says: i once saw a movie and a woman cut her lover's cock off and walked around town with it, or perhaps she ate it, i don't remember, and after that i saw a film by the same director about a woman who slept with an ape, i kept expecting to see the ape's cock, but i was out of luck, i expect they cut those frames out

(when the sun came up i suddenly really wanted to sleep, but a new life is beginning and you feel sorry for these minutes of the new, even though your eyes are glued together, you just have to put up with it and get on with it)

igor says: i was in the bathhouse, i am always embarrassed in there because i'm afraid my cock will get hard, and one guy, right, was walking around, so proud, because his cock was big, he was walking about waving it around, even when we went outside to smoke, everybody put towels round themselves, but he didn't bother

misha says: well one time I went into the bathhouse and there was this old geezer, about forty, he says let me give you a massage, and then he grabbed my cock and says: you do have a big one

(i don't know how to behave in certain situations, because i'm scared of everything, i'm embarrassed, and as they say in books, i can reveal the dark side of my soul only on paper. nobody publishes me, i have quarrelled with everyone, i don't eat anything, just smoke and drink water, it all began when they found I was hiv-positive, quite by chance, when i went to hospital with diarrhoea, perfectly ordinary diarrhoea, i'd drunk something that didn't agree with me, and they did a blood test, then everybody seemed to go mad, i don't want to tell you about it, i want to emigrate, will you help me? take me with you? i don't need to go far, anywhere)

katia says: i don't know why igor is so rude to me, it's as if i had poured salt on his cock

raia says: in porn films the men have very big cocks, i like jeff stryker films, and not just because he has a big cock, because he has such sad, piercing eyes, he must be very lonely, i could help him

igor says: when we were out at the dacha, all the boys were measuring their cocks with a pair of calipers to see whose was longest and thickest, and mine was biggest

liusia says: we'd had a bit to drink, you know, good wine, moldavian, with copper wire all wound round the bottle, and then he took his cock out and looked me in the eyes, i bent over, i was going to suck it and then i saw he had crabs in his pubes, i felt so ill i was sick all over his cock

(i never told anyone about my aids, i hid it and nobody could understand why i was so afraid of sex, i said i was tired, i was going through a difficult period in my life, i had a lot of things to think over, and then, evidently, rumours spread and people started phoning up threatening to kill me, saying i was a cunt, but i'd never done anything bad to anyone, then i saw *jeffrey*, everything turned out well for him in the end, i thought, maybe there's hope for me too, but one girl told me, don't get your hopes up, that's over in america everyone is so understanding, here we've just got scumbags, who're frightened for their own skin, and anyway it's all the same to them who they humiliate, who they dump their nastiness on)

there was this photographer photographed his cock, decorated it in different ways, he would wank it up and use an automatic camera to photograph it, then he made an exhibition and decided the tickets for the exhibition should be very expensive, and believe it or not, people paid up, some even came more than once, and he told us: i've got an admirer now and he wants to be my model, i looked at his cock but it wasn't very nice, mine is nicer, anyway, i'm telling you this because it isn't given to all of us to be an objet d'art

kostia drew a cock as a cactus in a bowl and gave me it

roma was very worried about his cock because he couldn't get it up, and the doctor told him it was all over, there was no hope, and roma was only twenty-five, all his life in front of him, although i reckon it saves a lot of problems

ira says: a boy came to her in the hostel, a bit of a dope, and she was laughing and he took all his clothes off and started coming on to her, so she hit his cock with a plimsoll, threw his clothes out the window and pushed him out the door, and he was outside with his erection but some boys had already run off with his clothes and he was walking around in the courtyard with his cock saluting

lera says: well i slept with a negro in the hostel, i was interested, but i didn't like it really because his cock was like an insect, actually he wasn't really a negro, more of an arab

tania says: well my girl friend told me a negro fucked her who had such a big cock that she was looking under her skirt for three weeks afterwards thinking he'd left something behind

(yesterday i got an email: 'cunt, you're dead, fuck off out of this town', someone has found out my email address, i haven't given it to any outsiders, so it must be one of my friends, smiling at me face to face, pretending they don't know anything, or sympathise, but then write letters like that, i didn't try to do anything, just changed my email address, it's a pity i can't go away, not because i don't have money, just because i'm scared, where could i go, would i be welcome, nobody needs me anywhere)

masha says: i've always been rather intrigued by circumcised cocks, but i saw my first one only quite recently and didn't at first realise that was what it was, and you know, it's really very neat, and they even say it's more hygienic

Credit: Genia Chef

then everybody talked at length about the *skoptsi* sect, but nobody really got down to the crux of the matter, its historical and ideological underpinning, the absence of a cock, the paradox of a voluntary repudiation of the cock, that is what was really animating those assembled, and it was the conversation that gave a lot of them a runny feeling somewhere inside in the region of their prostate

the *skoptsi* got everyone on to an even more interesting and intellectual conversation about farinelli the *castrato*, choirboys, holy fathers, numerous movie stars, but your clerk took a rest because he has always been a stickler for morality and political correctness

(i feel as if i am writing this novel from the next world and accordingly consider that i have the right to create such a text, it's hardly going to shock anyone or leave them not unmoved, as lena said after a cursory reading of *a different love*, i feel sorry for that person (the author), he lacked something in his life, i think that everyone reading these lines will be visited by an analogous thought and he will be one hundred per cent right, because at this moment i lack a great deal, namely myself, the self i was before this illness)

(it's a weird sensation a person experiences who cannot be alone, one to one with his own secret, and the feeling becomes even more weird when the secret, without his wishing it, becomes known to people he doesn't know, today again threats on my pager and i don't even try to change the number because these unknown morons will find it out anyway, last night when i went out to look at the fountains they were following me, two of them, one wearing a dracula mask and the other the mask of an enraged piglet, it seemed to me they had axes in their hands, they were waiting for me to attack them, to make the first aggressive move so they could hack me to pieces, so their conscience would be clear, after all even the wretchedest scumbag cannot always make up his mind to attack first, from cowardice, cannot always attack you from behind because of some sham feeling of honour, scumbags cannot be honourable, you will say, but you are wrong, just as i was wrong in the past)

(we should love and respect killers, if only because they have already done something which you personally could never bring yourself to do, although you might very much want to, sometimes you get this feeling, set off by other feelings: of revenge, outrage, hurt, madness, it comes like a lump into your aorta and you want to take an axe or a pistol in order never to see them again, not even a quiver, but then the feeling passes, you've lived through it and then you can't remember it at all, and they say that this unrealised wish gives birth to cancer cells, in the same way that the mythical energy of killing can't go away until it has killed, in the end you kill yourself, from inside, from your most vulnerable place)

liza says: my younger brother asked me, where does a fish keep its cock, i asked him who told you words like that, and he said my friend antosha told me in the nursery

lilia says: i'm gagging for a big cock

it's time to stop, everyone has realised that all this stuff about cocks was just a ploy to get you to read what i put in brackets, a little trap, a little trick, you would be reading about cocks, laughing, moving on and you would be sure to read every last bit (i know how bad you are), and you would at least glance through the most important thing, my complaints

i have never been abroad, everybody thinks i love spain, but actually i don't, i don't love spain or any other country, all those magical eldorados, i love the dirtiest, most vacuous country, the country populated by my clones

everybody says that i would never get on with one of my clones, perhaps, but at least i would know what he was going to say, what he was going to think, how he would like to come, and he wouldn't be hurt by my being ill perhaps the killers are trying to get hold of my hair, i have started noticing that my hair is falling out and disappearing without trace, so evidently someone wants it, but i am going bald, i want my hair myself

yesterday the killers shat just outside my door

i have always wished i could get my own cock in my mouth, but i can't bend enough, although i have seen other people managing it in movies, and i have a dream, a recurring dream, i suck my own cock, once i even saw my own face

lilia, rita, ira, igor and roma came round yesterday, they are not the killers, but they broke the dictaphone i was recording their conversations on, they tried to strangle me, but you can't strangle a corpse, they only managed to squeeze all the saliva out of me, they were all covered in my spit, my infected saliva, they broke my dictaphone, and there was a lot more on it about cocks, a lot that was funny and a lot that was revolting, but it's not difficult to make up stuff about cocks

my cock caused my illness

it's stinking of shit again, the killers have shat by my door again

it's very easy to recognise a killer in a crowd, from the gleam in his eyes, from the veins bulging on the back of his hands, from his bright red knob

the killer, the one in the enraged piglet mask, is standing under my window with a gleam in his eyes

i am a killer too, i want to go to bed with everyone who doesn't know nobody knows anything

the old woman on vasiliev island didn't die, she couldn't, vania the airman forgot how to write, now he can only write the word 'cock', well, as you know very well, that's all the military need

the old woman from vasiliev island, despite having an antique clock, was unhappy and this unhappiness was etched in her face, there were no bruises or livid spots there, but how can i explain it, you've never ridden on a diesel, in the vestibule between carriages, they have cancer cells right in the pupils of their eyes

i took the killers' shit to the clinic for analysis, it had intestinal worms and flecks of blood in it

i have forgotten how to cry: another symptom of my illness, it doesn't matter, i'll survive that, who needs crying

you will help me, just a one-way ticket, to a dirty country, in a third-class carriage, to wash my cock

warning: this text is infected, it is inadvisable to lick the letters with your tongue

my day job is as a newspaper editor, but at night i am a stripper, not for the money, for the image; a russian writer, suffering from aids, is dancing in calvin klein underpants to earn money for his medication

the killers are my clones, i know what they think, what they want, how they come, they have my face, especially my profile, only they dress differently, not in second-hand clothes i hope, i want them expensively dressed, no synthetics, the axe needs sharpening, i have to give samples tomorrow, i can't emigrate, there's nothing i can do, nothing

i dedicate this text to Rita Meklina, whom i do not know, and to all the other girls with a good heart who might have been mine ❏

Alexander 'Roach' Anashevich (born 1971) is a poet and dramatist. He also works as a journalist for his local newspaper in Voronezh

Translated by Arch Tait

CULTURE

Me and Sudie *by Steed Taylor, from* Share Your Vision, *an exhibition organised by Visual Aids in New York (October/November 2003) of work by HIV-positive artists with impaired sight. Credit: Steed Taylor*

DEFYING THE SILENCE

EDWARD LUCIE-SMITH

UNLIKE THEIR COUNTERPARTS IN OTHER
CREATIVE FIELDS, ARTISTS IN THE USA
HAVE SET OUT TO PORTRAY THOSE THINGS
ABOUT AIDS THAT GOVERNMENTS AND
SOCIETY CHOOSE TO IGNORE

'Aids art' is essentially an American invention. It has now manifested itself in
a large number of different locations, but is almost invariably based on a
model of artistic activity that evolved in the US – one that was a response to
the impact made by the epidemic on sections of US society. This means,
among other things, that the best-known artworks connected with Aids
have nearly always had homosexual themes. The social and economic effect
of heterosexually transmitted Aids in Africa has, by contrast, played a
distinctly minor role. Aids art enterprises in Africa – for example, in South
Africa with embroideries made by Zulu women; in Togo with T-shirts
printed with messages addressed to young people – have inevitably seemed
like paler copies of things that had already been done in the US. They have
also, much more than is the case with their US exemplars, seemed like
bourgeois enterprises with no lasting social impact at any deep level. This
was not so in the US, where artists, especially in the late 1980s and early
1990s, did undoubtedly call attention to things the government of the time
was attempting to ignore.

In the US, art about Aids was from the beginning didactic, and also from
the beginning polemical. It tried to enlighten the public about the true
nature of the epidemic. It protested against prejudice and sexual stereo-
typing, and at the same time it tried to put pressure on a reluctant Reagan
administration to do something both to help victims of this new and deadly
disease and to provide resources to find a cure. At a secondary level, it was
also an act of mourning.

The rise of Aids art coincided with the rise to power of the so-called
'rainbow coalition' in the US art world. While it was the German artist
Joseph Beuys who originally discovered the effectiveness of museums and
large exhibitions of contemporary art such as the Kassel Documenta as plat-
forms for minority political causes, it was the US, with its penchant for

single-issue political agitation, that made the fate of minorities a dominant theme in the world of contemporary art. This development culminated, more than a decade ago, with the 'politically correct' Whitney Biennial of 1991. A prominent feature of this was an 'Aids timeline' devised and presented by the radical artistic group General Idea. However, Aids was by no means the sole theme of this exhibition. In addition to art that tried to deal with Aids, it presented work by feminists, by African-Americans and by Latino artists.

The timeline was not something that appeared spontaneously. It was the culmination of a relatively slow process. The disease was first reported in 1981 and there had already been plays and films about it by the time the radical homosexual group ACT UP created an Aids emblem, with the slogan 'Silence = Death'. In the same year, 1987, an offshoot of ACT UP created an installation entitled *Let the Record Show* in the window of the New Museum of Contemporary Art on Lower Broadway – the first really visible link between the growing protest campaign and the world of contemporary art. This was not, however, nearly such a publicity-grabbing manifestation as the debut of the Names Project Quilt on Capitol Mall in Washington, which took place in the same year. The Names Project, where victims were commemorated by individual squares sewn by friends and relatives, eventually grew to nearly 11,000 items by the time of its second Washington showing in 1989. It was significant that it was a largely populist, amateur effort, rather than something generated by professional artists.

The year 1989 also saw the first really significant Aids art exhibit – *Witnesses: Against Our Vanishing*, at Artists Space in New York. The catalogue featured an angry essay by the artist David Wojnarowicz, himself an Aids victim, attacking the role of the Catholic Church. As a result, the National Endowment for the Arts withheld, but then was forced to reinstate, a grant promised to the exhibit.

In the same year the photographer Robert Mapplethorpe died. Mapplethorpe's retrospective exhibition, held at the Whitney Museum in 1988, though not officially an Aids event, in many ways functioned as such, since the photographer was already widely known to be suffering from the disease. His final *Self Portrait*, which shows him ravaged by Aids, holding a walking stick with a an ivory skull for a knob, is one of the best-known images linked to the early years of the epidemic.

This portrait is in artistic terms very conservative. It borrows its composition from Old Masters such as Van Dyck. What made it seem radical were the circumstances surrounding it. This is something that is often true of photography in general. It is also something that tends to be true of separatist gay art. What I mean by this is art that, like the drawings of Tom of Finland, addresses itself very directly to the gay community through its emphasis on homoerotic content.

In a sense, one of the things that the Aids epidemic did was to pull art with openly homosexual content towards the centre – to break down the wall of the ghetto that had hitherto contained it. Part of Mapplethorpe's own artistic ancestry can be found in this area – not only in the photography of George Platt Lynes, but in images made by the gay soft-porn studios that flourished in Los Angeles during the 1940s and 1950s – Bruce of LA often foreshadows Mapplethorpe, as does Bob Mizer of the Athletic Model Guild (who was also a source for David Hockney).

Many of the most affecting and effective of the artworks that refer to Aids are based on standard Christian archetypes, which is somewhat ironic, given the long-standing quarrel between Aids activists and the Roman Catholic hierarchy, and their equally bitter quarrel with the leaders of a number of Protestant fundamentalist denominations. Examples are two series, one American and one Swedish, based on the iconography of the Stations of the Cross. One, made up of paintings, is the work of the New Mexico-based artist Delmas Howe. The other, created by the Swedish lesbian photographer Elizabeth Ohlson, and one of the few really striking instances of Aids art produced in Europe, consists of carefully staged photographic tableaux. Ohlson's 'Ecce Homo' series, completed in 1998, is peopled by members of Stockholm's gay community. A touring exhibition in Sweden was seen by more than 250,000 people. One venue, at the invitation of the Archbishop, was Uppsala Cathedral, Sweden's premier church. The presence of the exhibition at Uppsala led to the cancellation of a proposed meeting between the Archbishop and Pope John Paul II.

Howe's series, completed in 2001, has recently been the subject of a documentary film, and his images, like those by Ohlson, are easily available on the web (www.delmashowe.com; www.ohlson.se/u_ecce.htm).

Both Howe and Ohlson put particular stress on the image of the *pietà* – in their versions the Christ figure becomes a universal symbol of those suffering from an incurable malady, who are at the same time scorned by much of the world for their misfortune.

Homosexual artists are not the only ones to have turned to established archetypes of this sort in recent times. They have also, for example, been employed by feminists, for rather similar reasons. The archetype placed in a gay or feminist context is both familiar and shocking: it communicates meaning with unrivalled efficiency.

Artists making reference to the Aids epidemic have also tried other strategies. Both the British duo Gilbert & George and the US painter Ross Bleckner have employed imagery derived from science – samples of blood or sperm seen through a high-powered microscope. Bleckner has also made use of a slightly unspecific imagery of chalices and flowers, with connotations of exaltation and mourning.

There is also the purely conceptual approach adopted by the Cuban-born artist Felix Gonzalez-Torres, who succumbed to Aids in 1996. Many of his installation pieces were made in memory of his lover Ross, who died before him. A typical example of his work is *Untitled: Placebo*, a piece where sweets are spread out on the floor and the public is encouraged to take them one at a time. The gradual diminution of the pieces of candy symbolises the gradual, inexorable diminution of the life of someone suffering from Aids.

The trouble with this, as with Bleckner's chalices, is that the imagery requires just a little too much explanation to be really effective. In an interview given very shortly before his death, Gonzalez-Torres spoke about the pleasure he got from a showing of *Placebo* at the Hirshhorn Museum, an institution more generally associated with figurative painting and sculpture:

> When I was at Hirshhorn and saw the show, there was one particular guard who was standing with the big candy floor piece *Untitled: Placebo*, and she was amazing. There was this suburban, white, middle-class mother with two young sons who came in the room and, in 30 seconds, this woman – who was a black, maybe church-going civil servant in Washington, in the middle of all this re-actionary pressure about the arts – there she was explaining to this mother and kids about Aids and what this piece represented, what a placebo was, and how there was no cure and so on. Then the boys started to fill their pockets with candies and she sort of looked at them like a schoolmistress and said, 'You're only supposed to take one.' Just as their faces fell and they tossed back all but a few she suddenly smiled again and said, 'Well, maybe two.' And she won them over completely! The whole thing worked because then they got the piece, they got the interaction, they got the generosity and they got her. It was great.

A touching story in itself, but also, in my opinion, one that gives the game away by demonstrating how inert the artistic element in all this actually is. It is the relationship between the museum guard and the group of visitors that is dynamic. And of course, what was actually there, what Gonzalez-Torres contributed to the occasion, could easily have been the subject of a large number of other, quite different explanations.

What Aids art currently struggles with, and here it is on a footing with many other varieties of contemporary art, is how to manage content: how to communicate both facts and emotion without at the same time surrendering its claim to avant-garde originality. This is one reason why essentially amateur enterprises, such as the Names Project Quilt, often seem more effective than the work produced by professional artists. ❏

Edward Lucie-Smith *is a poet and art critic. His most recent book is* Art Tomorrow *(Editions Pierre Terrail, Paris, 2002)*

USA 2001: The Triumph *and* The Stripping *from Delmas Howe's Stations of the Cross.* Credit: Delmas Howe

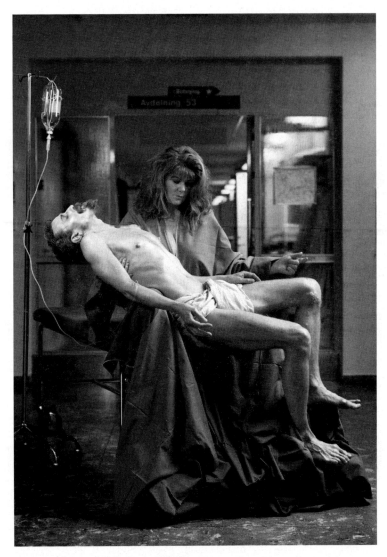

*Sweden 1998: Elizabeth Ohlson's Stations of the Cross,
featuring Stockholm's gay community.
Opposite:* Dignar under Korset; *above:* Pietà.
Credit: Elizabeth Ohlson

Above: USA from 1996: Joe's contribution to 'what it feels like to live with Aids/HIV' from the touring Movable Mural Project. Credit: Center for Community and Folk Art

Opposite: Life goes on *by Robert O'Donnell from the exhibition* Share Your Vision. *Credit: Robert O'Donnell*

Overleaf: Washington DC, 1993: exhibiting the Aids quilt. Credit: Leonard Freed / Magnum Photos

CARANDIRU

PATRICK WILCKEN

A BRAZILIAN CAUSE CÉLÈBRE
RAISES THE LID ON PRISON LIFE
AND BECOMES THE SUBJECT OF
A BOX-OFFICE HIT

On 3 October 1992, Brazil awoke to shocking news. After a fight between inmates had spun out of control, riot police had entered Cell Block 9 of São Paulo's Casa da Detenção, known as Carandiru, a sprawling 1950s-style concrete complex housing over 7,000 inmates, double the number it was built for. Hours later, 111 prisoners lay dead; not one of the riot police had been killed. More than 500 rounds had been fired into the block and, although the crime scene was substantially altered in the aftermath of the massacre by Colonel Ubiratan Guimarães, the commander of the operation, the inmates' wounds told the story. There were 37 shots to the back of the head, many in a downward trajectory, and more than 150 to the backs of arms, legs and in the back.

Untrained and undisciplined, Guimarães's men had panicked, firing blindly down corridors and into crowded cells. Many feared that they would be infected by the HIV virus if they came into contact with the prisoners; others claimed that the inmates had even threatened to infect them. 'If anyone squirts blood on me,' one policeman was reported as shouting, 'I'll kill them.' In a macabre coda, Guimarães ordered the surviving inmates to carry the bodies of their comrades and stack them in two-metre-high piles, so as to avoid blood contamination. The grimy black-and-white photos produced at the inquiry showed mounds of corpses dressed in football shorts and singlets piled up in filthy cells, images reminiscent of atrocities carried out under the cloak of war or dictatorship. But the killings took place in the very heart of a thrusting capitalist city, a tube stop away from downtown São Paulo.

Carandiru's status as a cause célèbre was cemented by the publication of the cancer specialist Dr Drauzio Varella's remarkable book *Estação Carandiru* (*Carandiru Station*), which was later made into a hit film by his friend and one-time patient, Hector Babenco. Back in 1987, Varella had embarked on an ambitious project. He had decided to research the incidence of HIV infection inside Carandiru – a confined, insanitary environment where anal sex and intravenous drug use were rife. Initial studies showed the overall rate to be 17 per cent, but among the 'prison women' (ie transvestites) this rose to a staggering 78 per cent. However, Varella's work would end up being much more than an epidemiological study – he became engrossed in Carandiru, the set-up, the inmates and their lives, and ended up volunteering his services each Monday for over a decade.

During this period, Varella was treating his long-time friend Babenco (director of *Kiss of the Spider Woman* and *Pixote*) for non-Hodgkin's lymphoma and, by telephone or at his bedside, he began telling Babenco of his experiences. Varella spoke of his initial fears and then slow acceptance within the prison. He talked about his work – how he had managed to get his safe-sex message across by bundling, somewhat incongruously, his film about Aids prevention with a pornographic video, and contracting the sex-bomb singer Rita Cadillac to perform in a consciousness-raising concert. For Babenco, Varella became 'a kind of alter ego', someone who was doing something creative and vital, at a time when the film director could do nothing. Babenco encouraged Varella to set down his experiences in book form. The outcome, *Estação Carandiru*, has sold over 400,000 copies to date, and was recently adapted into a BBC radio play.

Varella's book tells the story from the inside, introducing otherwise faceless inmates – the ageing transvestites, their bodies misshapen by back-street injections of industrial silicone, the drug addicts, murderers and petty criminals – as engaging personalities. It is a world peopled by characters with eccentric nicknames beloved of Brazilians: the transvestite 'Lady Di', the midget 'Mimimum Wage' and the philosophical 'No Chance'.

The tiny number of corrupt, poorly paid and badly trained guards (often no more than a dozen overseeing several thousand men) meant that power was effectively devolved to the prisoners themselves. The result was not so much chaos as a self-imposed order, a parallel social system. Carandiru was like a walled *favela*.

Sex was strictly policed by the inmates. In the very Latin culture of the prison, transvestites were treated well – as ladies – with cell-block marriages performed and recognised. During conjugal visits – a measure introduced to reduce tension in the prison – the men's wives were respected, the queue to use the bedroom orderly. There was no need to bang on the door; the punctuality was, according to Varella, 'British'.

Varella found that intravenous drug use was the principal vector for the spread of the HIV virus. Home-made syringes – needles burned on to plastic Bic pen encasements with plungers fashioned from flip-flop rubber – were passed around, perfunctorily rinsed out in a single, heavily contaminated glass. 'It was an HIV party,' concluded Varella, but one which, through his own efforts, was gradually coming under control. By January 1994, infection rates had dropped down to 13.7 per cent; four years later this had almost halved.

Varella's book was a big success in its own right, but its impact has been heightened by this year's release of Hector Babenco's film version. Parts of Babenco's *Carandiru* were shot inside the prison itself, a political embarrassment after the massacre and in the process of being decommissioned. The arrangements of the filming were strange, to say the least. 'I was handed a gigantic key by the governor,' explains Babenco 'after I had signed an agreement with the state authorities that I would be responsible for everything that happened during the six-week shoot.' Three thousand prisoners were still housed inside the complex, some of whom shouted abuse through their cell-window grilles while their actor doubles went through their paces. As the shoot got under way, there were death threats, rumours that prisoners were planning a massive breakout and that Babenco would be taken hostage at knife-point. Shooting the climactic massacre scene, the problems were

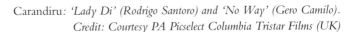

Carandiru: 'Lady Di' (Rodrigo Santoro) and 'No Way' (Gero Camilo).
Credit: Courtesy PA Picselect Columbia Tristar Films (UK)

more logistical: with 1,000 extras – some of whom were former inmates at Carandiru – horses, dogs and heavy weaponry, the prison yard was transformed into something like it might have been on the day of the killings: a maelstrom of orders shouted through megaphones, chaotic movements of people and general confusion.

Like Fernando Meirelles's ultra-violent gangland epic *City of God* (*Index* 1/03), *Carandiru* has done extremely well at the box office in Brazil, grossing even more than *Matrix Reloaded*. The audiences have cut across Brazil's gaping social divide from the poor whose life the film portrays to the wealthy, curious to know 'who these guys we fear so much are', says Babenco.

Meanwhile, the perpetrators of the Carandiru massacre have yet to face true justice. The commander of the operation, Colonel Ubiratan Guimarães, even managed to run for political office, his ballot ticket '111' a reference to the prison deathtoll. It was not until July 2001, after years of stalling and cover-ups, that he was finally brought to trial. He was duly sentenced to 632 years in prison, but is still free pending an appeal and remains unrepentant, lampooning Babenco's film in the press, even trying to block its release through the courts.

Carandiru itself is no more. On 12 August last year, 250 kilos of explosives were detonated at structural points around the compound. Politicians hope the demolition will efface the memory of Brazil's worst police massacre, but with the success of Varella's book and Babenco's film the tragedy of Carandiru will live on in the popular imagination.

ESTAÇÃO CARANDIRU
DRAUZIO VARELLA

IN THE AUDITORIUM During the first talks, Florisval, the director of security, positioned himself on the stage with his back to me, facing the audience. One day, I asked him not to bother coming and I stayed alone with the prisoners. It worked and I began to understand them better.

Sometimes I heard people talking at the back of the room while I was showing the Aids video. One morning, during the film, I decided to cross the darkened auditorium and sit there at the back among them, just to see if the chatter would stop.

I was moved by a feeling of trust, but I was frightened. I made my way across the auditorium slowly. When I reached the back rows, the conversation broke off. I sat on the floor, among the prisoners, watching the video, my hands cold and my heart racing. I had the sensation that someone would jump out from behind and strangle me. I controlled my fear and sat it out until the end. Then I stood up and returned at a leisurely pace to the stage. On the way back I noticed that the way I was walking was different: it had a streetwise air about it. Next week I went to the back of the auditorium again. The fear returned, but with much less intensity. The third time the fear had gone . . .

The task of getting hundreds of rogues out of bed before eight to watch an educational video followed by medical advice was thought to be unrealistic by the more experienced prison staff, but it was pushed forward by Hernani, a guy with flecked grey hair, a conman who specialised in borrowing money in the name of fake companies and then declaring them bankrupt:

'Doctor, waking up scoundrels is a difficult problem. Why don't you show an erotic video at the end of the screening? These guys are so desperate, it will pack the auditorium.'

We did a trial run. In the end, after I had left the room, an explicit erotic movie was brought in. The strategy of mixing music, preventative medicine and sex was unbeatable, a total success. It could work in other prisons, as long as two precautions are taken: don't allow people to watch only the last film, because the screening is a single package and, most important, the erotic film only starts after the doctor has left the room.

From the very first talks I was surprised by the consideration that the men showed towards me. In their questions they used terms such as 'anal sex', 'penetration', 'prostitution', 'homosexuals' or 'prison women' – never crude expressions; obscenities were definitely out of the question . . .

This aura of heartfelt respect around the personage of the doctor who was helping them gave me a heightened sense of responsibility. With more than 20 years' clinical experience, it was among those whom society looks on as scum that I saw most clearly the impact of the presence of the doctor on the human imagination, one of the mysteries of my profession.

'RICARDÃO'*   On the following night, a little fair-haired guy with light-coloured eyes, his belongings wrapped in newspaper, arrived at the assembly-point cell. He came in quietly and took up a place near the toilet bowl.

A little later, a swarthy man with a nasal voice lying down near the window recognised the fair-haired guy as his wife's lover.

It was a serious situation – going with an inmate's wife aroused the collective hatred of the prison. I have seen several killings caused by these love triangles: the husband is imprisoned, his wife goes with another man who later ends up in the same prison as his embittered rival . . .

The guy with the nasal voice shouted from the window:

'I know who you are, you jerk. You're my wife's "Ricardão". Now you're going to die!'

Zildenor [another inmate] described the incident like this:

It was an affair between 'Ricardão' and 'Dona Maria Faltosa'.**

The cuckold with the nasal voice went towards the fair-haired guy, but the group intervened:

'Forget it, mate, you're going to be banged up for years for this, you're not in for long. You can settle this score on the street.'

Their reasoning brought the betrayed husband to his senses, and he decided to avenge himself in a less radical way:

'OK, I won't kill the son-of-a-bitch 'Ricardão', but he will pay for what he did to my wife in the same currency. I'm going to take him from behind!'

The fair-haired guy, cowering, tried to talk him out of it.

'Don't do it, mate, I'm HIV-positive, it's not going to do you any good. I'm already going to die anyway, do you want to catch Aids as well?'

At this moment, a fat guy with no teeth stood up in the corner, a thief who had been in and out of prison:

'Leave the blondey to me. There's no problem, I'm HIV-positive as well!'

Sadly, the fair-haired guy was forced to go with the big bloke in the corner, Zildenor went on.

The next day, the fair-haired guy, seeing that Zildenor was a newcomer in the prison like him, came over looking for sympathy.

'Shit, man, I lied, I made up that story. I'm not HIV-positive.'

Zildenor comforted him: 'Don't get upset, neither was he.'

* A 'Ricardão' is someone who is full of himself, sleeps around and doesn't care about the consequences.
** A 'Dona Maria Faltosa' is a treacherous wife. ❑

Drauzio Varella, *excerpts from* Estação Carandiru *(Companhia das Letras, 1999). Translated by Patrick Wilcken*

MAKING INROADS

A huge country, with large urban slums and a crumbling health service, Brazil faced a potential catastrophe when HIV/Aids was first described in the 1980s. In 1993 the World Health Organisation (WTO) predicted that 1.2 million Brazilians would be infected by HIV by 2000. But today there are only around 600,000 carriers of the disease – a formidable achievement in a population of over 170 million. Life expectancy for Aids patients has climbed steadily, while admissions to hospitals for Aids-related illnesses have plummeted.

The key to success was early intervention. Pressured by NGOs working in the field, the government began to run ad campaigns, distribute condoms and treat drug addicts in the early 1990s. For those who had become infected, the Ministry of Health embarked on an aggressive policy of drug treatment with universal access to anti-retrovirals introduced in 1991.

But treatment proved expensive and with drug bills mounting, the Brazilian government went on the offensive. In 1997, they took on the multinational pharmaceutical companies by passing the controversial Article 68 of Brazil's patent law. The Article allowed the production of generic copies of anti-retrovirals if the drug company in question did not begin production in Brazil within three years of issuing their patent. The US tried to block the law at the WTO, but was eventually shamed into dropping the complaint in June 2001. Brazil has continued to champion the rights of developing countries to use generic copies of patented drugs, culminating in the November 2001 declaration at the WTO conference in Doha, Qatar, that the Trade-Related Aspects of Intellectual Property Rights (TRIPS) Agreement would not take precedence in public health emergencies.

Thanks to the production of cheap generic copies of Aids drugs and the lower prices now offered by pharmaceutical companies to pre-empt Brazil from breaking their patents, 100,000 people have been provided with anti-retrovirals free of charge. The Ministry of Health now produces eight out of 12 of the drugs cocktail for the treatment of Aids, and has bargained for anything up to an 80 per cent reduction on prices on imports from the West. Ten new pilot anti-retroviral plants are being set up, and Paulo Teixeira, the director of Brazil's Ministry of Health Aids programme, is now pushing the WTO to adopt a resolution allowing Brazil to export generic anti-retrovirals to countries that do not have the technology to produce

AIDS : ASSIM PEGA

AIDS PASSA DO HOMEM
PRA MULHER.
AIDS PASSA DA MULHER
PRO HOMEM.

AIDS PASSA PRA LÁ E
PASSA PRA CÁ.
VÍRUS NÃO RECONHECE
MACHEZA

QUEM TOMA BAQUE NA
VEIA VAI PEGAR O VÍRUS.
SE NÃO É HOJE VAI SER
AMANHÃ OU DAQUI A SEIS
MESES.

ASSIM NÃO PEGA

*Illustration from
Estação Carandiru
by Drauzio Varella.
Credit: Companhia
das letras*

their own and cannot afford to buy from the West. Teixeira is also working
with the WHO to scale up the Brazilian model to other parts of the world,
including transfers of drug production technologies to poorer countries such
as Guyana, Angola and Mozambique.

There are still enormous problems in Brazil. In poorer, more remote
regions, access to government programmes is uneven. The vast state of
Amazonas, for instance, has just one Aids clinic – in Manaus. Across Brazil's
overcrowded, insanitary prison system, it is estimated an average of 15–20
per cent of inmates are infected with the virus. Prejudice against the gay
community remains stubborn; conservative Church leaders have opposed
government initiatives. ❏

PW

OVERRATED AND UNDEREXPOSED

JIM D'ENTREMONT

COMMERCIAL PRESSURES HAVE
EMASCULATED AIDS-RELATED FILM
AND THEATRE PRODUCTIONS

Representations of HIV/Aids in theatre and film reflect parallel contagions of bigotry, erotophobia, cross-cultural blindness and denial. Since Aids was at first dismissed as a fringe affliction, the earliest dramatised references to the disease were destined to emerge from fringe theatre. The myth of Aids as a gay plague ensured that all media would approach the topic slowly, and with tongs.

The first play staged in the US or anywhere to deal with the rising epidemic appears to have been Robert Chesley's *Night Sweat*. The Meridian Gay Theatre production opened in New York on 24 May 1984, more than three years after the condition initially called GRID (Gay-Related Immune Deficiency) began appearing in that city. The play is a mordant cartoon about a suicide club called 'Coup de Grâce: the Experience', which offers doomed gay men a chance to choose their own deaths.

As Aids spread, its artistic indices entered the mainstream. In 1985, a year after *Night Sweat* premiered, the Circle Rep production of William Hoffman's *As Is* moved to Broadway, while Larry Kramer's *The Normal Heart* surfaced under the auspices of the New York Shakespeare Festival. Kramer, who co-founded Gay Men's Health Crisis, a pioneering Aids resource, built *The Normal Heart* around his anguished estrangement from that organisation. The play was a political outcry whose content galvanised some theatregoers, offended others and aged quickly. *As Is* may be a more broadly accessible act of mourning.

The plays raised divisive issues of sexually transmitted infection. Hoffman expressed nostalgia for the promiscuity Kramer reviled. Robert Chesley sparred with Kramer in the *New York Native*, a gay weekly, accusing him of 'gay homophobia and anti-eroticism'. In society at large, liberationists and abstentionists often condemned and sometimes censored one another, as if there were no middle ground.

By the mid-1980s, gay playwrights, screenwriters and directors felt enormous pressure to deal with Aids, while their heterosexual colleagues ducked the topic. Some gay artists countered the image of Aids as an efflorescence of depravity by typifying gay men as model citizens. Some simply floundered. 'So new is the concept of safe or unsafe sex that I still can't accept its reality,' Harvey Fierstein admitted in his introduction to the published script of *Safe Sex*, his 1987 triad of one-acts. Playwright Allan Bowne attempted to raise Aids awareness in his flawed *Beirut* (1987) by presenting the plight of quarantined heterosexuals in a future society wracked by an unnamed plague.

In the late 1980s, before the arrival of Tony Kushner's monumental *Angels in America* (1991–3), few noteworthy Aids plays were produced in the US. This is not to say that worthwhile scripts were unavailable. *Millennium Approaches*, the first part of Kushner's award-winning epic, had to receive the imprimatur of a 1992 production by the Royal National Theatre of Great Britain before American producers would touch it.

Film-makers, meanwhile, edged towards the subject. Stuart Marshall's 1984 documentary *Bright Eyes*, made in the UK for Channel Four, was the first Aids film of any consequence. In 1985, US film-maker Artie Bressan released *Buddies*, a low-budget feature film about a dying man's relationship with an Aids volunteer, and German director Rosa von Praunheim presented *Ein Virus kennt keine Moral*, an exuberant exercise in gallows humour. Marshall and Bressan later died of Aids-related illnesses; von Praunheim continues to address Aids issues in his politically charged work.

In November 1985, American commercial television broke ground limply with *An Early Frost*, in which a young lawyer infected by a male partner wins support from his well-groomed family. It was not until 1986, in the US independent production *Parting Glances*, that a fully dimensional character *living* with Aids, played by Steve Buscemi, appeared in American cinema. The film was the work of Bill Sherwood, who succumbed to the disease four years later.

By the end of the 1980s, the US National Endowment for the Arts (NEA) was supporting, either directly or through the American Film Institute, occasional independent films concerned with Aids. These included Todd Haynes's *Poison* (1990), in which a scientist unleashes a plague spread by kissing, and Greg Araki's anarchic *The Living End* (1992), which closes with a title blaming the deaths of thousands on the inaction of 'Republican fuckheads'. Such films helped fuel religious conservatives' efforts to abolish the NEA.

Longtime Companion (1990), produced by American Playhouse, a project of the US government-sponsored Public Broadcasting Corporation, drew

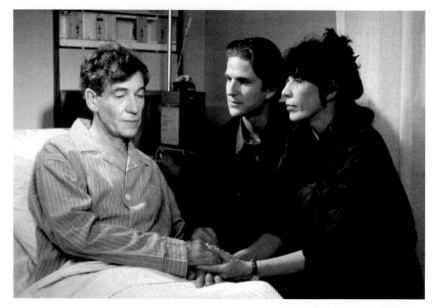

And the Band Played On, *1993: Ian McKellen, Matthew Modine and Lily Tomlin.*
Credit: Everett Collection / Rex Features

less opprobrium. Its medicinal scenario, by playwright Craig Lucas, portrays New York's gay population as a caring, sharing community, but one that cares not to share much of anything with the less affluent and the non-white.

And the Band Played On (1993) reached a broader audience. Produced by the cable service HBO after having been shunned by the leading US television networks, the 142-minute docu-drama is based on Randy Shilts's problematic non-fiction account of the early years of the epidemic. As its large cast finesses chunks of expository dialogue, the film touches controversy in its portrait of Dr Robert Gallo (Alan Alda), who may have usurped credit for isolating the human immunodeficency virus. Missing are the frequently astute opinions of medical authorities who think HIV may not be the cause of Aids, but rather a co-factor or a marker of infection.

And the Band Played On inspired a Canadian antidote, *Zero Patience*, John Greyson's musical film about Gaetan Dugas, the French-Canadian flight attendant luridly identified as 'Patient Zero', the 'Typhoid Mary' of Aids in Shilts's book and its celluloid counterpart. Greyson's impudent script pairs the ghost of Dugas with the still living Victorian polymath Sir Richard

Burton, who is working on a Hall of Contagion exhibit for the Toronto Museum of Natural History.

Among the 1993 spate of Aids films, the most overrated was Jonathan Demme's *Philadelphia*, a production embalmed in mass-audience palatability. The many flaws of this diagrammatic Hollywood movie include its non-depiction of the relationship between Aids sufferer Andy (Tom Hanks) and his partner Miguel (Antonio Banderas). Ron Nyswaner's screenplay censors out every Aids issue pertinent to gay couples; Andy and Miguel seem never even to have had sex. *It's My Party* (US, 1996), the personal work of a less imaginative director, Randal Kleiser, depicts Aids-besieged human relationships with greater honesty.

Aids may be rampant in the developing world, where its victims are typically heterosexual, but in American and European theatre, film and television most Aids-themed scripts approved for production describe the pain of white middle-class gay men, and aim to educate white middle-class heterosexuals without jeopardising their comfort. This is true even of *Angels in America*. Exceptions include the 1987 British television films *Intimate Contact* and *Sweet As You Are*, which examine the problems of non-gay people with Aids.

In 1995, two Hollywood films gave those problems some squeamish attention. *The Cure* condemns homophobic assumptions directed at Aids patients, while assuring audience members that its pubescent male leads are healthy, straight young men whose friendship has educational value. *Boys on the Side* threatens briefly to deal with the sexual options open to a seropositive woman, then becomes maudlin. In these movies, Aids makes everyone learn and grow and become a better person.

Few films concerned with heterosexual relations deal with sexual safety, especially US films trading in prurient prudery. Awareness of the issue does inform Cyril Collard's *Les nuits fauves* (France, 1993), whose bisexual, seropositive protagonist cruises the *quais* of Paris, then negotiates sex with a female lover. Another 1993 French film, François Magolin's *Mensonge*, depicts the plight of an HIV-positive pregnant woman; in Pedro Almodóvar's *Todo sobre mi madre* (Spain, 1999), the key Aids-infected figure is a pregnant nun.

Among the more discerning Aids films made in the UK is Nancy Meckler's *Indian Summer* (1996), whose concerns include transcendence of physical limitation. A more challenging work is Derek Jarman's *Blue* (1993), a visual artist's impassioned response to blindness and extinction. The film's audacious only image – a plain blue screen – appears for the 79-minute duration of a stream of verbal eloquence embedded in an evocative sound design. Blue was the last colour Jarman saw as cytomegalovirus destroyed his retinas; the film was the last fully realised effort he completed before his death.

Film often deals with Aids metaphorically, as in Luis Puenzo's botched reimagining of Camus's *La peste* (France/UK/Argentina, 1992). Beyond documentaries such as Tom Joslin's *Silverlake Life* (US, 1993), the literal horror of Aids is seldom shown. Scripts rarely portray the HIV health-care nightmare. *Before Night Falls* (US, 2000), Julian Schnabel's film about gay Cuban poet and novelist Reinaldo Arenas, glosses over the period when Arenas faced the medical emergencies of Aids in New York without health insurance.

Theatre might have applied sharper analytic powers to the pandemic, but the plays that followed *Angels in America* fell short. Paul Rudnick's 1992 off-Broadway comedy *Jeffrey*, filmed in 1995, submerged questions of sexual freedom in jokey uplift. Terrence McNally's 1995 Broadway success *Love! Valour! Compassion!* and its film adaptation slickly confronted gay men's struggles with friendship and mortality. Aids has figured in the musical *Rent* (1996); US playwright David Rabe's euthanasia play *A Question of Mercy* (1998); and, at opposite extremes of performance art, David Drake's re-assuring *The Night Larry Kramer Kissed Me* (1992) and Ron Athey's transgressive *Four Scenes from a Harsh Life* (1994).

Established playwrights have recently handled the subject with retrograde caution, though Craig Lucas, as if to atone for *Longtime Companion*, confronted the American film industry's censorship of Aids scripts in his 1998 play *The Dying Gaul*. For two decades, dramatic narratives focused on the disease have been expected to cosmeticise the image of its victims. Now that new drug protocols have begun prolonging life, resistance to letting Aids define the gay community has increased. American gay films have begun to resist alluding to Aids, while retaining Aids-inspired image-building strategies that help advance the conservative drift of Western culture. ❏

Jim D'Entremont *is a journalist, playwright and activist*

ROAD TO DAMASCUS

MALU HALASA

The nine-to-five or rather the eight-to-three in Beirut wasn't difficult to adjust to. It was the mornings and evenings I came to dread. First thing, the traffic was unbearable and the service, or shared, taxi drivers were fickle. If they didn't approve of my destination, they just dropped me off. The only public transportation that traversed the Christian and Muslim sides of the city without impunity was a rackety fleet of buses, which stopped for passengers every few feet or when anyone flagged them down. It brought new meaning to the word inclusiveness.

Some evenings provided other kinds of definitions. At a gracious dinner party in the mountains, a woman explained how she measured safety in her building during the Lebanese civil war. She made a point of asking after the health of her politician neighbour from his bodyguards. If he was well, she said that her family were safe because there was a bigger target in the building. Once, her husband and the politician, in search of the gastronomic speciality of raw liver in a particular village, found bodies and coffins on the streets instead. Throughout my stay, I met Beirutis who suffered terribly during the war, but only half alluded to their experiences. These conversations belonged to people who saw things they wish they hadn't.

During this mainly working trip, I was obsessed with the Hirj Sanaubar pine woods, the subject of a badly translated story commissioned for the Beirut new writing and images anthology I was co-editing with Roseanne Khalaf from the American University of Beirut. Historically, the woods acted as the city's green belt, separating Beirut's rich centre from its rural and suburban poor. After the murder and hasty burial of two Shi'ite brothers, within days of the official start of the civil war, the woods became a graveyard. The 1982 Israeli bombing destroyed what remained of them, in effect revealing how drastically the city had been changed by war. This unsettled past still lingers today, despite reconstruction and general gussying up.

It was a past I was trying to piece together for myself in the area around the Hotel Saint Georges. Twenty-three years ago, for a brief month in the summer of 1979, I lived in a nearby building that had intermittent water and electricity. I was waiting for Chairman Yasser Arafat, and interviewing his inner circle meanwhile. This included long conversations with children in camouflage combat gear, spouting PLO rhetoric. The city made me antsy, and I was prone to sudden decisions. In the middle of one night, I abruptly took my leave of Beirut, knowing full well I would have to return again and wait some more.

Damascus was my escape pod. I made several journeys there, usually at night, sometimes in the company of a fat Al Fatah general who was in love, or in one of those shared cabs. The drivers then weren't capricious. They were very careful on the winding roads or at the militia checkpoints. Since that summer, I have often wondered about the road between these two cities, but time has obscured most of my memories.

Now, a big yellow Cadillac or Buick, a whale of an American car, with a mauve velvet interior and curtains, was hurling me towards the Lebanese–Syrian border. A highway had replaced the circuitous mountain route, and the ride was smooth and uneventful until we reached the frontier. Despite the intervening years, I recognised it immediately. I had been there many times before, late, late at night. Sometimes it was a pit stop with other service passengers, or a shopping spree. The Al Fatah general took full advantage of the black market by stuffing his car boot with freshly baked bread, coffee, rice and cooking oil for his Romanian mistress. In the wee hours of the morning, during a war that continued for 17 long years, the emporiums glittered, a low-rent Las Vegas in the middle of absolutely nowhere.

Two hours later, we were ensnared in Damascene traffic. Since spring, when US Secretary of State Colin Powell lectured Syria on improving its record on terrorism, a deadline has hung over the country. For some, the Israeli bombing on 5 October was a nudge.

The last time Syria had been bombed by its neighbour was three decades ago, and Damascus was another city then, dour and Soviet. By 1979, various PLO factions operated openly, and no doubt operational training camps were located in the mountains or the Syrian Desert. The Russians were giving away Cold War scholarships, and my flatmates included rosy-cheeked scholarship winners doing work experience in the office of the Democratic Front for the Liberation of Palestine (DFLP) before university degrees in Odessa or Moscow.

This summer, I stayed with a good friend and his mother whose apartment was in the final throes of renovation. For as little as US$350, a state-of-the-art satellite dish which received 900 channels, hundreds of them pay-for-view porn, had been installed. Of course Iraq, even when it wasn't on BBC News 24, dominated everyone's conversation. One evening as he waited for an errant kitchen installer, the Palestinian house-painter watched emaciated catwalk models from Milan Fashion Week on satellite, and told me his story.

He had fought in Beirut during the civil war, but settled in the Syrian capital. When the US invaded Iraq in March, he had joined a small contingent of fighters who drove three cars across the Syrian–Iraqi border to fight them. He didn't know it then but his first engagement was not going to be against US troops. Every time he knocked on the door of a private residence and asked for a drink of water, he was told to go home. The Iraqis said they weren't going to fight, why should he?

This self-composed, assured house-painter, a man who seemed pretty much capable of anything, said he and his friends eluded the Americans and reached Baghdad two days before it fell. After restaurants and mosques refused them food and shelter, they left the next day. What we didn't discuss was the fact that there were obviously other fighters who had gone to Iraq and hadn't been turned away by the Iraqis but were helped and sheltered by them. And these men were highly trained. In the summer, the BBC reported the appearance in Baghdad of a string of bombs that had been tied together, a configuration used during the Lebanese civil war.

The balcony of my friend's apartment overlooked Jahlal Al-Bukhari Street. In the early morning, Uzbek women in distinctively coloured scarves walked towards the city centre, going to work either as cleaners or sellers of second-hand clothes. Coming from the opposite direction, an itinerant beggar slunk past the closed shutters of the Me and My Baby store, a household goods shop selling Moulinex appliances and a fast-food sandwich joint, towards the Qassioum slopes less than a mile away. Originally settled by the first refugees fleeing the Christian Crusaders who pillaged Jerusalem in the eleventh century, this neighbourhood was still reserved for the very poor.

Ironically, the only time Syria enjoys an economic boost or an influx of outside money is during war. According to the 1996 CIA fact book, the first Gulf war provided Syria with an aid windfall of nearly US$5 billion. Wartime makes the trickle-down effect easier. At a birthday party where young Syrian professionals boogied to the theme from *Peter Gunn* and Bob Dylan, I met Majid. His family-owned trucking company had transported thousands of tons of wheat flour and foodstuffs into Iraq for

Damascus, Syria, 2003: view from the balcony over Jahlal Al-Bukhari Street.
Credit: Malu Halasa

the international aid agencies. The roads were dangerous but Majid and his drivers avoided the trouble spots, such as Baghdad, which needed aid most. He was thankful that his economic sector was doing well, compared with his lawyer friends who complained about feeling stifled in a country trapped between the old and the new.

Despite a healthy showing of shoppers on the streets of Damascus, whether in the modern commercial district of Salahiyyeh with stores such as Naf Naf or Benetton, or in the ancient lanes of Al Hamidiyyeh souk, the Syrian economy is troubled. With the ruling Ba'ath Party firmly in charge, official corruption is rife. The Lebanese mobile phone explosion was lucrative for Syrian officials as well as Lebanese businessmen; Syria's recently enacted telecommunications reform could prove equally remunerative. It is a situation not lost on critics of official corruption who advocate economic reform. Last year, Aref Dalila – economist, university professor and founding member of the Committees for the Revival of Civil Society – joined countless pro-democracy dissidents in jail: he was found guilty of 'attempting to change the constitution by illegal means' and sentenced to ten years' imprisonment.

It is a situation that pits competing security services against each other and against government policies such as President Bashar Assad's amnesties for political prisoners. Once the 'red eye' – slang for surveillance – is on somebody, it's hard to shake it off. As an astute Syrian observed with a shrug, the security services are 'brutes but they are inefficient brutes'.

Yet Ba'athists are not oblivious to the fate of their co-party in Iraq, and are looking for ways to become, perhaps not less powerful, but less visible. The March parliamentary elections included Ba'athist as well as other candidates from seven other political parties under the banner of the Syrian National Progressive Front, an old slogan from the time of Hafez Assad. The Ba'ath Party is also trying to reach out to new, younger members.

Al Hamidiyyeh souk, Damascus, 2003: at the heart of a troubled economy.
Credit: Malu Halasa

Novelist and publisher Ammar Abdulhamid was invited to attend party talks on reform, but declined further involvement because of a lack of transparency. 'What's given in silence can be taken away in public,' said the publisher, who plans to translate Locke and Hume into Arabic for the first time.

Even once-dissident voices such as that of the cartoonist and satirist Ali Farzat have been silenced, whether through his own poor management of *Al-Doumari* (*Lamplighter*) newspaper or government-induced distribution woes. Two days before they were due to go to press, the offices were silent when I went to visit.

In a leafy public square nearby, Syrian Muslim and Christian families seek refuge from another gruelling 43-degree day. Religious pluralism is the main challenge facing countries in the region, not Western issues such as immigration or asylum seekers. In Beirut, those naturally shared spaces were shattered by war, and it remains to be seen if urban planning can recreate the right ambience. In Syria, the problem appears to have been solved, although the 1982 fate of the Muslim Brotherhood in Hama suggests that Assad's preferred method was brutal suppression. Some 20,000 are said to have died when Assad's now out-of-favour younger brother Rifaat and the Saraya Al-Difaah (Defence Companies), an elite Syrian army artillery, tank and helicopter unit, moved against the city. Hama, once a name never uttered in public, is now openly talked about.

Across the street from my friend's apartment, both veiled and unveiled women take their children to day care, which includes a crèche for the working mothers in the adjacent electricity board. At least women here are visible and vocal, a sign of something going well considering the ways in which women's lives have been badly affected by war and occupation from Kabul and Baghdad to Ramallah.

When I first visited Damascus as a teenager, there were no women on the streets during Ramadan, only uniformed men. In 1970, the city was heavily militarised; more so nine years later. Contrary to reports from US neo-conservatives and the Israelis, it is not like that now. The view over Jahlal Al-Bukhari Street may not be to everybody's liking, but at least the country is striving to take a good hard look at itself. ❑

Malu Halasa *is a writer and journalist. Her latest book is* Transit Beirut: New Writing and Images, *edited with Roseanne Khalaf (Saqi Books, London, 2004)*

Support for INDEX ON CENSORSHIP

It is the generosity of our friends and supporters which makes *Index on Censorship*'s work possible. *Index* remains the only international publication devoted to the promotion and protection of that basic, yet still abused, human right – freedom of expression.

Your support is needed more than ever now as *Index* and the Writers & Scholars Educational Trust continue to grow and develop new projects. Donations will enable us to expand our website, which will make access to *Index*'s stories and communication between free-speech activists and supporters even easier, and will help directly with our Sponsored Subscriptions Programme which provides free copies of the magazine to activists in the developing world and the former Soviet states.

Please help *Index* speak out.

The Trustees and Directors would like to thank the many individuals and organisations who support *Index on Censorship* and the Writers & Scholars Educational Trust, including:

IF YOU WOULD LIKE MORE INFORMATION ABOUT INDEX ON CENSORSHIP OR WOULD LIKE TO SUPPORT OUR WORK, PLEASE **CONTACT HUGO GRIEVE, DEVELOPMENT MANAGER, ON 020 7278 2313 OR EMAIL HUGO@INDEXONCENSORSHIP.ORG**

WWW.INDEXONCENSORSHIP.ORG
CONTACT@INDEXONCENSORSHIP.ORG
TEL: 020 7278 2313 • FAX: 020 7278 1878

SUBSCRIPTIONS (4 ISSUES PER ANNUM)
INDIVIDUALS: BRITAIN £32, US $48, REST OF WORLD £42
INSTITUTIONS: BRITAIN £48, US $80, REST OF WORLD £52
PLEASE PHONE 020 8249 4443
OR EMAIL TONY@INDEXONCENSORSHIP.ORG

Index on Censorship (ISSN 0306-4220) is published four times a year by a non-profit-making company: Writers & Scholars International Ltd, Lancaster House, 33 Islington High Street, London N1 9LH. *Index on Censorship* is associated with Writers & Scholars Educational Trust, registered charity number 325003 **Periodicals postage:** (US subscribers only) paid at Newark, New Jersey. Postmaster: send US address changes to *Index on Censorship* c/o Mercury Airfreight International Ltd Inc., 365 Blair Road, Avenel, NJ 07001, USA